AIR FRYER RECIPE COOKBOOK 2020-2021

The All-in-one Cookbook for Instant Vortex Plus Air Fryer, COSORI Air Fryer, NUWAVE Air Fryer and GoWISE USA, Chefman, Ninja, COMFEE', DASH, Innsky Air Fryer, Etc

By Jenny C. Amanda

Table of Content

Chapter 6: Mouth-watering Pork Recipes..117

Foreward

500+ Delicious, Affordable, and Easy-to-make Air Fryer Recipes Customized for Your Health and Appetite.

Are you on a hunt for **budget-friendly and tasty** air fryer meals?

Do you want **top-notch** air fryer meals that can be prepared with **easily accessible ingredients**?

Then this will be the book you're looking for. This cookbook would certainly **satisfy your needs** and more!

Be ready for the amazing resources available in the book. Here, we consider for you not only the practicability of the recipes, but also the health values of each meal. The very purpose of this cookbook is to help you eat trendily and nutritiously. We hope to help people who dream of having the fittest body while eating their hearts out to achieve their goals.

Sine you've got the ticket—an air fryer—to the journey, let's start our exploration. With the informative chapters in this book, you would be enlightened about multiple revolutionary healthy recipes which are notably effective for weight loss. The main contents in this well-structured book include:

- **A General Introduction to Air Fryers**
- **The Merits of Air Frying**
- **Step-by-Step Guide on Air Fryers:** Criteria for selecting a suitable air fryer, introduction of a typical Air fryer's components, and directions for operating an air fryer.
- **Tips and Tricks:** For maintenance and preparation of crispy meals.
- **500+ First-Class Recipes:** Healthy, easy-to-make, and inclusive (for ketogenic diet, paleo diet, vegan diet, etc.) recipes are offered. Each recipe consists of easily accessible ingredients, preparation time, cooking time & temperatures and servings.
- **Nutritional Info:** for calorie tracking and nutrient balancing.
- **Glossary:** to help refer to the recipes effectively.

With an Air Fryer, you can eat easy, eat healthy, and eat stylish.

Let's get cooking!

Introducing the Air Fryer

Equipped with highly sophisticated technologies, an Air Fryer is a helpful kitchen appliance that provides convenience to your lives. It makes use of a high-speed hot air circulation technology to cook the food by heating air to about 400°F. Consequently, the food can be evenly heated and come out tender and juicy with a crispy crust. Moreover, only minimal use of oil is required according to the recipes.

The air fryer has been constructed in a way that allows you to fry, roast, grill, bake, dehydrate and reheat cold food. As a result, you can save your kitchen's space by having one versatile Air Fryer.

Furthermore, the health benefits given by an air fryer cannot be overstated. Air Fryers are 90% healthier than traditional cooking appliances that require a lot of oil. What's more, you can have more free choices on the cooking time, temperature and other ingenious functions while cooking.

The Merits of Air Frying

This section will discuss the various reasons why cooking with an Air Fryer is the best choice. The most salient point that contributes to its rising popularity is the ability to make very low-fat meals. Technically, the Air Fryer makes use of the oil naturally contained in the ingredients and the heated air to cook your food evenly. Now, let us get informed with some other benefits.

- **The Air Fryer is versatile:**
  Air Frying allows you to prepare numerous dishes simultaneously through different methods since no limitation is set there. It's worth noting that roasted, baked, and grilled meals should be cooked separately. All in all, to make those five-star meals in the comfort of your home, all that is required is an Air Fryer. Therefore, go and add an air fryer to your cooking appliance shopping list right now!

- **The Air Fryer is very portable:**
  The Air Fryers have been designed with small, medium, and large sizes. Regardless of their size, Air Fryers can be easily taken with no matter where you go. You may take it for picnic outings, for instance. Moreover, being compact enough, Air Fryers do not occupy much space.

- **The Air Fryer reduces extra fat intake while keeping nutrients intact:**
  Air Frying is the healthiest cooking option on the block. Why? An Air Fryer reduces the oil and fat contained in meals by 80% while keeping the vitamins and minerals intact or enhanced thanks to the air circulation technology. For ovens and grillers,

either ruin the flavor of the food, or hurt the quality.

What is more, air frying is the perfect option for people conducting weight loss, portion control, and calorie-tracking.

- **Quite effortless to clean:**
  After every cooking session, food-debris and oil stains are inevitable. It is important to clean them up for the quality of the next dish. There are easy and relatively economical options (soap, water, and a washcloth) to keep your air fryer clean.

- **Air Fryer is incredibly time-saving:**
  Say goodbye to those days when you cannot prepare proper meals because of your stringent or unstable schedule. The Air Fryer cooks meals quickly and makes in minutes what would normally requires an hour. For example, bacon and eggs prepared in 10 minutes by an air fryer saves more time than the 30 minutes a gas cooker costs.

  Load the Air Fryer with the ingredients and set the time & temperature. Your meal should be ready before you are done with your shower and dressed for work.

- **Very safe and convenient to use:**
  Unlike normal pots, the Air Fryer does not need an open fire to heat up no matter how long the cooking time lasts or how high the temperature is.

  Furthermore, you don't need to worry about getting hurt by hot splatters from the air fryer while cooking.

Selection Criteria of a Perfect Air Fryer

Technically, all Air Fryer brands work to produce the same or similar results. However, some differences set them apart. The significant distinctions that we should inform you are the size, the temperature range of the Air Fryer, and your budget. Your choice can be driven by your needs in terms of the quantity and types of food you want. For this reason, let us talk about your options.

1. **Size options:** your choice here depends on the size of your family. Generally, there are three different sizes.
   - Small (ranging from 1 to 2 quarts): This is ideal for a person or at most two persons to fry a few pieces of chicken/meat, make fries, and other snacks.
   - Medium (ranging from 3 to 5.8 quarts): The medium-sized one is big enough to cater for at least 5 people. It can also cook a whole chicken (4 pounds) at a go. There is enough room to cook different dishes at once, thanks to the many cooking chambers and baking pans.
   - Large (ranging from 6.5 to 16 quarts): Now you can bring your party on! Make Pizzas, whole chickens, family-sized cakes, casserole, etc. with this size. The

room is completely enough.

2. **Technology options:**

- 3D Air Pulse: This Air Fryer technology requires a short pre-heating time and a tablespoon of oil to fry your snacks. Only the Tefal brand offers this technology, which makes your food crispier.
- Rapid Air: Some Philip Air fryers offer this technology among others. They also require only a tablespoon of oil for frying.
- TurboStar: It requires no pre-heating thanks to the superior heating element. It is the healthiest technology because it drains all the fat and residual oil produced during the cooking to the pan's base. This technology is the holy grail of the Philip fryer brand.
- Manual or Automatic Cooking Programs: Do you want to be able to walk away from your kitchen while cooking? The automatic cooking program allows you to pre-set the time and temperature as stated by the recipe, so you only have to take out the cooked food after the buzzer goes off. And the manual type requires many checks before the food is cooked.

The Components of a Typical Air Fryer and Their Functions

Here are some of the characteristic components of Air fryers:

- **Cooking Chamber:** Some Air Fryer brands have a bucket-like basket while others have a regular cooking basket. This is where all the cooking happens. It holds the pizza pans, cupcake pans, skewer racks for beautiful kebabs, dehydrating pans for the brands that can cook at as low as 120°F temperature, and other accessories used for cooking.
- **Fan & Heating Element:** The heating element is customarily above the cooking chamber. As air flows in through the air-inlet valve, the heating element heats it, and then the fan circulates it to every corner of the cooking basket.
- **Control Panel & Cooking Programs:** There are slight differences between different Air Fryer brands' cook settings. Consult the manuals for more details. Use the control panel to operate the Air Fryer by selecting the various cook settings (time and temperature buttons) and programs (dehydrate, grill, roast, bake, etc. buttons).
- **Timer:** It beeps (the sound will vary from different brands) when a cooking program is completed.
- **Parchment, Tongs, and Oven Mitts:** Line the cooking pans with parchment paper to collect oil and food crumbs. It helps to make the cleaning easier and faster. Use tongs and oven mitts to flip food and lift hot cooking pans from the cooking

basket.

Maintenance, Tips, and Tricks

Good maintenance, regular cleaning, and routine troubleshooting ensure the durability of your air fryer.

- Don't clean the air fryer when it is hot.
- We recommend that you wash the pans in hot water when you start to use them for the first time.
- Wipe the exterior and the heating element with a clean and damp cloth.
- Wash the cooking pans, baking pans, racks, pizza pans, etc. in warm soapy water using a soft sponge (to prevent scratches) or a dishwasher. Make sure to soak the pans in soapy water for a while before you wash them. Wipe the cooking chamber with hot water and a clean cloth. Use clean water to clean again and wipe off water with a dry cloth or air dry.
- Use healthy oils like Olive, Coconut, or Avocado oils. In fact, you only need very small quantities of oil when you cook with an air fryer, thus allowing you to save your budget.
- Make sure the air-outlet is not blocked when cooking your meal.
- Use brightly colored cooking pans and racks to avoid burns to your hands.
- To use your air fryer properly, you must carefully read through the manual provided with your chosen brand. A close reading over the troubleshooting procedures, safety issues, and systematic explanations in the manual is highly recommended.

Chapter 1: Breakfast Recipes

Air Fried French Toast

Air fried toast is a classic French cuisine that's quick, easy, and barely requires much effort to prepare.

Prep time and cooking time: 10 minutes| Serves: 2

Ingredients To Use:

- 4 thick bread slices
- 1/2 tsp. cinnamon
- 2 raw eggs
- 3/4 tsp. salt
- 3/4 tsp. ground cloves
- 2 tbsp. butter
- 3/4 tsp. ground nutmeg
- Maple syrup and icing sugar (serving)

Step-by-Step Directions to Cook It:

1. Set the Air Fryer to 350°F. Beat the eggs, nutmeg, cinnamon, cloves, and salt together in a bowl. Spread butter to each side of the bread slices and then cut into horizontal strips.
2. Dip the bread strips into the egg mixture.
3. Spray oil in a large skillet over medium heat and cook the bread strips for about 2 minutes.
4. Transfer the slightly brown bread strips to the Air Fryer and then cook till golden brown.
5. Serve the bread with maple syrup and icing sugar. Enjoy!

Nutritional value per serving:

Calories: 138kcal, Fat: 4g, Carb: 17g, Proteins: 8g

Rarebits and Eggs

If you are a lover of grilled cheese, you'd love this rarebits and egg recipe. It tastes amazing.

Prep time and cooking time: 10 minutes| Serves: 4

Ingredients To Use:

- 1/2 tsp. paprika
- 4 fried eggs, sunny side up
- 1-1/2 cups of mozzarella, grated
- 1 tsp. mustard powder
- 4 slices of sourdough
- 1/3 cup ale
- 2 tsp. Worcestershire sauce

Step-by-Step Directions to Cook It:

1. Preheat the Air Fryer to 350°F.
2. Mix the mustard powder, Worcestershire sauce, cheddar, ale, and paprika in a small-sized bowl.
3. Coat each side of the sourdough with the sauce mixture. Arrange the slices in the Air Fryer tray and cook until brown
4. Serve rarebits with fried eggs and sprinkle with pepper to taste.

Nutritional value per serving:

Calories: 256kcal, Fat: 23g, Carb: 21g, Proteins: 9g

Oat Muffins

Oat muffins are super easy to make, and nothing beats a warm air-fried muffin on a cold day.

Prep time and cooking time: 15 minutes | Serves: 6

- 2 large eggs
- 1/4 tsp. vanilla essence
- 1/2 cup icing sugar
- Cooking spray
- 3/4 tsp. baking powder
- 1 tbsp. raisins
- 3-1/2 oz. rolled oats
- 3 oz. butter, melted
- 1/2 cup flour

Step-by-Step Directions to Cook It:

1. Whisk the sugar and butter in a large bowl until soft. Combine the eggs and vanilla essence. Transfer the egg mixture into the butter and whisk until they form soft peaks.
2. In another large bowl, mix the oats, raisin, flour, and baking powder.
3. Grease the muffin molds with a light coating of oil spray. Set the Air Fryer to 350°F.
4. Mix the flour and egg mixture and then transfer it into the molds.
5. Place the molds into the Air Fryer tray. Cook for about 12 minutes and then serve.

Nutritional value per serving:

Calories: 202kcal, Fat: 9.5g, Carb: 7.8g, Proteins: 3.2g

Air Fryer Sandwich

Cooking a toasty and crunchy English sandwich just get a lot easier with an Air Fryer; you should try it out.
Prep time and cooking time: 13 minutes | Serves: 1

Ingredients To Use:

- 2 bacon slices
- 1 uncooked egg
- 1 English muffin

- Black pepper and salt to taste

Step-by-Step Directions to Cook It:

1. Whisk the egg in a soufflé cup and sprinkle with salt and pepper to taste.
2. Preheat the Air Fryer to 390°F and then arrange the bacon, soufflé cup, muffin, and bacon into the tray.
3. Cook for about 6-10 minutes.
4. Serve.

Nutritional value per serving:

Calories: 252kcal, Fat: 23g, Carb: 61g, Proteins: 22g

Crunchy Air Fryer Casserole

The Air Fryer casserole is perfect for breakfast, and it's also a great traditional holiday side dish.
Prep time and cooking time: 32 minutes | Serves: 4

Ingredients To Use:

- 4 raw eggs
- 1 cup of cheese, shredded
- Salt and pepper to taste
- 6 oz. of cooked sweet sausage.
- 1/2 cup bread crumbs

Step-by-Step Directions to Cook It:

1. Set the Air Fryer to 350°F.
2. Whisk the eggs in a large bowl until it forms soft peaks. Add half of the bread crumbs, sausage, and cheese into the egg. Season the mixture with pepper and salt.
3. Pour the mixture into a baking dish and top with the remaining cheese and bread crumbs.
4. Transfer the baking dish into the Air Fryer basket and cook for 20 minutes.
5. Serve.

Nutritional value per serving:

Calories: 217kcal, Fat: 37g, Carb: 27g, Proteins: 12g

Cottage Cheese Sandwich

For the maximum satisfaction, make sure the cottage cheese sandwich is well cooked. If the cheese doesn't melt in your mouth, then you need to cook it for a longer time.
Prep time and cooking time: 15 minutes | Serves: 1

Ingredients To Use:

- 1 cup cottage cheese, sliced
- 1 small capsicum, roasted and sliced
- 2 slices of bread
- 1 tbsp. melted butter

For Sauce:

- 1/2 tsp. olive oil
- 1/4 cup onion, chopped
- 1/4 tbsp. red chili sauce
- 1/2 clove garlic crushed
- 1/4 tbsp. Worcestershire sauce

Step-by-Step Directions to Cook It:

1. Cut the edges of the bread and then slice it horizontally.
2. Place a skillet over medium heat and cook the sauce ingredients until they thicken. Stir in the cheese and then cook for another 3 minutes. Spread sauce mixture on bread slices and then set aside.
3. Preheat the Air Fryer to 300⁰F. Place the sandwiches into the Air Fryer basket and cook for about 15 minutes at 250⁰F. Flip slices in between the cooking. Serve in a parchment-lined basket with ketchup.

Nutritional value per serving:

Calories: 246kcal, Fat: 29g, Carb: 31g, Proteins: 21g

Creamy Semolina Cutlets

This recipe is healthy and can be served as breakfast or tea time snack. It's also easy to make.
Prep time and cooking time: 60 minutes | Serves: 2

Ingredients To Use:

- 12 oz. of mixed vegetables, chopped
- 1/2 tsp. salt
- 3 tbsp. vegetable oil
- 1 cup of smooth semolina
- 1/2 tsp. black pepper, ground
- 2-1/2 lbs. milk

Step-by-Step Directions to Cook It:

1. Heat the milk in a shallow saucepan over medium heat. Add the mixed vegetables and cook for about 3 minutes, until tender.
2. Season the vegetable mixture with pepper and salt. Stir in the semolina and then cook for another 10 minutes, until the mixture thickens
3. Pour the semolina mixture into a greased pan. Refrigerate the mixture for about 4-6 hours.
4. Preheat the Air Fryer to 350°F.
5. Take out the refrigerated mixture and cut into any desired shape. Brush the cutlets with oil and then arrange into an Air Fryer basket. Cook for about 10 minutes and serve hot.

Nutritional value per serving:

Calories: 246kcal, Fat: 12g, Carb: 22g, Proteins: 8g

Spicy Yam Kebab

Air fried yam kebab requires zero oil, which is great for your health. The recipe also provide the carbs that keep you going for the day.

Prep time and cooking time: 30 minutes | Serves: 2

- 4 tbsp. coriander, chopped
- 3 tbsp. cream
- 1-1/2 Tsp. salt
- 3 tsp. lemon juice
- 3 tbsp. capsicum, chopped
- 3 eggs
- 2 cups of sliced yam
- 2 medium-sized onions, chopped
- 5 green chilies, chopped
- 1-1/2 tbsp. ginger powder
- 1-1/2 tsp. garlic powder
- 1 medium cucumber, sliced

Step-by-Step Directions to Cook It:

1. Mix the onion, ginger, garlic, lemon juice, coriander, and cream to form a paste in a small-sized bowl.
2. In another bowl, whisk the egg and seasonings with salt.
3. Coat the yam slices with lemon paste before dipping into the egg mixture.
4. Skewer vegetables and yam into wooden skewers.
5. Preheat the Air Fryer to160⁰F for about 10 minutes.
6. Cook the yam for about 25 minutes, until tender.

Nutritional value per serving:

Calories: 322kcal, Fat: 10g, Carb: 32g, Proteins: 4g

Chicken Sandwich

The chicken is crispy and terrifically delicious. It's stuffed in toasted hamburger buns and can be served with fries.
Prep time and cooking time: 40 minutes| Serves: 4

Ingredients To Use:

- 2 boneless chicken breast, pounded
- 1/2 cup of milk
- 1 tbsp. sugar
- Cooking oil spray
- 1/2 tsp. garlic powder
- 1 cup all-purpose flour
- 1 tsp. paprika
- 1 tsp. kosher salt
- 1/2 tsp. freshly ground pepper
- 4 toasted hamburger buns
- Pickle slices(optional)

Step-by-Step Directions to Cook It:

1. Marinate chicken in pickle juice and refrigerate for about 30 minutes.
2. Preheat the Air Fryer to 340⁰F
3. Beat the egg and milk until soft peaks are formed.
4. Combine sugar, paprika, salt, pepper, garlic, and flour in a small-sized bowl.
5. Take out the marinated chicken and discard the juice.
6. Coat the marinated chicken in egg mixture before dipping in all-purpose flour.
7. Spray Air Fryer basket with cooking oil and then place the chicken into the basket.
8. Cook the chicken for about 15 minutes, until tender. Flip the chicken in between the cooking and spray oil lightly whenever necessary.
9. Turn up the Air Fryer temperature to 400⁰F and continue cooking until the chicken is crispy. Remove the chicken from Air Fryer, allow it to cool and then stuff it in between the buns.

Nutritional value per serving:

Calories: 245kcal, Fat: 36g, Carb: 32g, Proteins: 14g

Air fried Crunchy Granola

It's healthy, crunchy, and customizable. And air frying only takes half the time that a conventional oven needs. Fantastic!
Prep time and cooking time: 30 minutes | Serves: 4

Ingredients To Use:

- 1 cup chopped dried fruits
- 1/4 cup almonds, sliced
- 1/4 cup chopped pecans
- 1 cup rolled oats, uncooked
- 1/4 cup flaked coconut
- 1 tsp. vanilla extract
- 3 tbsp. vegetable oil
- A pinch of salt
- 3 tbsp. maple syrup

Step-by-Step Directions to Cook It:

1. In a medium-sized bowl, mix the nuts, coconut, and oats.
2. In another bowl, stir in the oil, maple syrup, vanilla, and salt. Add the oat mixture and stir to combine well.
3. Line the Air Fryer basket with parchment paper. Spread the oat mixture evenly in the basket. Bake at 300ºF for 15 minutes and stir in between the cooking until well done.
4. Remove the granola from the oven and mix in dried fruits.
5. Store in an airtight container.

Nutritional value per serving:

Calories: 199kcal, Fat: 11g, Carb: 23g, Proteins: 4g

Spicy Bacon

This recipe is a sweet-spicy low carb breakfast that's worth every bite. It can also be served as a snack or as a meal.
Prep time and cooking time: 20 minutes|

Serves: 4

Ingredients To Use:

- 1/4 tsp. black pepper
- 1-1/2 tbsp. brown sugar
- 1/4 tsp. cayenne pepper
- 1 lb. thick-cut bacon, sliced into three equal sections

Step-by-Step Directions to Cook It:

1. Combine the sugar and pepper in a large bowl. Coat the bacon slices with the pepper mixture and leave for about 5 minutes.
2. Place the bacon slices in the Air Fryer basket and bake at 350ºF for about 10 minutes. Cook in batches if necessary.

Nutritional value per serving:

Calories: 125kcal, Fat: 9g, Carb: 5g, Proteins: 8g

Prosciutto and Cheese Strata

This stratum is baked to a cheesy golden perfection with a crusty layer and soft inner texture.
Prep time and cooking time: 20 minutes|
Serves: 2

Ingredients To Use:

- 1-1/2 cup of whole wheat bread, cut into cubes
- 1 large egg, lightly beaten
- 1/2 cup whole milk
- 1/2 cup grated cheddar cheese, divided
- Kosher sea salt
- Black pepper
- 1 thin slices prosciutto, cut into 1-inch square
- 3 asparagus spears, cut horizontally
- 1 tbsp. chopped chives

Step-by-Step Directions to Cook It:

1. Arrange the bread cubes in a baking pan

that fits the air fryer.

2. Whisk the eggs and milk in a large bowl until soft peaks are formed. Add half of the cheese, sprinkle in salt and pepper. Drizzle in 3/4 of the egg mixture over the bread cubes.
3. Arrange the prosciutto and asparagus spears over the coated bread and transfer the pan to the air fryer.
4. Top with the cheese and egg mixture, then put into the air fryer.
5. Bake the cheese strata at 330⁰F for about 15 minutes.
6. Allow to cool and then serve with chopped chives.

Nutritional value per serving:

Calories: 221kcal, Fat: 9g, Carb: 12g, Proteins: 16g

Creamy Strawberry French Toast

The French cream cheese toast has a strawberry flavor that makes a perfect relaxing breakfast with a cup of coffee.
Prep time and cooking time: 15 minutes|
Serves: 4

Ingredients To Use:

-   8 slices bread, white sandwich
-   3 tbsp. milk
-   1/3 cup of powdered sugar
-   Cream cheese, cut into thin slices
-   8 strawberries, sliced thinly
-   2 raw egg
-   1 tsp. ground cinnamon

Step-by-Step Directions to Cook It:

1. Use a rolling pin to flatten the bread.
2. Cover the surface go the bread with cheese and then top with strawberries.
3. Fold the bread tightly and repeat the process with the remaining bread slices.
4. Mix the egg and milk in a shallow bowl.

5. Dip the folded bread into the egg mixture and then place it on a tray. Sprinkle powdered sugar atop the coated bread.
6. Place the bread in an oil-coated Air Fryer basket. Cook at 330⁰F for 5 minutes.

Nutritional value per serving:

Calories: 322kcal, Fat: 34g, Carb: 18g, Proteins: 4g

Croissant Delight

Who can miss an air fried croissant with eggs and vegetables? This recipe is fluffy and baked much to your delight.
Prep time and cooking time: 13 minutes|
Serves: 1

Ingredients To Use:

-   1 cup shredded cheddar cheese
-   1/2 cup salad greens, packed
-   1 croissant, homemade or store-bought
-   3 slices honey ham
-   4 honey cherry tomato, halved
-   4 small button mushrooms, quartered
-   1 large egg

Step-by-Step Directions to Cook It:

1. Spray the baking dish with cooking oil.
2. Arrange the ingredients on two even layers inside the baking dish. Insert the cheese into the middle and top layers. Pour the egg in the center of the ham.
3. Season with salt and pepper. Sprinkle in rosemary and then place the dish on the Air Fryer basket alongside the croissant.
4. Bake at 325⁰F for 4 minutes. Remove the croissant and bake for another 4 minutes.
5. Serve the croissant with baked egg and greens.

Calories: 226kcal, Fat: 40g, Carb: 32 g, Proteins: 20g

Crunchy French Toast

French toast made with sourdough bread gives it a crunchy, delicious, fun twist that's hard to resist.

Prep time and cooking time: 10 minutes| Serves: 4

Ingredients To Use:

- 2 slices of sourdough bread
- Wild blueberries
- 3 raw eggs
- 1 tbsp. softened butter
- 1 tsp. vanilla syrup
- 3 tsp. maple syrup

Step-by-Step Directions to Cook It:

1. Set the Air Fryer to 356°F.
2. Whisk the egg and vanilla in a small bowl.
3. Butter the edges of the bread and dip in the egg mixture.
4. Place the bread into the Air Fryer basket and cook for about 6 minutes. Flip the bread in between the cooking.
5. Serve with a drizzle of maple syrup and top with berries.

Nutritional value per serving:

Calories: 129kcal, Fat: 10g, Carb: 27g, Proteins: 8g

Thai Fried Fluffy Omelette

This recipe is made in a traditional Thai style with a crispy and tender texture. It's loaded with protein and can be stuffed in toasted buns.

Prep time and cooking time: 10 minutes| Serves: 2

Ingredients To Use:

- 1 cup onion, chopped
- 1 tbsp. fish salt
- 1/2 cup minced pork
- 2 large eggs

Step-by-Step Directions to Cook It:

1. Beat the eggs until it is light and fluffy. Set the Air Fryer to 280°F.
2. Combine all ingredients in a bowl and then transfer the mixture into the Air Fryer tray.
3. Cook the omelet to a golden brown.

Nutritional value per serving:

Calories: 205kcal, Fat: 15g, Carb: 4g, Proteins: 10g

Air Fried Fritters

The recipe is laced with spices ranging from apples and cinnamon to every other things savory.

Prep time and cooking time: 15 minutes | Serves: 2

Ingredients To Use:

- 2 medium-sized apples, peeled, cored, sliced
- 1-1/2 tsp. of ground cinnamon, divided
- 1/2 cup rice flour
- 2 tbsp. cornstarch
- 1 tsp. baking powder
- 1/2 cup club soda
- 1/2 cup and 2 tablespoons sugar
- 1 cup rolled oats
- 1 medium egg

Step-by-Step Directions to Cook It:

1. Mix half of the sugar and cinnamon in a medium-sized bowl.
2. Set the Air Fryer to 350°F.
3. Pulse the oat to smooth using a food processor. Transfer the oat to the bowl

and add salt, rice flour, cornstarch, baking powder, cinnamon, and the rest of the sugar.
4. Stir in eggs and soda until smooth.
5. Dump the apple rings into the mixture and then pour into an Air Fryer tray. Cook for about 5 minutes. Cook in batches if necessary.

Nutritional value per serving:

Calories: 296kcal, Fat: 2.1g, Carb: 64g, Proteins: 5.5g

Glazed Pancake

The orange-flavored pancake accompanied by a drizzle of maple syrup makes a tempting sweet breakfast that nobody can resist.
Prep time and cooking time: 10 minutes| Serves: 2

Ingredients To Use:
- 2 tsp. dried basil
- 2 tsp. dried parsley
- Salt and pepper to taste
- 3 tbsp. softened butter
- 1 medium-sized orange (zested)
- 1-1/2 cups almond flour
- 3 large eggs
- 1 tbsp. maple syrup

Step-by-Step Directions to Cook It:
1. Preheat the Air Fryer to 250⁰F
2. Combine all the ingredients in a medium-sized bowl.
3. Spray the pancake mold with cooking oil.
4. Cook the pancakes for about 3 minutes and then serve with a drizzle of maple syrup.

Nutritional value per serving:

Calories: 216kcal, Fat: 14g, Carb: 21g, Proteins: 3g

Air Fried Apricot Pudding

The recipe is an old-fashioned breakfast that can also be served as a dessert. It's also perfect with flavored ice cream.
Prep time and cooking time: 20 minutes| Serves: 2

Ingredients To Use:
- 2 cups apricot, chopped
- 2 cups almond flour
- 2 cups of milk
- 3 tbsp. unsalted butter
- 2 tbsp. custard powder
- 3 tbsp. sugar

Step-by-Step Directions to Cook It:
1. Heat the milk and sugar in a saucepan and thicken the mixture with almond and custard powder. Add apricots and then stir with a spatula.
2. Preheat the Air Fryer to 300⁰F for about 5 minutes.
3. Line the Air Fryer basket with parchment paper and then coat with butter.
4. Pour the mixture into the lined basket. Cook for about 10 minutes and serve with fruits.

Nutritional value per serving:

Calories: 178kcal, Fat: 10g, Carb: 11g, Proteins: 3g

Chocolate Waffle

The recipe is a combination of intense flavors which is sweet and savory. It's the perfect meal for breakfast.

Prep time and cooking time: 8 minutes| Serves: 2

Ingredients To Use:

- 1 tbsp. cocoa powder
- 2 egg
- 3/4 tsp. dried basil
- 3/4 tsp. dried parsley
- Salt and pepper to taste
- 3 tbsp. butter
- 1/2 cup chocolate chips
- 1-1/2 tsp. coconut flour

Step-by-Step Directions to Cook It:

1. Preheat the Air Fryer to about 250⁰Fahrenheit.
2. In a small-sized bowl, mix all the ingredients except for the chocolate chips. Ensure that the mixture is smooth.
3. Spray a waffle mold with cooking spray. Pour the batter into the mold and then place it into the Air Fryer basket for about 4 minutes. Garnish with chocolate chips and serve.

Nutritional value per serving:

Calories: 192kcal, Fat: 12g, Carb: 10g, Proteins: 5g

Cinnamon Roll Waffle

The cinnamon roll waffle is of aromatic flavors and can be enjoyed with a cup of coffee or tea.
Prep time and cooking time: 10 minutes| Serves: 2

Ingredients To Use:

- 1/2 tsp. cinnamon
- 2 eggs
- 2 strawberries, sliced (serving)
- 1/2 cup butter or shredded cheese
- 1 tbsp. heavy cream
- 2 tsp. flour

Step-by-Step Directions to Cook It:

1. In a small sized-bowl, combine all the ingredients.
2. Set the Air Fryer to a temperature of

250⁰F. Transfer the batter into a mold and transfer it to the Air Fryer. Cook until golden brown. Serve with strawberries.

Nutritional value per serving:

Calories: 256kcal, Fat: 14g, Carb: 7g, Proteins: 11g

Zucchini pancake

Zucchini pancake is an easy recipe that's also great for vegetable lovers. Fill, cook, serve. No stress, right?
Prep time and cooking time: 8 minutes | Serves: 2

Ingredients To Use:

- 2 tsp. dried parsley
- Salt and pepper to taste
- 2 tsp. dried basil
- 3 tbsp. butter
- 2 medium-sized zucchinis (shredded)
- 1-1/2 cups of almond flour
- 3 medium eggs

Step-by-Step Directions to Cook It:

1. Preheat the Air Fryer to 250⁰F.
2. In a shallow bowl, mix and stir all the ingredients until smooth.
3. Spray a pancake mold with cooking oil and pour the batter into the mold.
4. Place the mold in an Air Fryer basket. Cook for about 5 minutes, until golden brown.
5. Serve.

Nutritional value per serving:

Calories: 120kcal, Fat: 4g, Carb: 14g, Proteins: 7g

Vanilla Flavoured Pudding

This creamy and flavored recipe is nostalgic and easy. The homemade vanilla pudding is best served with berries and ice cream.

Prep time and cooking time: 15 minutes|
Serves: 2

- 2 cups vanilla powder
- 3 tbsp. powdered sugar
- 3 tbsp. unsalted butter
- 2 cups of milk
- 1 cup oats
- 2 tbsp. corn flour

Step-by-Step Directions to Cook It:

1. Heat the milk and sugar in a saucepan over medium heat. Thicken the mixture with flour ingredient.
2. Preheat the Air Fryer to 300⁰F. Pour the batter into the dish and place it in the Air Fryer basket.
3. Cook for about 10 minutes. Serve.

Nutritional value per serving:

Calories: 232kcal, Fat: 9g, Carb: 29g, Proteins: 29g

Nut Brownies

Who don't love homemade fudgy brownies that can be prepared in half of the usual time? Get hooked with this Air Fryer baked recipe, and don't forget to top it up with whipped cream.
Prep time and cooking time: 30 minutes|
Serves: 2

Ingredients To Use:

- 3 tbsp. melted dark chocolate
- 1/2 cup condensed milk
- 1 cup all-purpose flour
- 1/2 cup chopped nuts
- 1 tbsp. unsalted butter
- 2 tbsp. water

Step-by-Step Directions to Cook It:

1. In a medium-sized bowl, whisk all the ingredients till smooth.

2. Line a cakepan with parchment paper and brush the lining with butter.
3. Preheat the Air Fryer to 300⁰F
4. Place the pan into the Air Fryer bask and cover with aluminum foil.
5. Cook the brownies for about 15 minutes.
6. Allow cooling before slicing.

Nutritional value per serving:

Calories: 185kcal, Fat: 18g, Carb: 54g, Proteins: 6g

Baked Yoghurt

Yogurt baked in an Air Fryer is healthy and requires simple ingredients. Here's how to make the savory recipe.
Prep time and cooking time: 15 minutes |
Serves: 3

Ingredients To Use:

- 2 cups fresh cream
- 2 cups condensed milk
- 2 cups yogurt
- Fresh berries (garnish)
- Sugar and water (garnish)

Step-by-Step Directions to Cook It:

1. Combine all ingredients to form a paste.
2. Transfer the mixture to a baking bowl. Ensure not to overfill the bowl.
3. Preheat the Air Fryer to 300⁰F.
4. Transfer the bowl into the Air Fryer basket and cover with parchment paper. Cook for about 15 minutes.
5. Refrigerate the mixture and garnish with berries and sugary liquid.
6. Serve chilled.

Nutritional value per serving:

Calories: 160kcal, Fat: 20g, Carb: 32g, Proteins: 6g

Blackberry Pancake

This pancake recipe is fluffy and made from scratch. It's also thick and very filling.
Prep time and cooking time: 10 minutes|
Serves: 2

- 1-1/2 cups almond flour
- Salt and pepper to taste
- 3 tbsp. butter
- 3 medium eggs
- 2 tsp. dried basil
- 2 cups blackberry, minced
- 2 tsp. dried parsley

Step-by-Step Directions to Cook It:

1. Preheat the Air Fryer to 250⁰F.
2. Stir all ingredients together in a small bowl.
3. Grease the pancake molds with butter and pour in the batter. Place it in the Air Fryer and cook on both sides till golden brown.
4. Serve with honey.

Nutritional value per serving:

Calories: 152kcal, Fat: 10g, Carb: 22g, Proteins: 5g

Tuna Sandwich

This jazzed-up tuna recipe melts right in your mouth. It's also hot and spicy, which makes it a perfect breakfast for a cold day.
Prep time and cooking time: 15 minutes|
Serves: 2

Ingredients To Use:

- 1 tin tuna
- 1 tbsp. softened butter
- 1 small capsicum, peeled, roasted, and sliced
- 2 slices of white bread

Sauce Ingredients:

- 1/4 cup chopped onion
- 1/2 cup of water
- 1/2 tsp. olive oil
- 1/4 tsp. mustard powder
- Salt and black pepper to taste
- 1 garlic clove, crushed
- 1/4 tbsp. red chili sauce
- 1/4 tbsp. Worcestershire sauce
- 1/2 tbsp. sugar
- 1 tbsp. tomato ketchup

Step-by-Step Directions to Cook It:

1. Cut out edges of the bread and then slice horizontally.
2. Cook sauce ingredients in a saucepan over medium heat. Add the tuna to the sauce and cook until fragrant.
3. Mix the capsicum with sauce and spread the mixture on bread slices.
4. Preheat the Air Fryer to 300⁰F for 5 minutes. Arrange the sandwich side by side into the Air Fryer basket. Cook both sides to a golden brown for about 15 minutes.
5. Serve.

Nutritional value per serving:

Calories: 102kcal, Fat: 8g, Carb: 4g, Proteins: 12g

Bread with Ham and Egg

This recipe is a cross between homemade French toast and ham sandwich, making you excited for the day.
Prep time and cooking time: 30 minutes|
Serves: 1

Ingredients To Use:

- 2 bread slices (brown or white)
- 1/2 lb. sliced ham, cooked
- 1 egg white
- 1 tsp. sugar

Step-by-Step Directions to Cook It:

1. Cut the bread slices diagonally.
2. Beat the egg whites and sugar in a small bowl.
3. Dip the bread into the egg mixture.
4. Preheat the Air Fryer to 350⁰F.
5. Transfer the coated slices into the Air Fryer basket and cook to golden brown on both sides.
6. Serve with slices of ham and cheese(optional)

Nutritional value per serving:

Calories: 232kcal, Fat: 25g, Carb: 28g, Proteins: 18g

Strawberry Tart

Tart filled fruits are very common in some countries like Morocco. The recipe is topped with colourful strawberries that make the tart stunning.
Prep time and cooking time: 30 minutes|
Serves: 2

Ingredients To Use:

- 2 tbsp. powdered sugar
- 1-1/2 cup of plain flour
- 3 tbsp. unsalted butter
- 2 cups cold water

Fillings:

- 1 cup fresh cream
- 3 tbsp. butter
- 2 cups sliced strawberries

Step-by-Step Directions to Cook It:

1. Combine all ingredients apart from fillings in a large bowl. Knead the dough with fresh cold milk and wrap it up with a plastic bag for about 10 minutes.
2. Stir in the filling ingredients in another bowl. Using a rolling pin, roll out the dough into pie and spoon the strawberry

mixture in between. Press pie edges with a fork. Spray the tart with cooking spray.
3. Preheat the Air Fryer to 300⁰F for 5 minutes.
4. Transfer the tart to an Air Fryer basket. Cook to a golden brown and serve with candy sprinkles.

Nutritional value per serving:

Calories: 229kcal, Fat: 9g, Carb: 39g, Proteins: 2g

Almond Milk

The recipe is a creamy, custardy dessert that has a soft texture. It melts when it hits your tongue and can be served with strawberries or dried fruit.
Prep time and cooking time: 10minutes |
Serves: 4

Ingredients To Use:

- 1 tsp. gelatin
- 2 tbsp. custard powder
- 3 tbsp. powdered sugar
- 2 cups almond powder
- 2 cups of milk

Step-by-Step Directions to Cook It:

1. Heat the milk and sugar in a saucepan over medium heat. Thicken the mixture with almond powder, custard powder, and gelatin.
2. Preheat the Air Fryer to 300⁰F.
3. Place the saucepan containing the milk mixture into the Air Fryer.
4. Cook for about 10 minutes and then allow to cool.

Nutritional value per serving:

Calories: 148kcal, Fat: 1.6g, Carb: 28.8g, Proteins: 4.7g

Honey Glazed Donut

This is just the first of many awesome doughnut recipes you will come across in this book. Doughnuts are delicious, soft, and lip-smacking, and this particular recipe requires simple ingredients that can be easily available on your pantry.
Prep time and cooking time: 25 minutes|
Serves: 8

Ingredients To Use:

- 1-1/2 cups powdered sugar
- 2 tsp. honey
- 2 tbsp. milk
- 1 can large flaky-style biscuit dough
- 1/4 cup butter, melted

Step-by-Step Directions to Cook It:

1. Cut out the dough into eight biscuits. Make a hole in the middle of the biscuits using a round cutter. Brush butter on both sides of the biscuits and place them on a parchment or cookie sheet.
2. Place the biscuits in a preheated Air Fryer and bake at 330⁰F for 12 minutes.
3. Transfer the donuts to a cooling rack and allow to cool.
4. In a large-sized bowl, combine honey and powdered sugar. Add milk until the desired consistency is reached. Dunk donuts in the honey mixture.
5. Serve.

Nutritional value per serving:

Calories: 207kcal, Fat: 7g, Carb: 31g, Proteins: 3g

Baked Eggs in Brioche

This classic recipe consists of a perfectly baked egg nestled in the middle of a French bread. It's soft and tasty.
Prep time and cooking time: 15 minutes|

Serves: 3
Ingredients To Use:

- 3 slices cheddar cheese
- 3 medium eggs
- 1 tbsp. chives
- 3 brioche rolls (about 3 × 3 inches in size)
- 3 tbsp. butter, melted
- Salt and pepper, to taste

Step-by-Step Directions to Cook It:

1. Remove the top of the brioche (1 inch) to make a hole using a round cutter. Brush the edges with butter and place cheese inside the brioche.
2. Crack one egg into each brioche and sprinkle in salt, chives, and pepper.
3. Arrange the brioche into the Air Fryer basket and bake for 10 minutes at 330⁰F.
4. Serve.

Nutritional value per serving:

Calories: 140kcal, Fat: 7g, Carb: 15g, Proteins: 3g

Air Fried Creamy Hash Brown Casserole

This easy cheesy breakfast recipe will wholly satisfy you. The casserole is filled with creamy and tasty ingredients.
Prep time and cooking time: 30 minutes|
Serves: 2

Ingredients To Use:

- 1 cup shredded cheddar cheese
- 1/2 cup breadcrumbs
- 2 tbsp. butter, melted
- 10.5 oz. chicken soup
- 1/2 cup sour cream
- 1/2 tsp. salt
- 1-1/2 cups shredded hash brown potatoes
- 1/3 cup chopped onion

1. In a large bowl, combine the cream and soup. Season with salt. Add the onions, hash brown, and cheese. Spoon the mixture into a baking dish and set aside.
2. In another bowl, combine the breadcrumbs and butter. Add the bread mixture evenly into the baking dish.
3. Place the dish into the preheated Air Fryer and bake at 300⁰F for 15 minutes.
4. Serve when cool.

Nutritional value per serving:

Calories: 280kcal, Fat: 20g, Carb: 15g, Proteins: 5g

Greek Feta Baked Omelette

The Greek feta omelette is loaded with Greek flavors that are irresistible. Get the eggs cracking!
Prep time and cooking time: 10 minutes | Serve: 2

Ingredients To Use:

- 1/8 tsp. oregano
- 3 eggs, lightly beaten
- 6 cherry tomatoes, quartered
- 3 tbsp. frozen leaf spinach, thawed and drained
- 2 tbsp. crumbled feta cheese

Step-by-Step Directions to Cook It:

1. Coat the inside of a baking dish with cooking oil. Stir in eggs and add cheese, spinach, and oregano.
2. Place the dish into a preheated Air Fryer.
3. Bake at 330⁰F for 6 minutes.

Nutritional value per serving:

Calories: 207kcal, Fat: 14g, Carb: 6g, Proteins: 16g

Air Fried Garlic Bacon and Potatoes

The golden-brown air-fried potatoes are baked with bacon to make delicious and crispy bites.
Prep time and cooking time: 30 minutes| Serve: 4

Ingredients To Use:

- 2 sprigs of rosemary
- 4 medium-sized Yukon Gold potatoes, peeled and cut into halves
- 4 strips of streaky bacon
- 6 cloves of garlic, smashed
- 3 tsp. vegetable oil

Step-by-Step Directions to Cook It:

1. Preheat the Air Fryer to 390°F.
2. Mix all the ingredients in a large bowl.
3. Roast them in an Air Fryer basket for 25 minutes.
4. Serve.

Nutritional value per serving:

Calories: 226kcal, Fat: 12g, Carb: 28g, Proteins: 10g

Air Fried Sausage

The Air Fryer makes the golden-brown sausage patties by using no stovetop oil. So you don't have to worry about the oil splatter.
Prep time and cooking time: 20 minutes| Serves: 6

Ingredients To Use:

- 1 tsp. salt
- 1 tsp. paprika
- 1 tsp. dried thyme
- 2 tsp. fennel seed
- 1 tsp. maple syrup
- 2 lbs. ground turkey
- 2 tsp. dry rubbed sage

Step-by-Step Directions to Cook It:

1. Combine all ingredients in a large size bowl.
2. Spoon the mixture into a ball, and then make patties using your palm.
3. Place the patties into the Air Fryer basket.
4. Cook at 350⁰F for about 10 minutes. Cook in batches if necessary.
5. Serve.

Nutritional value per serving:

Calories: 170kcal, Fat: 15g, Carb: 10g, Proteins: 6g

Crunchy carrot

Air fried carrot can be added to your breakfast menu, especially if you are a big fan of veggies. Enjoy with honey or maple syrup.
Prep time and cooking time: 22 minutes| Serves: 2

Ingredients To Use:

- 4 carrots, sliced horizontally
- 1 tbsp. olive oil
- Salt to taste

Step-by-Step Directions to Cook It:

1. Coat the carrot with olive oil and season with salt.
2. Preheat the Air Fryer to 360⁰F
3. Cook the carrot until tender.
4. Serve.

Nutritional value per serving:

Calories: 22kcal, Fat: 3g, Carb: 0g, Proteins: 0g

Grilled Cheese

It's super easy to create a crispy delight by spreading the cheese and butter mixture on a toasted bread.

Prep time and cooking time: 15 minutes| Serves: 2

Ingredients To Use:

- 1/2 cup cheddar cheese
- 4 slices white bread
- 1/4 cup butter softened

Step-by-Step Directions to Cook It:

1. Preheat the Air Fryer to 360°F.
2. Spread the butter on each bread.
3. Cover each bread with another slice. Stuff cheese in between the bread slices and place them into the Air Fryer.
4. Cook for about 5 minutes to a golden brown.

Nutritional value per serving:

Calories: 490kcal, Fat: 23g, Carb: 14g, Proteins: 0g

Mini Sausage Roll

Sausage is rolled in flatbread before air fried to golden brown. The good part about this recipe is that it can be served at parties.
Prep time and cooking time: 20 minutes| Serves: 4

Ingredients To Use:

- 1 packet of flatbread
- 10 mini beef sausage

Step-by-Step Directions to Cook It:

1. Slice the bread into triangles. Roll each sausage in the triangular bread until all are well wrapped.
2. Preheats our Air Fryer to 356°F and place the rolls in the fryer basket. Bake them for 15 minutes until crispy, and flip the rolls in between the cooking.

Nutritional value per serving:

Calories: 182kcal, Fat: 12 g, Carb: 8g, Proteins: 6g

Air Fryer Bacon and Egg

This recipe is a total bomb! It's easy to make and cheesy on the inside. The best part is that it requires few ingredients.
Prep time and cooking time: 50 minutes | Serves: 8

Ingredients To Use:

- 1/4 tsp. pepper
- 1 can buttermilk biscuits (5 biscuits)
- 2 oz. cheddar cheese, cut into cubes
- 4 slices bacon, cut into 1/2-inch pieces, cooked to crispy
- 1 tbsp. butter
- 2 eggs, beaten and fried
- 1 egg

Step-by-Step Directions to Cook It:

1. Use a cutter to cut around a parchment paper to make it fit the Air Fryer. Place it in the Air Fryer and spray with cooking oil.
2. Cut out dough into five biscuits and further cut each biscuit into two layers. Spoon the egg and bacon into the center and pinch edges to seal.
3. Mix one egg and water in a small bowl. Coat the biscuit with egg wash using a brush.
4. Place the biscuits in the Air Fryer.
5. Set to 325^{0}F and cook for 10 minutes.
6. Cook for a longer time if necessary.

Nutritional value per serving:

Calories: 200kcal, Fat: 12g, Carb: 17g, Proteins: 7g

Hard-Boiled Egg

You can get a well-done hardboiled egg ready with an Air Fryer. It requires little energy and also saves water. Superb!
Prep time and cooking time: 20 minutes| Serves: 6

Ingredients To Use:

- 6 large eggs

Step-by-Step Directions to Cook It:

1. Preheat the Air Fryer to 270^{0}F.
2. Carefully place the eggs in the Air Fryer and cook for 15 minutes.

Nutritional value per serving:

Calories: 77kcal, Fat: 5g, Carb: 0.5g, Proteins: 3g

Soft Boiled Egg

Low carbs and very easy to cook. Soft boiled eggs can be enjoyed with varieties of the other air-fried recipes in this book, such as Almond Milk and Air Fried Sausage.
Prep time and cooking time: 20 minutes| Serves: 4

Ingredients To Use:

- 4 large eggs

Step-by-Step Directions to Cook It:

1. Preheat the Air Fryer to 270^{0}F.
2. Carefully place the eggs in the Air Fryer and cook for 10 minutes.
3. Allow to cool and enjoy.

Nutritional value per serving:

Calories: 70kcal, Fat: 4g, Carb: 0.5g, Proteins: 4g

Breakfast Potatoes

Air fried breakfast potatoes are loaded with ingredients ranging from bell pepper to onions, potatoes, and cloves. It's worth a try.
Prep time and cooking time: 30 minutes| Serves: 4

Ingredients To Use:

- 1 tbsp. olive oil
- 1/4 tsp. pepper
- 1/2 tsp. salt

- 1/2 tsp. paprika
- 1-1/2 lbs. potatoes, diced and sakes in water
- 1/4 onion (chopped)
- 1 green bell pepper, washed chopped, and soaked in water.
- 2 garlic cloves (minced)

Step-by-Step Directions to Cook It:

1. Combine all ingredients in a bowl and place them in the Air Fryer basket.
2. Cook in the Air Fryer at 350⁰F for 25 minutes. Shake the basket at a 10 minutes interval till it completely cooked. Serve.

Nutritional value per serving:

Calories: 153kcal, Fat: 15g, Carb: 18g, Proteins: 3g

Toast Sticks

There are different ways to make a French toast recipe by using an Air Fryer. In this recipe, you get to try one of those methods.
Prep time and cooking time: 40 minutes|
Serves: 6

Ingredients To Use:

- 2 large eggs
- Kosher salt
- 6 thick slices Pullman, sliced into thirds
- Honey or maple syrup, for serving
- 1/3 cup of heavy cream
- 1/3 cup of whole milk
- 3 tbsp. granulated sugar
- 1/4 tsp. ground cinnamon
- 1/2 tsp. pure vanilla extract

Step-by-Step Directions to Cook It:

1. Whisk all ingredients in a bowl except for the Pullman slices.
2. Dunk in the slices and arrange in an Air Fryer basket.
3. Cook in the Air Fryer at 375⁰F for 8 minutes.
4. Serve with honey or maple syrup.

Nutritional value per serving:

Calories: 192kcal, Fat: 15g, Carb: 10g, Proteins: 8g

Air Fried Mozzarella Sticks

The homemade mozzarella cheese is healthier than the store-bought, and the best part is that all the ingredients can be gotten in the pantry and fridge.
Prep time and cooking time: 55 minutes|
Serves: 6

Ingredients To Use:

- 12 oz. package mozzarella cheese sticks, cut into halves
- 1/4 cup mayonnaise
- 1/2 tsp. garlic powder
- 1 large egg
- 1/4 cup all-purpose flour
- 1/4 cup fine, dry breadcrumbs
- 1/2 tsp. onion powder

Step-by-Step Directions to Cook It:

1. Freeze the cheese sticks for 30 minutes.
2. Beat the egg and mayonnaise in a bowl. Add the onions, breadcrumbs, onion, and garlic powder.
3. Dip the mozzarella sticks in the egg mixture and then in the flour mixture. Place them in the Air Fryer and cook for 5 minutes at 370⁰F.
4. Cook in batches if necessary
5. Serve with sauce.

Nutritional value per serving:

Calories: 232kcal, Fat: 20g, Carb: 10g, Proteins: 6g

Air Fried Beignets

There's so much more you can make with an Air Fryer, and beignet is one of them. Pull out your Air Fryer and start cooking.
Prep time and cooking time: 20 minutes|
Serves: 4

- 1-1/2 tsp. melted butter
- 1/2 tsp. baking powder
- 1/2 tsp. vanilla extract
- 1 pinch salt
- 2 tbsp. confectioners' sugar
- cooking spray
- 1/2 cup all-purpose flour
- 1/4 cup white sugar
- 1/8 cup of water
- 1 large egg, separated

Step-by-Step Directions to Cook It:

1. Preheat the Air Fryer to 370°F.
2. Using a cooking spray to grease the silicon egg mold.
3. Combine all ingredients except the egg white.
4. Use an electric mixer to mix the egg white until soft peaks are formed. Fold into batter.
5. Fill the mixture in a silicon mold and then place it into the Air Fryer.
6. Cook for 10 minutes and remove it from the mold.
7. Place it on a parchment sheet and replace it into the Air Fryer. Cook for another 4 minutes. Sprinkle sugar on the beignets and serve.

Nutritional value per serving:

Calories: 88kcal, Fat: 1.7g, Carb: 16g, Proteins: 1.8g

Air Fried Caramelized Banana

This gooey snack can be served with a cup of warm milk. It's also very healthy and customizable.
Prep time and cooking time: 7 minutes|
Serves: 1

Ingredients To Use:

- 1 tbsp. coconut sugar
- Yogurt as toppings
- 2 bananas, peel and slice lengthwise
- 1/4 lemon, juiced

Step-by-Step Directions to Cook It:

1. Drizzle the lemon juice and sprinkle sugar atop banana.
2. Place the banana on a round parchment paper and put it into an Air Fryer.
3. Cook for 8 minutes at 400°F.
4. Top with yogurt.

Nutritional value per serving:

Calories: 60kcal, Fat: 10g, Carb: 6g, Proteins: 10g

Donut Sticks

This customized sugar-coated donut recipe is cooked in the Air Fryer, and best served warm.
Prep time and cooking time: 35 minutes|
Serves: 8

Ingredients To Use:

- 1 oz. refrigerated roll dough, cut into 1/2 inch lengthwise
- 1/2 cup sugar
- 1/2 cup flavored fruit jam
- 2 tsp. ground cinnamon
- 1/4 cup butter, melted

Step-by-Step Directions to Cook It:

1. Dunk the donut sticks in butter and arrange in an Air Fryer basket.

2. Set the Air Fryer to 380⁰F and cook the sticks for about 5 minutes.
3. Combine the cinnamon and sugar in a small bowl. Coat the air-fried donut in the cinnamon mixture.

Calories: 266kcal, Fat: 11.8g, Carb: 37.6g, Proteins: 2.2g

Stuffed Bell Pepper

To start your day with a low carb meal rich in protein, try out the tenderly cooked stuffed bell pepper.
Prep time and cooking time: 20 minutes| Serves: 2

Ingredients To Use:

- 1 tsp. olive oil
- 4 eggs
- Salt and pepper to taste
- 1 bell pepper, halved and seeded

Step-by-Step Directions to Cook It:

1. Brush oil on bell pepper edges.
2. Crack two eggs into the bell pepper with the sunny side facing up. Season with salt and pepper.
3. Arrange the bell pepper into the Air Fryer basket.
4. Set the Air Fryer to 390F and cook for 13 minutes.
5. Serve.

Nutritional value per serving:

Calories: 164kcal, Fat: 10g, Carb: 4g, Proteins: 11g

Parmesan Baked Eggs

Air fried parmesan baked eggs make a tasty breakfast, and it's also time-saving when cooked in ramekins.
Prep time and cooking time: 10 minutes| Serves: 3

Ingredients To Use:

- 6 medium eggs
- 3 tbsp. Parmesan cheese, grated
- 3 tbsp. butter
- 1 shallot, minced
- 6 tsp. heavy cream
- 1 tbsp. minced fresh rosemary
- 1/2 tbsp. minced fresh thyme
- Salt and pepper, to taste

Step-by-Step Directions to Cook It:

1. Evenly divide the butter, thyme, rosemary, and shallot into three small ramekins.
2. Preheat the Air Fryer to 350⁰F.
3. Transfer the ramekins to an Air Fryer basket and cook for about 2 minutes, until the butter melts.
4. Carefully move out from the Air Fryer basket. Add cream and egg into the ramekins. Sprinkle in cheese atop the eggs and bake for 10 minutes.
5. Remove the ramekins from the oven and allow to cool before serving. Sprinkle in salt and pepper.

Nutritional value per serving:

Calories: 165kcal, Fat: 28g, Carb: 12g, Proteins: 10g

Chapter 2: Poultry Recipes

Air Fried Chicken Fillets

This recipe is versatile and perfect for a quick protein fix. The breadcrumbs also add texture to the chicken.

Prep time and cooking time: 30 minutes| Serves: 3

Ingredients To Use:

- 2 eggs, whisked
- 1/2 tsp. salt
- 12 oz. chicken fillets
- 4 oz. flour
- 1 tsp. ground black pepper
- 2 tbsp. vegetable oil
- 8 tbsp. breadcrumbs

Step-by-Step Directions to Cook It:

1. Preheat the Air Fryer to 330°F.
2. Mix the oil, pepper, and salt in a small bowl.
3. Crack the eggs and put the flour in separate bowls, and set aside.
4. Dip the chicken in the flour and then in the egg. Coat with the bread crumbs and oil mixture afterward.
5. Arrange the chicken into the Air Fryer basket and cook for 10 minutes at 390⁰F, until golden brown.

Nutritional value per serving:

Calories: 165kcal, Fat: 3.6g, Carb: 5g, Proteins: 31g

Prawn Seasoned Chicken Drumsticks

This seasoned prawn recipe gives the chicken a lovely seafood taste that will amaze your friends and family.

Prep time and cooking time: 3o minutes| Serves: 3

Ingredients To Use:

- 3/4 tsp. sugar
- 10-1/2 oz. chicken drumsticks
- 3 tsp. prawn paste
- 1/2 tsp. Shaoxing wine
- 1 tsp. sesame oil
- 1 tsp. ginger juice
- 6 tsp. vegetable oil

Step-by-Step Directions to Cook It:

1. Prepare the marinade by mixing the prawn paste, Shaoxing wine, ginger, oil, and juice in a small bowl.
2. Marinate the chicken for about 4 hours in the refrigerator.
3. Preheat the Air Fryer for about 5 minutes at 356⁰F.
4. Coat the chicken with cooking spray and then place it in the Air Fryer. Cook the chicken for about 15 minutes and flip at intervals until golden brown.

Nutritional value per serving:

Calories: 282kcal, Fat: 10g, Carb: 12g, Proteins: 20g

Honey Lemon Chicken

The sweet, tangy taste boosts the flavor of the chicken. Marinate the chicken for longer hours if desired.

Prep time and cooking time: 7 hours| Serves: 4

Ingredients To Use:

- 1/4 tsp. white pepper powder
- 1/2 tsp. sea salt

- 1/2 black pepper, crushed
- 2 tbsp. fresh lemon juice
- 16 chicken wings; washed & pat dry
- 2 tbsp. pure honey
- 2 tbsp. light soy sauce

Step-by-Step Directions to Cook It:

1. Mix all the marinade ingredients into a shallow bowl. Marinate the chicken and put it in the refrigerator for 8 hours.
2. Remove the chicken and discard the marinade. Allow the chicken to rest for half an hour and arrange into the Air Fryer basket. Cook in the Air Fryer for about 15 minutes at 350°F and serve with lemon wedges.

Nutritional value per serving:

Calories: 299kcal, Fat: 24g, Carb: 13g, Proteins: 7g

Air Fried Chicken Breast

This air-fried chicken breast is a classic recipe. It's juiced up with vinaigrette and fork-tender.
Prep time and cooking time: 2hours 30 minutes | Serves: 4

Ingredients To Use:

- 3 tbsp. red wine vinegar
- 1 tbsp. shallot, chopped
- 1 tsp. kosher salt
- 2 tsp. rosemary leaves, chopped
- 2/3 cup olive oil
- 2 garlic clove, chopped
- 1/4 tsp. pepper flakes, crushed
- 1/3 cup green olives, chopped
- 2 tbsp. capers
- 4 boneless chicken breast, skinned, cut into half

Step-by-Step Directions to Cook It:

1. Combine all the vinaigrette ingredients in a small bowl until an emulsion is formed. Dip the chicken in half of the vinaigrette and marinate in a refrigerator for 2 hours.
2. Preheat the Air Fryer to 380°F.
3. Spray cooking oil on the Air Fryer basket.
4. Cook the chicken for 15 minutes. Flip to the other side after half the time.
5. Add olives and capers into the remaining vinaigrette and serve with the air fried chicken.

Nutritional value per serving:

Calories: 205kcal, Fat: 22 g, Carb: 2g, Proteins: 17g

Garlic Chicken Nuggets

It's easy to make air-fried homemade chicken nuggets without coming to a store. Spice with garlic for a better flavor
Prep time and cooking time: 40 minutes| Serves: 2

Ingredients To Use:

- 1/2 lb. of flour
- 3 tbsp. of garlic powder
- 1 tbsp. of black pepper
- 1 tsp. of salt
- 1 egg, whisked
- 2 chicken breast, boneless, skinless, and cut into pieces

Step-by-Step Directions to Cook It:

1. Combine the garlic, pepper, salt, and flour in a shallow dish. Whisk the egg and transfer to another shallow bowl.
2. Set the Air Fryer to 356°F.
3. Coat the chicken with eggs and then flour mixture.
4. Arrange the chicken into the Air Fryer basket and cook for about 20 minutes.

Nutritional value per serving:

Calories: 275kcal, Fat: 15g, Carb: 25g, Proteins: 18g

Mustard Chicken

The recipe provides you with a lip-smacking meal that's perfect for a quick get together.
Prep time and cooking time: 45 minutes|
Serves: 4

Ingredients To Use:

- 1/2 tsp. ground pepper
- 1/4 cup of Dijon mustard
- 1 tsp. dried tarragon leaves, crushed
- 4 boneless chicken breast, skinned
- 2 tsp. olive oil

Step-by-Step Directions to Cook It:

1. Preheat the Air Fryer to 350⁰F.
2. Mix all the ingredients in a large-sized bowl.
3. Place the chicken in the Air Fryer basket.
4. Cook the chicken for about 20 minutes.
5. Enjoy.

Nutritional value per serving:

Calories: 225kcal, Fat: 15g, Carb: 0g, Proteins: 19g

Chicken Salad Sandwich

Air fried chicken adds a good flavor and texture to your salad sandwich. It's a perfectly healthy breakfast.
Prep time: 2 hours | Cook time: 30 minutes | Serves: 2

Ingredients:

- 2 tbsp. olive oil
- 1/2 tbsp. garlic powder
- 2 toasted onion rolls
- 2 chicken breast
- Salt to taste

Chicken salad ingredients:

- 2 smoked chicken breast chopped
- 1 tsp. chimichurri
- 2 tbsp. mayo
- 1 tbsp. chopped peppadews

- Salt and lime to taste

Step-by-Step Directions to Cook It:

1. Combine the chicken and garlic, salt, and olive oil in a glass bowl. Marinate for about two hours in the refrigerator.
2. Preheat the Air Fryer to 340⁰F. Place the marinated chicken inside the Air Fryer basket and then cook for about 30 minutes.
3. In a large bowl, combine the mayo and chimichurri. Add the peppadews, salt, chopped chicken, grilled corn, and lime. Mix and stuff into toasted buns or bread.
4. Serve.

Nutritional value per Serving:

Calories: 277.7kcal, Carbs: 65g, Fat: 51g, Protein: 25g

Air Fried Chicken and Pecan Salad

This is another healthy air fried recipe that's almost irresistible.
Prep time and cooking time: 2 hours 50 minutes | Serves: 4

Ingredients To Use:

- 1 cup sweet pickle brine
- 2/3 cup of cooked wheat berries
- 12 oz. chicken breast, boned and skinned
- 2/3 cup chopped sweet gherkins
- 1 tsp. ground black pepper
- 1/2 tsp. kosher salt
- 1/2 cup chopped pecans
- 1/2 cup mayonnaise
- 1/4 cup cider vinegar
- 1 tsp. dried dill
- 1/4 tsp. celery seed
- 1 cup finely chopped celery
- 2 large tomatoes, sliced

1. In a medium-sized bowl, combine the chicken and brine. Marinate the chicken in the refrigerator for at least 2 hours.
2. Preheat the Air Fryer to 380⁰F.
3. Take out the chicken and air fry for about 20 minutes, until golden brown.
4. Remove the chicken from the Air Fryer and allow it to cool. Shred the chicken with a fork.
5. In a large serving bowl, combine the chicken with the remaining ingredients. Serve.

Nutritional value per serving:

Calories: 280kcal, Fat: 20 g, Carb: 10g, Proteins: 16g

Chicken Sliders

This Air Fryer recipe is done so nicely and tenderly that it melts against the roof of your mouth.
Prep time and cooking time: 50 minutes| Serves: 2

Ingredients To Use:
- 1-1/2 lbs. chicken thighs, boned
- 8 hamburger buns, split

Sauce ingredients:
- 1/2 cup root beer
- 1/2 tsp. garlic powder
- 2 tbsp. fresh lemon juice
- 1/8 tsp. ground cayenne pepper
- 1 tsp. prepared chili powder
- 1 tbsp. olive oil
- 1/2 cup yellow onion, chopped
- 2/3 cup ketchup

Step-by-Step Directions to Cook It:
1. Sauté the sauce ingredients in a large skillet over medium heat until fragrant.

2. Spray the Air Fryer basket with cooking oil.
3. Dip the chicken in the sauce ingredients and cook on both sides for about 15 minutes.
4. Place the chicken on a plate and shred it with a fork.
5. Place the shredded chicken in between the buns and serve with coleslaw.

Nutritional value per serving:

Calories: 192kcal, Fat: 5g, Carb: 8g, Proteins: 20g

Garlic Turkey Rolls

This recipe provides you with a savory lunch that's tastier than the traditional plain turkey sandwich.
Prep time and cooking time: 55 minutes| Serves: 4

Ingredients To Use:
- 1-1/2 tsp. of ground cumin
- 1/2 tsp. of ground chili
- 1-1/2 oz. of parsley, finely chopped
- 1 tsp. of cinnamon
- 1 clove of garlic, crushed
- 1 small sized onion, finely chopped
- 1 tsp. of salt
- 1 lb. of turkey breast fillets, cut into 2/3 horizontal strip length.
- 6 tsp. of olive oil

Step-by-Step Directions to Cook It:
1. Combine the chili, cinnamon garlic, cumin, pepper, olive and salt in a medium bowl. Take out about one tablespoon of the mixture and set aside.
2. Sprinkle the parsley and onion into the pepper mixture and stir.
3. Preheat the Air Fryer to 356°F.
4. Spoon the herb mixture on the meat and then roll firmly from the shorter end. Tie

the roll with a butcher's string and then brush it with the remaining spice mixture.
5. Arrange the rolls in the Air Fryer and cook for 40 minutes.

Nutritional value per serving:

Calories: 287kcal, Fat: 17.1g, Carb: 16.6g, Proteins: 16.9g

Chicken with Ginger

This ginger chicken recipe produces perfectly cut pieces of chicken which is coated in aromatic spices and air fried to perfection.
Prep time and cooking time: 3 hours| Serves: 2

Ingredients To Use:

- Melted butter
- 1/4 cup lemon juice
- 1/2 tsp. dried thyme
- Kosher salt
- Ground chili pepper
- 1 tbsp. ginger, grated
- 1 tsp. garlic clove, minced
- 2 tbsp. olive oil
- 1 bay leaf
- 3 lbs. chicken, sliced

Step-by-Step Directions to Cook It:

1. In a small shallow bowl, combine the garlic, salt, ginger, lemon, thyme, and pepper.
2. Pour the marinade over the chicken in a large bowl and put it in the refrigerator for at least 2 hours. Discard the marinade and oil the Air Fryer basket.
3. Preheat the Air Fryer to 350⁰F and cook the chicken for about 25 minutes, until golden brown on both sides.
4. Drizzle the melted butter over the chicken and serve.

Nutritional value per serving:

Calories: 310 kcal, Fat: 16 g, Carb: 6 g, Proteins:37 g

Spiced Drumsticks

The recipe does not require marination; all it takes is medium heat and balanced spices.
Prep time and cooking time: 30 minutes| Serves: 4

Ingredients To Use:

- 6 tsp. of Montreal chicken spices
- 6 tsp. of chicken seasoning
- 6 tsp. of ground black pepper
- 1 tsp. of olive oil
- 1 tsp. of salt
- 4 chicken drumsticks

Step-by-Step Directions to Cook It:

1. Combine all the spices and seasonings in a large bowl. Coat the chicken with olive oil.
2. Use your palms to rub the spices on the chicken.
3. Preheat the Air Fryer to 200°F. Place the chicken into the Air Fryer and allow it to cook for 10 minutes.
4. Lower the heat to 150°F and cook for another 8 minutes.

Nutritional value per serving:

Calories: 180kcal, Fat: 2g, Carb: 5g, Proteins: 20g

Buffalo Chicken Bowl

It's easy to throw together a chicken bowl It's loaded with veggies and also topped with irresistible tangy blue cheese.
Prep time and cooking time: 20 minutes | Serves: 4

Ingredients To Use:

- Blue cheese, for topping

- 2 tbsp. wing sauce
- 6 oz. cooked chicken breasts, diced
- 1-1/2 oz. blue cheese, crumbled
- 12 wonton wrappers
- 1/4 cup softened cream cheese
- 2 tbsp. ranch salad dressing

1. In a medium-sized bowl, combine the hot wing sauce, softened cream cheese, chicken cheese, and ranch dressing.
2. Line the inside of the mini muffin pan with a piece of wonton wrapper each.
3. Fill each pan with the chicken mixture and ensure it doesn't get filled to the top.
4. Set the Air Fryer to 330⁰F.
5. Place the pan in the Air Fryer and bake for 10 minutes, until golden brown.
6. Top with blue cheese and serve.

Nutritional value per serving:

Calories: 249kcal, Fat: 14g, Carb: 18g, Proteins: 11g

Chicken and Potatoes

This crispy chicken is served over hearty air-fried purple potatoes.
Prep time and cooking time: 30 minutes|
Serves: 2

Ingredients To Use:

- 1/2 cup purple sweet potato, peeled and rinsed
- 1/2 cup of salad green
- 1/2 portion of chicken, halved, rinsed, and pat dry
- 1 tsp. olive
- 1 tbsp. herbs chicken spices

Step-by-Step Directions to Cook It:

1. Combine the spices and olive oil in a large bowl. Dip in the chicken and marinate for at least 8 hours in the refrigerator.
2. Set the Air Fryer to 350°F.
3. Spray the Air Fryer basket with cooking oil and cook the potatoes in the Air Fryer for about 10 minutes.
4. Add the chicken into the Air Fryer basket and cook for about 12 minutes, until brown, nicely colored, and tender.
5. Serve with greens.

Nutritional value per serving:

Calories: 255kcal, Fat: 12g, Carb: 23g, Proteins: 16g

Chicken Nachos

Chicken nachos are arranged in a nice pile and topped with a tasty blend of Mexican shredded cheese, tomatoes, and beans.
Prep time and cooking time: 30 minutes|
Serves: 4

Ingredients To Use:

- 2 medium tomatoes, seeded and diced
- 15 oz. can black beans, rinsed and drained
- 1 tsp. garlic powder
- 1 tsp. salt
- 4 scallions, chopped
- 3/4 cup chopped fresh cilantro
- 8-oz. shredded cheese, Mexican blend
- 2 tsp. chili powder
- 2 tsp. ground cumin
- 2 cups chopped or shredded cooked chicken breasts
- Tortilla chips
- 1 jalapeño, chopped

Step-by-Step Directions to Cook It:

1. Combine the chili powder, garlic powder, cumin, and salt in a small bowl.
2. Add the chicken into the mixture and toss evenly to coat.
3. Line the Air Fryer basket with aluminum foil. Arrange the chips inside the Air

Fryer basket and top with the chicken, beans, tomatoes, scallion, and cheese.
4. Set the Air Fryer to 300⁰F and bake for 15 minutes. Garnish with cilantro and jalapeño.

Nutritional value per serving:

Calories: 295kcal, Fat: 15g, Carb: 10g, Proteins: 8g

Turkey Breast

The turkey breast is cooked to tender and then served with a mixture of sauce, sages, lemon juice, cumin pepper butter, and chives.
Prep time and cooking time: 1 hour | Serves: 4

Ingredients To Use:
- 4 tbsp. butter
- Ground pepper
- 2 tbsp. olive oil
- 1/4 tsp. ground cumin
- 1 tsp. Worcestershire sauce
- A handful of sage, chopped
- 1 lb. turkey breast steaks, pound and slice to pieces
- Kosher salt
- 1 tbsp. fresh lemon juice
- 1/4 cup chives, chopped

Step-by-Step Directions to Cook It:
1. Oil the Air Fryer basket and set the temperature of the Air Fryer to 350⁰F.
2. Season the turkey with pepper and salt.
3. Pulse the cumin, lemon juice, salt, sauce, chives, and salt in a blender.
4. Air fry the turkey and serve with the chives mixture.

Nutritional value per serving:

Calories: 250kcal, Fat: 10g, Carb: 5g, Proteins: 15g

Glazed Rosemary Chicken

This rich flavored glazed rosemary recipe takes your chicken to a whole new savory level.
Prep time and cooking time: 20 minutes| Serves: 2

Ingredients To Use:
- 1 spring rosemary, roughly chopped
- 1/2 tsp. red pepper flakes
- 2 tsp. honey
- 2 chicken breasts, rinsed and pat dry
- 1 tsp. olive oil
- ground pepper, to taste
- kosher salt, to taste

Step-by-Step Directions to Cook It:
1. Brush the chicken with olive oil. Season the chicken (skin-side up) with pepper, salt, red pepper, honey, and rosemary.
2. Preheat the Air Fryer to 330⁰F and bake the chicken for 15 minutes, until tender.

Nutritional value per serving:

Calories: 220kcal, Fat: 18g, Carb: 9g Proteins: 9g

Air Fried Butter Milk Chicken

The chicken is firstly marinated with seasoned buttermilk before air fried to crispy tenderness.
Prep time and cooking time: 8 hours 40 minutes| Serves: 4

Ingredients To Use:
- 2 chicken breasts

Marinade
- 2 cups buttermilk
- 2 tsp. salt
- 2 tsp. black pepper
- 1 tsp. cayenne pepper

Seasoned Flour

- 2 cups flour
- 1 tbsp. baking powder
- 1 tbsp. garlic powder
- 1 tbsp. paprika powder
- 1 tsp. salt
- 1 tsp. pepper

Step-by-Step Directions to Cook It:

1. To prepare the marinade, combine the pepper, salt, and chicken pieces in a large bowl. Add the buttermilk and refrigerate for at least 8 hours.
2. In another separate large bowl, mix the flour, paprika, salt, pepper, baking powder, and garlic powder. Take out the marinated chicken and discard the marinade. Coat the marinated chicken with the seasoned flour mixture.
3. Transfer the coated chicken into the Air Fryer basket and cook in a 370⁰F preheated oil-coated Air Fryer.
4. Cook the chicken for about 30 minutes and spray cooking oil at intervals.
5. Serve.

Nutritional value per serving:

Calories: 294kcal, Fat: 15g, Carb: 10g, Proteins: 18g

Sauced Chicken Wings

A simple blend of sweet-based sauces, honey, and sour wine makes funky savory glazed wings.
Prep time and cooking time: 1 hour 10 minutes| Serves: 8

Ingredients To Use:

- 1-1/2 cup of honey
- 21 pieces of chicken wings, washed and pat dry
- 1-1/2 oz. of canola oil
- 1 tsp. light soy sauce
- 3 tsp. oyster sauce

- 3 tsp. dark soy sauce
- 1/2 tsp. pepper
- Huo Tiao Chinese Wine

Step-by-Step Directions to Cook It:

1. To prepare the marinade, combine the soy sauces, Huo Tiao wine, oyster sauce, oil, pepper, and honey.
2. Transfer the marinade and chicken wings to a ziploc bag and marinate in the refrigerator for about 30 minutes. Line the Air Fryer basket with aluminum foil and arrange the chicken into it.
3. Preheat the Air Fryer to 392°F. Cook the chicken for about 30 minutes, until golden brown.

Nutritional value per serving:

Calories: 290kcal, Fat: 17g, Carb: 14g, Proteins: 19g

Chicken Jerks

This distinctive seasoned jerk recipe is made with aromatic spices that adds a lovely flavor to the chicken.
Prep time and cooking time: 1 hour |Serves: 5

Ingredients To Use:

- 1 tsp. of white pepper
- 3 tsp. of chopped fresh thyme
- 6 cloves of garlic, finely diced
- 1 tsp. of cinnamon
- 4 green onions, finely chopped
- 2-1/2 ounces of lime juice
- 1 tsp. cayenne pepper
- 6 tsp. of sugar
- 30 chicken wings
- 8 tablespoons of red wine vinegar
- 6 tsp. of soy sauce
- 1 tsp. of salt
- 6 tsp. of vegetable oil
- 3 tsp. of grated ginger

- 1 habanera pepper, seeded and finely chopped

1. Mix all the ingredients in a large glass bowl and then toss with chicken pieces. Place the bowl in the refrigerator and marinate for at least 6 hours.
2. Preheat the Air Fryer to 390⁰F.
3. Take out the wings and discard the marinade.
4. Cook the chicken in the Air Fryer for about 20 minutes.
5. Drizzle ranch dressing atop chicken and serve.

Calories: 220kcal, Fat: 18g, Carb: 19g, Proteins: 24g

Teriyaki Chicken Wings

If you are a lover of well-flavored chicken wings, you'll love this recipe. This teriyaki chicken wing recipe is great for parties, day out, and a big game day.
Prep time and cooking time: 50 minutes|
Serves: 6

- 24 chicken wings, steamed
- 5 tbsp. chopped cilantro, chopped

- 3 tbsp. rice wine vinegar
- 1/4 cup brown sugar
- 5 garlic cloves, minced
- 1 cup of soy sauce
- 1 cup of grapefruit juice
- 1/4 cup hoisin sauce
- 2 tbsp. ketchup
- 2 tbsp. fresh and grated ginger

1. Preheat the Air Fryer to 330⁰F.

2. Transfer the steamed wings into the Air Fryer and bake for about 30 minutes. Coat with cooking oil and flip at intervals.
3. Mix the sauce ingredients in a saucepan and cook over medium heat until a paste is formed.
4. Serve the chicken with sauce and sprinkle in cilantro.
5. Serve.

Calories: 271.9kcal, Fat: 9.8g, Carb: 19.9g, Proteins: 24.7g

Tabasco Chicken

This tabasco chicken recipe is loaded with great flavor and made of simple ingredients easily accessible at the local grocery store.
Prep time and cooking time: 30 minutes |
Serves: 4

- 6 chicken legs, tip trimmed off

- 1 tbsp. Tabasco sauce
- 1 tbsp. ketchup
- 1 tbsp. soy sauce
- 1 tbsp. cider vinegar

1. Combine the marinade ingredients in a small bowl and toss the chicken legs into it.
2. Preheat the Air Fryer to 330⁰F.
3. Cook the chicken for about 20 minutes on both sides until golden brown.

Calories: 295cal, Fat: 12g, Carb: 0.6 g, Proteins: 15g

Turkey Fritters

This easy homemade recipe is a great idea when you have a leftover turkey that needs to be used up.

Prep time and cooking time: 30 minutes|
Serves: 4

- 2 or 3 green chilies finely chopped
- 1-1/2 tbsp. lemon juice
- Salt and pepper to taste
- 1 lb. minced turkey
- 3 tbsp. ginger finely chopped
- 1-2 tbsp. fresh coriander leaves

Step-by-Step Directions to Cook It:

1. Combine the ingredients in a clean bowl.
2. Shape the mixture into round and flat patties using your palms.
3. Wet the patties slightly with water.
4. Set the Air Fryer to160⁰F.
5. Cook the patties in the Air Fryer basket for about 30 minutes until evenly cooked.
6. Serve.

Nutritional value per serving:

Calories: 196kcal, Fat: 10g, Carb: 6g, Proteins: 15g

Duck Fingers

The recipe is another twist to the traditional chicken recipe which is loved by kids and adults.

Prep time and cooking time: 30 minutes|
Serves: 4

Ingredients To Use:

- 1 cup of milk
- 3 medium eggs
- 1 cup of rice flour
- 1 tsp. garlic powder
- Salt and pepper to taste
- 1 tsp. chili powder
- 2 duck breast, cut into strips

Step-by-Step Directions to Cook It:

1. Combine the eggs and milk in a large bowl and toss the duck strips into the bowl.
2. Mix all the remaining ingredients in another bowl and transfer the duck into the mixture.
3. Preheat the Air Fryer to 220⁰F and cook the duck fingers for about 20 minutes until golden brown.
4. Serve.

Nutritional value per serving:

Calories: 195kcal, Fat: 10g, Carb: 12g, Proteins: 8g

Turkey Burger Cutlets

The turkey burger cutlet is a must-try for burger lovers. The patties can also be stored in a refrigerator overnight.

Prep time and cooking time: 30 minutes |
Serves: 4

Ingredients To Use:

- 1/2 lb. minced turkey
- 1/2 cup breadcrumbs
- A pinch of salt to taste
- 1/4 tsp. ginger finely chopped
- 1 green chili finely chopped
- 1 tsp. lemon juice
- 1 tbsp. Fresh coriander leaves, chopped
- 1/4 tsp. red chili powder
- 1/2 cup of boiled peas
- 1/4 tsp. cumin powder
- 1/4 tbsp. dried mango powder

Step-by-Step Directions to Cook It:

1. Mix all the ingredients in a large bowl. Shape the mixture into cutlets using your palms.
2. Preheat the Air Fryer to 250⁰F.
3. Cook the cutlets for about 15 minutes and stuff them in between the toasted

buns.

Nutritional value per serving:

Calories: 237kcal, Fat: 15g, Carb: 10g, Proteins: 12g

Pesto Chicken

Chicken air fried with pesto is great for parties, holidays, picnics, and birthdays.
Prep time and cooking time: 40 minutes|
Serves: 4

Ingredients To Use:

- 2 tbsp. olive oil
- 1/4 cup of basil pesto
- Kosher salt
- Ground cayenne pepper
- 1-1/2 lbs. chicken breast

Step-by-Step Directions to Cook It:

1. Preheat the Air Fryer to 320°F.
2. In a small-sized bowl, combine the pesto and oil. Set the mixture aside.
3. Oil the chicken and season it with pepper and salt.
4. Cook in the Air Fryer for about 20 minutes, until tender.
5. Serve.

Nutritional value per serving:

Calories: 180kcal, Fat:12 g, Carb: 0g, Proteins: 22g

Chicken Wrapped in Bacon

The chicken remains moist and savory wrapped in bacon and cheese before it is cooked in the Air Fryer.
Prep time and cooking time: 20 minutes |
Serves: 4

Ingredients To Use:

- 1 tbsp. garlic soft cheese
- 6 Rashers unsmoked back bacon
- 1 chicken breast, chopped

Step-by-Step Directions to Cook It:

1. Spread out the bacon and lay some cheese atop it.
2. Arrange the chicken atop the bacon and cheese. Roll them up and tie up with a butcher string or a cocktail stick.
3. Place the rolled-up chicken in the Air Fryer and cook for about 15 minutes at 356°F.

Nutritional value per serving:

Calories: 198kcal, Fat: 7.9g, Carb: 1.5g, Proteins: 30.3g

Chicken Kiev

Be ready to savor one of the most flavourful chicken you've ever tasted with this recipe
Prep time and cooking time: 35 minutes |
Serves: 2

Ingredients To Use:

- Breadcrumbs
- 1 medium chicken breast, flattened and chopped.
- 1/2 cup soft cheese
- 1/4 tsp. garlic puree
- 1tsp. parsley
- Medium egg (beaten)
- Salt and pepper, as desired

Step-by-Step Directions to Cook It:

1. Combine ½ of the parsley, garlic, and soft cheese in a small bowl.
2. Stuff the mixture in between the chicken.
3. In another small bowl, combine the salt, pepper, parsley, and bread crumbs.
4. Coat the chicken in beaten eggs and then in the bread crumbs mixture.
5. Cook the chicken in the Air Fryer at 350°F for about 30 minutes.

6. Serve.

Nutritional value per serving:

Calories: 322kcal, Fat: 19g, Carb: 28g, Proteins: 21g

Garlic Herb Turkey

The Air Fryer cooks this turkey recipe to a nice juicy fork-tender. For this year's Thanksgiving, don't forget to use an Air Fryer for a yummy buttery turkey.
Prep time and cooking time: 1 hour 10 minutes | Serves: 6

Ingredients To Use:

- 3 cloves garlic, minced
- 1 tsp. freshly chopped thyme
- 2 lb. turkey breast, rinsed and pat dry
- Kosher salt and pepper to taste
- 4 tbsp. butter, melted
- 1 tsp. freshly chopped rosemary

Step-by-Step Directions to Cook It:

1. Season the turkey with pepper and salt.
2. Mix the thyme, rosemary and butter in a small bowl.
3. Transfer the turkey to oil-coated Air Fryer basket and cook at 380ºF for about 40 minutes.
4. Flip the turkey at intervals and cook until fork-tender.
5. Rest on a platter before serving.

Nutritional value per serving:

Calories: 226kcal, Fat: 19g, Carb: 5g, Proteins: 34g

Chicken Breast with Tarragon Mustard Paste

This recipe is a no-brainer weekend dinner delight. You can boost its flavor by marinating the chicken breasts.
Prep time and cooking time: 20minutes|

Serves: 4

Ingredients To Use:

- 1 cup Dijon mustard
- 2 tbsp. olive oil
- 1/2 tsp. ground pepper
- 4 chicken breast, halved, boned, and skinned
- 1 tbsp. dried tarragon leaves

Step-by-Step Directions to Cook It:

1. Combine all the ingredients and then set aside.
2. Preheat the Air Fryer to 320ºF.
3. Transfer the chicken to the Air Fryer and cook for about 10 minutes, and flip the chicken to the other side at intervals.
4. Serve.

Nutritional value per serving:

Calories: 202kcal, Fat: 8g, Carb: 4g, Proteins: 18g

Hoisin Glazed Chicken Thighs

The sauce gives the chicken thighs a sweet, smoky flavor. The recipe is best served with rice.
Prep time and cooking time: 20 minutes| Serves: 4

Ingredients To Use:

- 8 chicken thighs
- Olive oil
- Sea salt
- Ground black pepper
- 1-1/2 hoisin ginger sauce

Step-by-Step Directions to Cook It:

1. Rinse the chicken thighs and pat dry with a paper towel. Season them with pepper and salt. Coat the chicken with oil and transfer to a preheated Air Fryer.
2. Brush the sauce atop chicken and cook for about 15 minutes at 320ºF.

3. Brush the sauce atop chicken frequently at intervals until fork-tender.
4. Serve.

Calories: 242kcal, Fat: 15g, Carb: 5g, Proteins: 19g

BlackBerry Glazed Chicken

This fruit-infused chicken recipe is rich in antioxidants, giving you a healthy and tasty experience.
Prep time and cooking time: 30 minutes|
Serves: 4

Ingredients To Use:

- 6 oz. fresh blackberries
- 1/4 cup of water
- 2 tbsp. white wine vinegar
- 1 tbsp. sugar
- 2 tbsp. cold butter
- 1 tbsp. whole-grain mustard
- 4 chicken thighs, rinsed and pat dried
- 4 drumsticks, rinsed and pat dried
- Sea salt and ground black pepper to taste
- Fresh, flat-leaf parsley

Step-by-Step Directions to Cook It:

1. Preheat the Air Fryer to 340⁰F.
2. Spray the Air Fryer basket with cooking oil.
3. In a small-medium skill, add berries, water, sugar, and vinegar. Cook for about 10 minutes and mash the berries with a potato masher. Continue cooking until half of the liquid is vapored. Add the mustard and cold butter. Set aside.
4. Dip the chicken into the berry mixture and cook in the Air Fryer to fork-tender. Baste the chicken occasionally while cooking.
5. Enjoy!

Nutritional value per serving:

Calories: 182kcal, Fat: 8g, Carb: 4g, Proteins: 12g

Popcorn Chicken

Cut into a bite-size, the air fired chicken is always welcomed by kids. Enjoy with the dipping sauce!
Prep time and cooking time: 10 minutes |
Serves: 4

Ingredients To Use:

- 1-1/2 lbs. chicken thighs, boneless and skinless
- 1 egg
- 1 cup of flour
- 1 tsp. baking powder
- 1 cup canola oil
- 1 cup of pickle brine
- Salt to taste

Step-by-Step Directions to Cook It:

1. Marinate the chicken in pickle juice and refrigerate for some hours.
2. Whisk the egg and milk in a bowl.
3. Combine the flour, salt and baking powder in a large bowl.
4. Coat the chicken in the egg and milk before dipping in the flour mixture.
5. Shake the chicken to remove the excessive flour.
6. Fry the chicken in the Air Fryer for 3 minutes at 350⁰F.
7. Serve.

Nutritional value per serving:

Calories: 327kcal, Fat: 22g, Carb: 10g, Proteins: 25g

Keto Fried Chicken

Are you looking for a recipe that allows you

to enjoy fried chicken? Then you have to try out this recipe.

Prep time and cooking time: 4 hours 10 minutes | Serves: 4

Ingredients To Use:

- 1-1/2 lb. chicken drumsticks
- 1 tsp. paprika
- 2 eggs
- Canola oil
- 1/4 tsp. cayenne pepper
- 1 cup almond flour
- Salt to taste
- 3/4 cup of whipping cream

Step-by-Step Directions to Cook It:

1. Combine the chicken and whipping cream in a bowl. Refrigerate for about 4 hours.
2. Preheat the Air Fryer to 350⁰F.
3. Mix the almond flour, salt, and pepper in a bowl.
4. Dip the chicken in the egg mixture and then flour mixture.
5. Air fry the chicken for 10 minutes until golden brown.

Nutritional value per serving:

Calories: 312kcal, Fat: 18g, Carb: 1g, Proteins: 25g

Onion and Parsley Turkey Rolls

This recipe will amazingly vitalize you turkey.

Prep time and cooking time: 45 minutes| Serves: 4

Ingredients To Use:

- 1 small sized onion, finely chopped
- 1 tsp. of salt
- 1/2 tsp. of ground chili
- 1 lb. of turkey breast fillets, cut horizontally into 2/3 length
- 6 tsp. of olive oil
- 1 tsp. of cinnamon
- 1 clove of garlic, crushed
- 1-1/2 oz. of parsley, finely chopped
- 1-1/2 tsp. of ground cumin

Step-by-Step Directions to Cook It:

1. Combine the garlic, cumin, cinnamon, salt and chili in a large bowl.
2. Add the olive oil and set aside one spoon of the mixture.
3. Sprinkle in the parsley and onion into the mixture.
4. Preheat the Air Fryer to 356⁰F.
5. Spread the herb mixture on the turkey breast and roll firmly. Tie up the rolls with a butcher's string.
6. Cook the rolls for about 40 minutes until golden brown.
7. Serve.

Nutritional value per serving:

Calories: 285kcal, Fat: 12g, Carb: 8g, Proteins: 10g

Chicken and Sweet Potatoes

The combo of creamy flavored chicken and potatoes is everything you want in a comforting meal.

Prep time and cooking time: 40 minutes | Serves: 4

Ingredients To Use:

- 5 oz. chicken breast
- 3 tsp. of vegetable oil
- Salt and pepper to taste
- 1/4 cup of flour, seasoned with salt and pepper
- 1 cup of buttermilk
- 1 tsp. of garlic, finely chopped
- 1 egg, whisked
- 1/2 tsp. of pepper
- 7 oz. of breadcrumbs

- 2 medium-sized sweet potatoes, peel, and slice into chips.
- 3 tsp. of smoked paprika

1. Combine the garlic, buttermilk, and pepper into the bowl of chicken breasts.
2. Marinate the chicken in the fridge for at least 6 hours.
3. Set the Air Fryer to 374⁰F.
4. Remove the marinated chicken and discard the marinade.
5. Coat the chicken in flour, egg, and seasoned bread crumbs.
6. Transfer the chicken into the Air Fryer and cook for about 10 minutes. Set aside.
7. Cook the potatoes in an Air Fryer for about 6 minutes and then season with salt and pepper.
8. Serve the chicken with chips.

Calories: 298kcal, Fat: 12g, Carb: 18g, Proteins: 16g

Chicken with Buttered Pecan

Pecan adds floral and woodsy aroma to the recipe. It's also loaded with iron, fiber, and calcium.

Prep time and cooking time: 45 minutes|
Serves: 4

- 2 tbsp. packed brown sugar
- Zest of 1 lemon
- 1/2 tsp. ground cayenne (optional)
- 1 tsp. freshly ground black pepper
- Cooking spray
- 3 1/2 cups of pecans, finely chopped
- 4 tbsp. butter, melted, divided
- 2 large eggs
- 1 1/4 lb. chicken breast, chopped
- 1/4 cup of all-purpose flour

- 1/2 tsp. kosher salt

1. Preheat the Air Fryer to 425°F. Spray the Air Fryer basket with cooking oil.
2. Put the chopped pecans in a bowl and set aside.
3. In another bowl, combine the sugar, lemon zest, pepper, melted butter, and egg.
4. Dip the chicken in the flour mixture and dredge in the egg mixture.
5. Roll the pecans on the chicken and transfer the chicken to the Air Fryer basket.
6. Cook for about 15 minutes and brush butter on the chicken at intervals.
7. Season with salt. Garnish with parsley and drizzle honey mustard atop it.

Calories: 222kcal, Fat: 15g, Carb: 8g, Proteins: 18g

Chicken Salad

Fresh herbs give this recipe a fun twist. You can either poach the chicken or air fry it to your taste.

Prep time and cooking time: 30 minutes |
Serves: 4

- 1/2 cup of mayonnaise
- 1/2 cup small dill pickle, chopped
- 2 tbsp. pickle brine
- Kosher salt and freshly ground black pepper
- 2 stalks celery, sliced
- 2 tbsp. chopped fresh flat-leaf parsley
- 2 tbsp. chopped fresh dill
- 1-1/2 lb. boneless, skinless chicken breast

1. Preheat the Air Fryer to 340⁰F.
2. Coat the Air Fryer basket with cooking oil.
3. Season the chicken breast with pepper and salt.
4. Cook the chicken in the Air Fryer till fork-tender and then shred into pieces. Set aside and allow to cool.
5. Combine all the remaining ingredients in a small bowl.
6. Add the shredded chicken and serve.

Calories: 196kcal, Fat: 13g, Carb: 6g, Proteins: 12g

Air Fried Chicken with Tomatoes and Fennel Seed

The air fried chicken is cooked with lots of flavourful and colorful veggies that are hard to resist.
Prep time and cooking time: 1 hour 10 minutes | Serves: 4

Ingredients To Use:

- 1 tbsp. lemon zest
- 3 tbsp. lemon juice
- 4 lbs. chicken, flattened and bone removed
- 3 tbsp. lemon juice
- 1 cup grape tomatoes, rinsed
- 1 cup pitted olives
- 8 oz. sourdough bread, shredded into 1-inch pieces
- 3 cup baby kale
- 2 fennel bulbs, cored and sliced
- 1 garlic clove, crushed
- 3 tbsp. olive oil
- Kosher salt and freshly ground pepper to taste
- 1 tbsp. fennel seeds, crushed
- 1 tbsp. coriander seeds, crushed

Step-by-Step Directions to Cook It:

1. Preheat the Air Fryer to 450°F. Line the Air Fryer tray with aluminum foil. Combine the garlic, fennel, garlic, and one spoonful of oil inside the Air Fryer tray. Sprinkle in salt and pepper.
2. Brush the chicken with oil and then add the spice mixture.
3. Lower the Air Fryer temperature to 360⁰F. Place tomatoes and olives into the Air Fryer tray and arrange the chicken atop them. Cook for about 30 minutes.
4. Mix the bread and the remaining oil in a bowl. Add salt and pepper. Sprinkle the bread mixture into air fried chicken and continue cooking till fork-tender.
5. Place the chicken on a platter and serve with kale. Drizzle some lemon juice if desired.

Nutritional value per serving:

Calories: 216kcal, Fat: 14g, Carb: 6g, Proteins: 18g

Curry Chicken Salad

The recipe gets its bright color from the traditional curry spice. Pack this homemade meal for a nice sunny picnic day.
Prep time and cooking time: 30 minutes | Serves: 4

Ingredients To Use:

- 2 scallions, thinly sliced
- 1/4 cup of fresh cilantro, chopped
- 1/4 cup low-fat sour cream
- 2 tbsp. mayonnaise
- 1 tsp. lemon zest
- 2 tbsp. fresh lemon juice
- 1 tbsp. curry powder
- Kosher salt and freshly ground black pepper

- 1/2 cup of golden raisins
- 1-1/2 lb. boneless, skinless chicken breast, chopped

1. Preheat the Air Fryer to 340ºF.
2. Coat the Air Fryer basket with cooking oil.
3. Season the chicken breast with pepper and salt.
4. Cook the chicken in the Air Fryer till fork-tender and then shred into pieces. Set aside and allow to cool.
5. Combine all the remaining ingredients in a small bowl.
6. Add the shredded chicken and serve.

Nutritional value per serving:

Calories: 112kcal, Fat: 14g, Carb: 4g, Proteins: 12g

Air Fried Cornflakes Crusted Chicken

Cornflakes add a fun crunchy texture to chicken recipes. The air fried chicken is extra crispy and also requires no extra oil.
Prep time and cooking time: 1 hour 30 minutes | Serves: 4

Ingredients To Use:

- 4 small bone-in chicken thighs, skin removed
- 1 cup all-purpose flour
- 1/2 tsp. cayenne pepper
- Sea salt and ground black pepper to taste
- 4 small chicken drumsticks, skin removed
- 4 cup crunchy cornflakes cereal, crushed
- 1 tsp. celery seed, divided

Step-by-Step Directions to Cook It:

1. Preheat the Air Fryer to 360°F. Add the garlic powder, celery seed, buttermilk, salt, and cayenne seed in a glass bowl. Toss the mixture with chicken and marinate for 30 minutes in a refrigerator.
2. Line the Air Fryer tray with aluminum foil and coat with oil.
3. Mix pepper, salt flour, and the remaining celery seed in a bowl and set aside.
4. Pour the remaining buttermilk in another bowl and do the same for cornflakes.
5. Take out the chicken from the marinade and coat firstly in flour, buttermilk, and then crushed cornflakes.
6. Arrange the coated chicken in the Air Fryer basket and cook for about 30 minutes until fork-tender.
7. Serve.

Nutritional value per serving:

Calories: 222kcal, Fat: 8g, Carb: 15g, Proteins: 16g

Spiced Chicken Cutlets

The spiced grit gives the chicken cutlet recipe a southern sensibility that keeps your family members raving about it.
Prep time and cooking time: 1 hour | Serves: 6

Ingredients To Use:

- 2 large eggs
- 2 1/4 cup stone-ground grits
- 1 tsp. ground cinnamon
- 1/4 tsp. ground nutmeg
- Sea salt and ground black pepper
- 1 cup all-purpose flour
- 1-1/2 tsp. baking powder
- 6 chicken breast cutlets
- 3/4 cup canola oil
- 2 tbsp. olive oil
- 1 1/2 lb. green beans, trimmed

- 1/2 cup thinly sliced red onion
- 2 tsp. lemon zest
- 3 tsp. lemon juice
- 1/4 cup fresh parsley
- 2 oz. feta, crumbled
- 1 tsp. ground coriander
- 1 tsp. ground cardamom
- 1 tsp. ground turmeric

Step-by-Step Directions to Cook It:

1. Mix the baking powder, coriander, cinnamon, flour, turmeric, cardamom, and nutmeg in a bowl.
2. Preheat the Air Fryer to 250⁰F.
3. Combine the egg and a quarter cup of water in a bowl. Put grits in another separate bowl.
4. Add oil into a skillet over medium heat. Add beans and cook until tender. Season with salt and pepper.
5. Coat the chicken in the flour mixture, egg mixture, and then the grit mixture.
6. Transfer into the Air Fryer and cook for 5 minutes, until tender.
7. Serve the chicken with beans, and the remaining ingredients.

Nutritional value per serving:

Calories: 196kcal, Fat: 12g, Carb: 10g, Proteins: 14g

Chicken Thighs and Chick Peas

What a colorful meal for a warm weeknight date. The recipe is easy and healthy.
Prep time and cooking time: 45 minutes | Serves: 4

Ingredients To Use:

- 2 cans chickpeas, rinsed
- Fresh thyme leaves, For serving
- Sea salt and ground black pepper
- 3 tsp. canola oil
- 1-1/2 tsp. smoked paprika

- 1/2 tsp. ground cumin
- 1 cup grape tomatoes
- 8 small bone-in, skin-on chicken thighs
- 1/2 medium onion, chopped
- 3 cloves garlic, chopped

Step-by-Step Directions to Cook It:

1. Preheat the Air Fryer to 365°F. Season the chicken with salt and pepper. Spray cooking oil in the Air Fryer basket. Cook the chicken for about 15minutes, until golden brown.
2. Heat the oil in a large skillet over medium heat. Sauté the garlic, cumin, paprika, and onion, until fragrant.
3. Add tomatoes, chickpeas, and the air fried chicken. Stir and cook for another 5 minutes.
4. Serve.

Nutritional value per serving:

Calories: 225kcal, Fat: 12g, Carb: 6g, Proteins: 18g

Crispy Chicken with Herbs and Carrots

Loads of fresh mints, pepitas, carrots, and herbs are topped on the air-fried fork-tender chicken.
Prep time and cooking time: 45 minutes| Serves: 4

Ingredients To Use:

- Salt and pepper to taste
- 2 tsp. canola oil
- 12 oz. small carrots
- 1 box of olive oil and herb couscous, cooked according to package direction
- 1/3 cup chopped fresh parsley
- 1/4 cup chopped fresh mint
- 1 finely chopped garlic clove

- 1 tbsp. olive oil
- 1 tbsp. lemon juice
- 4 boneless chicken thighs
- 1/3 cup roasted salted pepitas
- 2 tsp. lemon zest

Step-by-Step Directions to Cook It:

1. Preheat the Air Fryer to 380°F. Sprinkle chicken thighs with salt and pepper.
2. Cook the chicken in the Air Fryer until golden brown. Season carrot with salt and pepper and thread on skewers. Cook for about 2 minutes in the Air Fryer.
3. On a large skillet, combine the parsley, couscous, garlic, oil, pepitas, lemon juice, and zest. Stir fry over medium heat.
4. Serve with the air fried chicken and carrots.

Nutritional value per serving:

Calories: 267kcal, Fat: 12g, Carb: 8g, Proteins: 14g

Chicken Tenders

In this recipe, the potatoes and peas upgrade the cornflakes-coated chicken to a whole new level. Don't hesitate to try this out!

Prep time and cooking time: 30 minutes| Serves: 4

Ingredients To Use:

- 1 chopped shallot
- 2 tbsp. butter
- 1 1/2 cup thawed frozen green peas
- 1 tbsp. fresh lemon zest
- 1 1/4 pound of chicken tenders
- 2 cup cornflakes, finely crushed
- 2 tbsp. extra virgin olive oil
- 16-oz. packaged baby Idaho potatoes
- 1 tbsp. lemon-pepper seasoning
- 1/3 cup grated Parmesan

- 1/3 cup plain Greek yogurt
- Salt and black pepper, as desired
- 1/4 cup of torn mint leaves
- Lemon wedges, for garnish

Step-by-Step Directions to Cook It:

1. Preheat the Air Fryer to 360⁰F.
2. Mix the yogurt and lemon pepper in a small bowl. Dredge the chicken inside the mixture and set aside for a minute. Coat the chicken in parmesan, oil, and then cornflakes.
3. Spray the Air Fryer basket with cooking oil.
4. Transfer the chicken into the Air Fryer and cook for about 15 minutes, until tender.
5. Melt the butter in a large skillet under medium heat.
6. Add the rest of the ingredients and cook for 10 minutes.
7. Serve alongside the chicken.

Nutritional value per serving:

Calories: 201kcal, Fat: 14g, Carb: 10g, Proteins: 18g

Jerk Chicken and Mango Lettuce Ball

The recipe is sweet, low carb, and has quite a nice blend of texture. Get your jerk chicken to a whole new level!

Prep time and cooking time: 40 minutes| Serves: 4

Ingredients To Use:

- 1-1/2 tbsp. soy sauce
- 2 tsp. jerk seasoning
- 2 chopped garlic cloves
- 1 tsp. jarred fresh ginger
- 3/4 cup chopped mango
- 1/4 cup chopped fresh cilantro leaves

- 1 cup of basmati rice, cooked
- 1 cup chicken stock
- Kosher salt and black pepper to taste
- 1 lb. ground chicken
- 1/2 red onion, chopped
- 1/2 red bell pepper, chopped
- 1 tbsp. canola oil
- Butter lettuce leaves, for serving

Step-by-Step Directions to Cook It:

1. Line the Air Fryer basket with aluminium foil.
2. Combine the ground chicken, red bell pepper, and onion in a bowl. Season with salt and spray cooking oil atop it. Cook in the Air Fryer for about 20 minutes at 250°F, until golden brown.
3. Meanwhile, heat the canola oil in a large skillet. Add the soy sauce, clove, jerk seasoning, and ginger. Cook until fragrant and season with pepper.
4. Fold the sauce mixture into mango and cilantro. Stuff the chicken and rice in buttercup leaves. Serve.

Nutritional value per serving:

Calories: 195kcal, Fat: 12g, Carb: 6g, Proteins: 19g

Kale and Chicken Pita Salad

The pita just adds a great layer of crunchiness to the Mediterranean kale chicken salad recipe.
Prep time and cooking time: 30 minutes| Serves: 4

Ingredients To Use:

- 1 chopped garlic clove
- 5-oz. container baby kale
- 2 cup lightly crushed pita chips
- 2 sliced scallions
- 1-1/2 lb. chicken tenders
- 2 tsp. salt-free Greek seasoning

- Kosher salt and black pepper
- 3-1/2 tbsp. olive oil
- 3 tbsp. fresh lemon juice
- 2 tbsp. tahini
- 2 sliced Persian cucumbers
- 5 thinly sliced radishes
- 1 cup halved grape tomatoes

Step-by-Step Directions to Cook It:

1. Preheat the Air Fryer to 340°F.
2. Coat the Air Fryer basket with cooking oil.
3. Season the chicken breast with pepper and salt.
4. Cook the chicken in the Air Fryer till fork-tender and then shred into pieces. Set aside and allow to cool.
5. Combine all the remaining ingredients in a small bowl.
6. Add the shredded chicken and serve.

Nutritional value per serving:

Calories: 175kcal, Fat: 8g, Carb: 12g, Proteins: 22g

Peppered Chicken with Quinoa

The peppered chicken dish just gets refreshing with this spiced up quinoa. Savory and healthy combo all in one serving.
Prep time and cooking time: 1 hour 5 minutes | Serves: 4

Ingredients To Use:

- 3 radishes, halved and thinly sliced
- 1 small carrot, grated
- 3 oz. feta, crumbled
- 1/4 cup fresh basil leaves, chopped
- 1/4 cup olive oil, divided
- 8 small bone-in, skin-on chicken thighs
- Kosher salt
- Freshly ground pepper
- 1 cup quinoa, rinsed and cooked according to package directions

- 2 tbsp. unseasoned rice wine vinegar
- 4 scallions, sliced

1. Preheat the Air Fryer to 350⁰F.
2. Season the chicken with salt and pepper. Brush oil atop the chicken and cook in the Air Fryer until golden brown.
3. Combine the rest of the ingredients in a large bowl and serve with the air fried chicken.

Nutritional value per serving:

Calories: 187kcal, Fat: 10g, Carb: 18g, Proteins: 26g

Chicken with Fruit Salsa

Add a nutritious profile to your chicken with fruit salsa. The recipe gets a nice flavor lift with the marinade ingredient.
Preparation time and cooking time: 2 hours 40 minutes | Serves: 4

Ingredients To Use:

- Freshly ground black pepper
- 4 boneless, skinless chicken breast halves
- 1/2 jalapeño, seeded and chopped
- 1 garlic clove, chopped
- 1 tsp. chili powder
- 1/4 cup extra-virgin olive oil, divided
- 1 tbsp. lime zest
- 2 cup sweet cherries, pitted and chopped
- 1 small shallot, chopped
- 1/4 cup lime juice
- Kosher salt
- 1/4 cup chopped fresh cilantro
- 1 avocado, chopped

Step-by-Step Directions to Cook It:

1. Mix the chili powder, three tablespoons oil, lime zest, salt, pepper, and lemon juice in a glass bowl.
2. Marinate the chicken in the mixture and refrigerate for about 30 minutes.
3. Mix the shallot, cilantro, cherries, jalapeño in a small bowl. Sprinkle in salt and pepper. Fold the mixture into the avocado.
4. Preheat the Air Fryer at 350⁰F.
5. Cook the marinated chicken until tender.
6. Serve with fruit salsa.

Nutritional value per serving:

Calories: 200kcal, Fat: 10g, Carb: 9g, Proteins: 14g

Stuffed Chicken

Treat your family to a nice weeknight's stuffed chicken recipe. You can't go wrong with this on the table.
Prep time and cooking time: 35 minutes| Serves: 4

Ingredients To Use:

- 8 oz. boneless, skinless chicken breasts, cut "2-x-4" pocket into the chicken breast
- 3/4 cup chopped green olives
- 1/4 cup toasted sliced almonds
- 1-1/2 tbsp. chopped fresh dill
- 1 tbsp. lemon zest

Step-by-Step Directions to Cook It:

1. Combine the remaining ingredients in a mixing bowl and stuff inside the chicken.
2. Sprinkle in salt and pepper. Brush oil atop the chicken and set aside.
3. Preheat the Air Fryer to 360⁰F.
4. Place the chicken in the Air Fryer basket and cook until golden brown.
5. Serve.

Nutritional value per serving:

Calories: 182kcal, Fat: 9g, Carb: 6g, Proteins:

25g

Cheese Stuffed Chicken

Cheesy chicken is a fantastic dish that'll wow your guest right away. The recipe is a sure take-home-to-mama.

Prep time and cooking time: 35 minutes|
Serves: 4

Ingredients To Use:

- 1 cup quartered cherry tomatoes
- 2 oz. crumbled goat cheese
- 2 tbsp. toasted pine nuts
- 2 tbsp. chopped fresh basil
- 8 oz. boneless, skinless chicken breasts, cut "2-x-4" pocket into the chicken breast

Step-by-Step Directions to Cook It:

1. Combine the remaining ingredients in a mixing bowl and stuff inside the chicken.
2. Sprinkle in salt and pepper. Brush oil atop the chicken and set aside.
3. Preheat the Air Fryer to 360°F.
4. Place the chicken in the Air Fryer basket and cook until golden brown.
5. Serve.

Nutritional value per serving:

Calories: 185kcal, Fat: 12g, Carb: 6g, Proteins: 12g

Chapter 3: Fish and Seafood Recipes

Tilapia and Chives Sauce

Tilapia and chives sauce is a delicious and crusty meal that's great for dinner. Also, it can be prepared in a short time.

Prep time and cooking time: 18 minutes|
Serves: 4

Ingredients To Use:

- 4 medium tilapia fillets
- 2 tbsp. chopped chives
- 1/4 cup Greek yogurt
- 2 tsp. honey
- Juice from 1 lemon
- Salt and black pepper to taste
- Cooking spray

Step-by-Step Directions to Cook It:

1. Preheat the air fryer to 3500F.
2. Season the fish with salt and pepper, spray with cooking spray. Transfer to the air fryer and cook for 8 minutes, and flip the fish in between the cooking.
3. In a bowl, mix the yogurt, chives, honey, salt, lemon juice, and pepper. Whisk until thoroughly combined.
4. Serve the fish with the chives sauce. Enjoy!

Nutritional value per serving:

Calories: 261kcal, Fat: 4g, Carb: 16g, Proteins: 21g

Thyme and Parsley Salmon

Thyme and parsley salmon is an easy and delicious meal. All the ingredients used to spice the salmon infuse the meal with tons of flavors.

Prep time and cooking time: 25 minutes|

Serves: 4

Ingredients To Use:

- 4 salmon fillets (boneless)
- 3 tbsp. extra virgin olive oil
- Juice from 1 lemon
- 4 thyme sprigs
- 1 yellow onion (diced)
- 3 tomatoes, sliced
- 4 parsley sprigs
- Salt and black pepper to taste

Step-by-Step Directions to Cook It:

1. Preheat the air fryer to 360^0F.
2. Drizzle 1 tbsp. of oil in a pan layered with the sliced tomatoes, which can fit into the air fryer. Add salt, pepper, and drizzle with more oil. Add the fish, season with salt and pepper, drizzle with the rest of the oil. Add the rest of the ingredients.
3. Transfer to the air fryer and close the lid, set the time for 12 minutes.
4. Serve and enjoy!

Nutritional value per serving:

Calories: 180kcal, Fat: 5g, Carb: 8g, Proteins: 26g

Creamy Salmon

The name of this recipe says it all. The meal is creamy and tasty!

Prep time and cooking time: 20 minutes|
Serves: 4

Ingredients To Use:

- 4 salmon fillets
- 1/2 cup coconut cream
- 1/3 cup grated cheddar cheese
- 1 tbsp. olive oil

- 1 and 1/2 tsp. mustard
- Salt and black pepper to taste

1. Preheat the air fryer to 320^{0}F.
2. Season the salmon with salt and black pepper, drizzle with oil. In a bowl, add coconuts and all the ingredients, stir well. To a pan that fits into the air fryer, add the salmon and top with the coconut mix.
3. Transfer to your air fryer and close the lid. Set the time to 10 minutes.
4. Serve hot and enjoy!

Nutritional value per serving:

Calories: 170kcal, Fat: 3g, Carb: 10g, Proteins: 17g

Cod fillets and Peas

The cod fillets and peas is an excellent meal for dinner; it contains everyday ingredients that can be prepared in no time.
Prep time and cooking time: 20 minutes| Serves: 4

Ingredients To Use:

- 4 cod fillets (boneless)
- 4 tbsp. wine
- 2 tbsp. chopped parsley
- 1/2 tsp. dried oregano
- 2 garlic cloves (minced)
- 2 cups peas
- 1/2 tsp. paprika
- Salt and pepper to taste

Step-by-Step Directions to Cook It:

1. Preheat the air fryer to 360^{0}F.
2. In a food processor, add the garlic, wine, paprika, oregano, parsley, salt, and pepper, pulse until smooth.
3. Coat the fillets with the mixture and transfer to the air fryer. Close the lid and cook for 10 minutes.
4. Meanwhile, place a pot over medium heat, add peas and fill with water. Cook for 10 minutes, drain.
5. Serve the fish with the peas.

Nutritional value per serving:

Calories: 241kcal, Fat: 6g, Carb: 10g, Proteins: 22g

Trout and Butter Sauce

The recipe is nice and tasty and can serve as a good lunch or a main course. Not only is it easy to prepare, but it also requires simple ingredients.
Prep time and cooking time: 20 minutes| Serves: 4

Ingredients To Use:

- 4 trout fillets (boneless)
- 2 tbsp. olive oil
- 6 tbsp. butter
- 3 tsp. grated lemon zest
- 2 tsp. lemon juice
- 3 tbsp. chives
- Salt and pepper to taste

Step-by-Step Directions to Cook It:

1. Preheat the air fryer to 320^{0}F.
2. Season the trout with salt, pepper, and oil. Transfer to the air fryer and cook for 10 minutes.
3. Meanwhile, heat the butter in a pan over medium heat, add all the ingredients. Whisk and cook for 2 minutes. Remove from heat.
4. Serve the fish with the sauce, enjoy!

Nutritional value per serving:

Calories: 200kcal, Fat: 6g, Carb: 19g, Proteins: 21g

Cod Steaks with Plum Sauce

The taste and flavor of the plum sauce are irresistible. You will love it!

Prep time and cooking time: 30 minutes|
Serves: 2

Ingredients To Use:

- 2 cod steaks
- 1 tbsp. plum sauce
- 1/4 tsp. turmeric powder
- 1/2 tsp. ginger powder
- 1/2 tsp. garlic powder
- Salt and black pepper to taste
- Cooking spray

Step-by-Step Directions to Cook It:

1. Preheat the air fryer to 360°F.
2. Season cod steaks with salt, garlic, ginger, turmeric, and pepper. Spray with cooking oil. Transfer the steak to the air fryer and cook for 15 minutes, flip after 7 minutes.
3. Place a pan over medium heat, add the plum sauce and stir. Cook for 2 minutes.
4. Serve the cod with the plum sauce, Enjoy!

Nutritional value per serving:

Calories: 250kcal, Fat: 5g, Carb: 10g, Proteins: 12g

Tabasco Shrimps

The fragrance of this recipe is enticing and will leave you wanting more.

Prep time and cooking time: 20 minutes|
Serves: 4

Ingredients To Use:

- 1 lb. shrimps (peeled and deveined)
- 2 tbsp. olive oil
- 1/2 tsp. parsley
- 1 tsp. dried oregano
- 1/2 tsp. smoked paprika
- 1 tsp. red pepper flakes
- 1 tsp. tabasco sauce
- 2 tbsp. water
- Salt and black pepper to taste

Step-by-Step Directions to Cook It:

1. Preheat the air fryer to 370°F.
2. In a bowl, mix all the ingredients with the shrimps. Transfer to the air fryer and cook for 10 minutes.
3. Serve and enjoy!

Nutritional value per serving:

Calories: 180kcal, Fat: 3g, Carb: 10g, Proteins: 9g

Cod Fillets with Fennel and Grapes Salad

This recipe creates a highly nutritious and flavorful meal. The grape introduces its subtle yet delicious flavor to create a tasty fish.

Prep time and cooking time: 25 minutes|
Serves: 2

Ingredients To Use:

- 2 black cod fillets (boneless)
- 1 fennel bulb, thinly sliced
- 1 tbsp. olive oil
- 1 cup grapes (cut into halves)
- 1/2 cup pecans
- Salt and black pepper

Step-by-Step Directions to Cook It:

1. Preheat the air fryer to 400°F.
2. Season the fish with salt and pepper, drizzle with oil. Transfer to the air fryer basket and close the lid. Set the time to 10 minutes, remove and set aside.
3. Meanwhile, in a bowl, mix the fennel, pecans, grapes, oil, salt, and pepper. Add to a pan that fits into your air fryer, cook for 5 minutes.
4. Serve the cod with the grapes and the

fennel mix. Enjoy!

Calories: 270kcal, Fat: 3g, Carb: 22g, Proteins: 21g

Butter Shrimps Skewer

Buttered shrimps are crispy and delicious; the mouth-watering aroma will leave you wanting for more. Enjoy!
Prep time and cooking time: 16 minutes| Serves: 2

Ingredients To Use:

- 8 shrimps (peeled and deveined)
- 1 tbsp. melted butter
- 4 garlic cloves (minced)
- 1 tbsp. chopped rosemary
- 8 green bell pepper slices
- Salt and black pepper to taste

Step-by-Step Directions to Cook It:

1. Preheat the air fryer to 360⁰F.
2. In a bowl, add the butter, garlic, rosemary, salt, pepper, bell pepper, and shrimps. Toss to coat and let marinate for 10 minutes. Arrange the shrimps with bell pepper on the skewer.
3. Transfer to the air fryer cooking basket and cook for 6 minutes.
4. Serve and enjoy.

Nutritional value per serving:

Calories: 120kcal, Fat: 1g, Carb: 10g, Proteins: 7g

Asian Salmon

Salmon is a versatile and healthy ingredient in any meal, and so is this recipe. This meal is easy to prepare.
Prep time and cooking time: 1hour 15 minutes| Serves: 2

Ingredients To Use:

- 2 medium salmon fillets
- 3 tsp. mirin
- 6 tbsp. honey
- 6 tbsp. light soy sauce
- 1 tsp. water

Step-by-Step Directions to Cook It:

1. Preheat the air fryer to 360⁰F.
2. In a bowl, add the mirin, water, soy sauce, honey, and whisk. Add the salmon to the mixture and toss to coat. let marinate in the refrigerator for 1 hour.
3. Transfer the fillets to the air fryer and close the lid. Set the time for 15 minutes (flip the fillets at 7minutes).
4. In a bowl, place a pan over medium heat: Add the soy sauce marinade and whisk. Cook for 2 minutes or until thick; remove from heat.
5. Drizzle the marinade over the salmon, enjoy!

Nutritional value per serving:

Calories: 260kcal, Fat: 7g, Carb: 4g, Proteins: 21g

Salmon and Blackberry Glaze

A delicious way to enjoy a meal rich in antioxidants! It is delicious, and you can have it on your table in no time.
Prep time and cooking time: 43 minutes| Serves: 4

Ingredients To Use:

- 4 medium salmon fillet (skinless)
- 1 cup of water
- 1/4 cup of sugar
- 1 tbsp. olive oil
- 1-inch ginger (grated)
- 12 oz. blackberries
- Juice from 1/2 lemon
- Salt and black pepper to taste

1. Heat a pot of water over medium heat, add the ginger, blackberries, lemon juice, and stir. Cook for 4-5 minutes, drain the water and return to heat. Add sugar and stir, bring to a simmer and lower the heat. Cook for 20 minutes and remove from heat.
2. Preheat the air fryer to 350^{0}F.
3. Allow to cool, brush the salmon fillets with the sauce, and season with salt and pepper. Brush with olive oil, transfer to the air fryer, and cook for 10 minutes, flip once.
4. Serve and enjoy!

Nutritional value per serving:

Calories: 281kcal, Fat: 3g, Carb: 10g, Proteins: 14g

Snapper Fillets and Veggies

Everyone loves the nutritious veggies added to a meal; this combination of fish and veggies creates an exotic, healthy, and tasty meal
Prep time and cooking time: 24 minutes|
Serves: 2

Ingredients To Use:

- 2 red snapper fillets (boneless)
- 1 tsp. dried tarragon
- 1/2 cup chopped red pepper
- 1/2 cup chopped leeks
- 1 tbsp. olive oil
- 1/2 cup chopped green pepper
- 1/4 cup white wine
- Salt and pepper to taste

Step-by-Step Directions to Cook It:

1. Preheat the air fryer to 350^{0}F.
2. In a pan fitting the air fryer, mix all the ingredients, including the fillets. Transfer to the air fryer and cook for 14 minutes,

flip halfway.
3. Serve and enjoy!

Nutritional value per serving:

Calories: 250kcal, Fat: 12g, Carb: 12g, Proteins: 20g

Lemon Sole and Swiss Chard

Lemon sole and Swiss chard is a tasty meal that can be served as a light lunch or dinner.
Prep time and cooking time: 24 minutes|
Serves: 4

Ingredients To Use:

- 4 sole fillets
- 4 white bread slices (quartered)
- 4 tbsp. butter
- 1/4 cup. grated parmesan
- 1/4 cup lemon juice
- 1/4 cup chopped walnut
- 2 garlic cloves
- 1 tsp. grated lemon zest
- 2 bunch of Swiss chards (chopped)
- Salt and pepper to taste
- 3 tbsp. capers
- 4 tbsp. olive oil

Step-by-Step Directions to Cook It:

1. In a food processor, add the walnut, bread, cheese, lemon zest, and pulse well. Add the olive oil and pulse. Set aside.
2. Preheat the air fryer to 350^{0}F.
3. Heat the butter in a pan over medium heat, add the lemon, juice, capers, salt, and pepper, stir. Add the fillet and toss to coat, transfer to the air fryer. Spread the bread mixture on top and cover with the lid. Set the time for 14 minutes.
4. Meanwhile, in a pan, heat the oil and add the Swiss chard, garlic, salt, pepper, and stir. Cook for 2 minutes and remove from heat.

5. Serve the fish with the Swiss chards and enjoy it!

Calories: 301kcal, Fat: 6g, Carb: 23g, Proteins: 13g

Air Fried Branzino

Air fried branzino is a healthy and low carb recipe that can be easily prepared on a busy weekday. It's also flavourful and tasty.
Prep time and cooking time: 20 minutes|
Serves: 4

Ingredients To Use:

- 4 branzino fillets
- Zest from one lemon (grated)
- Zest from one orange (grated)
- 2 tbsp. olive oil
- 1/2 cup parsley
- Juice from 1/2 lemon
- Juice from 1/2 orange
- Pinch of red pepper flakes (crushed)
- Salt and black pepper to taste

Step-by-Step Directions to Cook It:

1. Preheat the air fryer to 350⁰F.
2. In a bowl, mix fish fillets with all the ingredients, toss to coat, transfer to the air fryer basket, and set the time for 10 minutes, flip in between the cooking.
3. Serve and enjoy!

Nutritional value per serving:

Calories: 261kcal, Fat: 8g, Carb: 19g, Proteins: 16g

Marinated Salmon

The filets are infused with tasty flavor after being marinated. Air-frying provides you with a crusty and flaky fish dish that's worth trying.
Prep time and cooking time: 1hour 20 minutes| Serves: 6

Ingredients To Use:

- 1 whole salmon
- 1 tbsp. garlic (minced)
- Juice from 2 lemons
- 1 tbsp. chopped dill
- 1 lemon sliced
- 1 tbsp. chopped tarragon
- Pinch of salt and black pepper

Step-by-Step Directions to Cook It:

1. Preheat the air fryer to 350⁰F.
2. In a large bowl, mix the fish with lemon juice, salt, and pepper. Leave to marinate for 1 hour in the refrigerator. Stuff the fish with lemon and garlic, transfer to the air fryer basket, and set the time for 20 minutes.
3. Serve with coleslaw, Enjoy!

Nutritional value per serving:

Calories: 300kcal, Fat: 8g, Carb: 12g, Proteins: 23g

Trout Fillets in Orange Sauce

The trout fillets in orange sauce create with a sweet and tangy taste can be enjoyed as a main course or light lunch.
Prep time and cooking time: 20 minutes|
Serves: 4

Ingredients To Use:

- 4 trout fillet (skinless and boneless)
- 1 tbsp. ginger (minced)
- 4 spring onions (chopped)
- Juice and zest from 1 orange
- 1 tbsp. olive oil
- Salt and black pepper to taste

Step-by-Step Directions to Cook It:

1. Preheat the air fryer to 360⁰F.
2. Season fillets with salt, pepper, and oil. Put in a pan that fits into the air fryer, add the ginger, orange zest, green

onions, orange juice, and mix. Transfer to the air fryer and close the lid, set the time for 10 minutes.

3. Serve and enjoy!

Calories: 239kcal, Fat: 10g, Carb: 1823g, Proteins: g

Italian Barramundi Fillets and Tomato Salsa

Italian delicacies are known for their flavors and spices, and this dish gives you an authentic Italian flavor.

Prep time and cooking time: 18 minutes|
Serves: 4

Ingredients To Use:

- 2 barramundi fillets
- 1/4 cup. chopped green olives
- 2 tbsp. lemon zest
- 1/4 cup of black olives (pitted)
- 1 tbsp. plus 2 tsp. olive oil
- 2 tbsp. lemon juice
- 2 tsp. Italian seasoning
- 1/4 cup cherry tomatoes, chopped
- 2 tbsp. chopped parsley
- Salt and black pepper to taste

Step-by-Step Directions to Cook It:

1. Preheat the air fryer to 360^0F.
2. Season the fillets with salt, pepper, Italian seasoning, and olive oil. Transfer to the air fryer basket and cook for 8 minutes, flipping halfway.
3. Meanwhile, in a bowl, add tomatoes, lemon zest, green olives, lemon juice, black olives, pepper, parsley, salt, and 1 tbsp. Olive oil. Mix thoroughly.
4. Serve the fish with the tomato salsa.

Nutritional value per serving:

Calories: 270kcal, Fat: 4g, Carb: 16g, Proteins: 24g

Cod and Vinaigrette

Cod and vinaigrette is a favorite for people who love a fancy taste; it possesses a subtle but enticing flavor and a firm but flaky texture.

Prep time and cooking time: 25 minutes|
Serves: 4

Ingredients To Use:

- 4 cod fillets
- 2 tbsp. lemon juice
- 1 bunch basil, chopped
- 12 cherry tomatoes, halved
- 2 tbsp. olive oil
- 8 black olives (pitted and roughly chopped)
- Salt and black pepper to taste
- Cooking spray

Step-by-Step Directions to Cook It:

1. Preheat the air fryer to 360^0F.
2. Season the fillets with salt and pepper, transfer to the air fryer cooking basket and cook for 10 minutes, flip in between the cooking.
3. Heat oil in a saucepan over medium heat, add olives, tomatoes, lemon juice, and stir. Bring to a simmer, add salt, pepper, and basil, remove from heat.
4. Serve the fish with the sauce.

Nutritional value per serving:

Calories: 230kcal, Fat: 5g, Carb: 8g, Proteins: 10g

Spanish Salmon

Spanish salmon is a dish that is full of vibrant flavors that you will never fail to enjoy. It is tasty and yummy!

Prep time and cooking time: 25 minutes|
Serves: 6

Ingredients To Use:

- 6 salmon fillets
- 3 red onions (cut into medium wedges)
- 2 tbsp. chopped parsley
- 1/2 tsp. smoked paprika
- 3/4 cup pitted green olives
- 5 tbsp. olive oil
- 3 red pepper cut into medium wedges
- 2 cups bread croutons
- Salt and black pepper to taste

Step-by-Step Directions to Cook It:

1. Preheat the air fryer to 356°F.
2. In a pan that fits into the air fryer, add croutons, paprika, bell pepper, olives, and olive oil. Stir well and transfer to the air fryer, cook for 7 minutes.
3. Meanwhile, sprinkle the salmon with oil, and transfer to the air fryer with the veggies. Turn up the temperature to 360°F. Set the time for 8 minutes.
4. Serve the fish with the veggies.

Nutritional value per serving:

Calories: 311kcal, Fat: 8g, Carb: 21g, Proteins: 22g

Delicious Red Snapper

The herbs and vegetables complement the nutty flavor of the red snapper, creating a mouth-watering dish.
Prep time and cooking time: 45 minutes|
Serves: 4

Ingredients To Use:

- 1 big red snapper
- 1 jalapeno (chopped)
- 3 cloves garlic (minced)
- 1 red bell pepper (chopped)
- 1 tbsp. butter
- 2 tbsp. white wine
- 2 tbsp. chopped parsley
- 1/2 lb. chopped okra

- Salt and pepper to taste

Step-by-Step Directions to Cook It:

1. In a bowl, mix the jalapeno, wine, and stir. Rub the snapper with the mixture and season with salt and pepper. Leave to marinate for 30 minutes.
2. Preheat the air fryer to 400°F.
3. Heat the butter in a pan over medium heat, add okra, and bell pepper. Stir and cook for 5 minutes. Stuff the red snapper with the okra mixture and parsley. Rub with olive oil and transfer to the air fryer basket, close the lid, and set the time for 15 minutes.
4. Serve and Enjoy!

Nutritional value per serving:

Calories: 261kcal, Fat: 7g, Carb: 21g, Proteins: 18g

Shrimp and Crab Mix

What can be better than the combination of crabs and shrimps? This recipe creates a meal packed full of delicious taste and nutrients.
Prep time and cooking time: 35 minutes|
Serves: 4

Ingredients To Use:

- 1 lb. shrimps (peeled and deveined)
- 1 cup chopped green bell pepper
- 1 cup flaked crabmeat
- 1 cup chopped celery
- 2 tbsp. breadcrumbs
- 1 cup mayonnaise
- 1/2 cup yellow onions (chopped)
- 1 tbsp. melted butter
- 1 tsp. Worcestershire sauce
- 1 tsp. sweet paprika
- 1 cup chopped celery
- Salt and black pepper

1. Preheat the air fryer to 320°F.
2. In a pan that fits into the air fryer, mix all the ingredients. Transfer to the air fryer and set the time for 25 minutes.
3. Serve and enjoy!

Nutritional value per serving:

Calories: 200kcal, Fat: 11g, Carb: 1519g, Proteins: g

Creamy Shrimps and Veggies

This dish takes shrimp dishes to a whole new level with its attractive look and flavorful tastes.

Prep time and cooking time: 40 minutes|
Serves: 4

Ingredients To Use:

- 1 lb. shrimp (peeled and deveined)
- 1 cup heavy cream
- 1 spaghetti squash (halved)
- 1 bunch of asparagus (chopped)
- 1 cup grated parmesan cheese
- 2 tbsp. olive oil
- 1/4 cup melted butter
- 2 garlic cloves (minced)
- 1 yellow onion (chopped)
- 2 tsp. Italian seasoning
- 1 tsp. red pepper flakes (crushed)
- 8 oz. mushroom (chopped)
- Salt and pepper to taste

Step-by-Step Directions to Cook It:

1. Preheat the air fryer to 390°F, place the squash halves in the air fryer basket. Close the lid and cook for 17 minutes. Transfer to a board and scoop the inside into a bowl.
2. Boil enough water in a pot over medium heat, add asparagus for 2-3 minutes. Transfer to a bowl containing ice water and set aside. Heat oil in a pan that fits

into the air fryer; add onions, mushroom, and cook for 7 minutes.
3. Add the remaining ingredients, and transfer to the air fryer, reduce to 360°F. Set time to 6 minutes.
4. Serve and enjoy!

Nutritional value per serving:

Calories: 311kcal, Fat: 6g, Carb: 12g, Proteins: 16g

Salmon and Avocado Salsa

Salmon and avocado salsa is one of the best vegetable recipes available. It is healthy and full of flavors.

Prep time and cooking time: 40 minutes|
Serves: 4

Ingredients To Use:

- 4 salmon fillets
- 1 tsp. garlic powder
- 1 tbsp. olive oil
- 1/2 tsp. sweet paprika
- 1 tsp. ground cumin
- 1/2 tsp. chili powder
- Salt and pepper to taste

For the Salsa:

- 2 tbsp. chopped cilantro
- 1 red onion (chopped)
- Juice from 2 limes
- 1 avocado (peeled and chopped)
- Salt and black pepper to taste

Step-by-Step Directions to Cook It:

1. Preheat the air fryer to 350°F.
2. In a medium bowl, add the onion powder, pepper, salt, chili powder, cumin, and paprika. Mix well and rub the salmon with the mixture, drizzle with oil. Transfer to the air fryer and cook for 5 minutes.
3. Meanwhile, in a bowl, add all the salsa ingredients and toss well.

4. Serve and enjoy.

Nutritional value per serving:

Calories: kcal, Fat: g, Carb: g, Proteins: g

Salmon and Greek Yogurt Sauce

The salmon and Greek yogurt sauce are creamy, tasty, and delicious. It can be easily prepared.
Prep time and cooking time: 30 minutes|
Serves: 2

Ingredients To Use:

- 2 salmon fillets
- 1 cup Greek yogurt
- 1 tbsp. chopped basil
- 1/2 tsp. chopped cilantro
- 6 lemon slices
- 1/2 tsp. chopped mint
- 2 tsp. curry powder
- 1 garlic clove (pressed)
- Pinch of cayenne pepper
- Salt and pepper to taste

Step-by-Step Directions to Cook It:

1. Preheat the air fryer to 400^{0}F.
2. Place each salmon fillet on parchment paper, make 3 slits, and stuff with basil. Season the fillets with salt and pepper, top each with a slice of lemon. Fold parchment paper and seal, transfer to the air fryer and bake for 20 minutes.
3. Meanwhile, in a bowl, add the yogurt, pepper, cayenne pepper, curry, garlic, mint, cilantro, and salt. Mix well.
4. Serve the fish drizzled with the yogurt sauce.

Nutritional value per serving:

Calories: 242kcal, Fat: 1g, Carb: 2g, Proteins: 8g

Asian Halibut

The Asian halibut is mouth-watering and delicious. It is best served with steamed rice.
Prep time and cooking time: 40 minutes|
Serves: 3

Ingredients To Use:

- 1 lb. halibut Steaks
- 1/4 cup sugar
- 1/2 cup mirin
- 2/3 cup soy sauce
- 2 tbsp. lime juice
- 1/4 cup orange juice
- 1 garlic clove (minced)
- 1/4 tsp. red pepper flakes (crushed)
- 1 tsp. grated ginger

Step-by-Step Directions to Cook It:

1. Place a pot over medium heat and add the soy sauce and other ingredients except for the fish. Bring to a boil and remove from heat. Pour half of the marinade into a bowl, add the halibut, and stir. Leave to marinate in the refrigerator for 30 minutes.
2. Preheat the air fryer to 390^{0}F.
3. Transfer to the air fryer and cook for 10 minutes, flip in between the cooking. Serve the halibut with the rest of the sauce.
4. Enjoy!

Nutritional value per serving:

Calories: 251kcal, Fat: 5g, Carb: 14g, Proteins: 23g

Flavour Air Fried Salmon

Salmon is an everyday favorite with its subtle flavor and great taste. Cooking this with an air fryer for a healthy meal.
Prep time and cooking time: 1 hour 8 minutes| Serves: 2

- 2 salmon fillets
- 1/3 cup brown sugar
- 2 tbsp. lemon juice
- 1/3 cup water
- 1/2 tsp. garlic powder
- 1/3 cup brown sugar
- 3 scallions, chopped
- 2 tbsp. olive oil
- Salt and black pepper to taste

Step-by-Step Directions to Cook It:

1. In a bowl, add the sugar, water, garlic, lemon juice, soy sauce, salt, pepper, and oil. Whisk until well combined; add the salmon fillets and mix. Leave to marinate for 1 hour.
2. Transfer the salmon fillets to your air fryer and cook for 8 minutes, flip in between the cooking.
3. Serve garnished with scallions, enjoy!

Nutritional value per serving:

Calories: 160kcal, Fat: 8g, Carb: 20g, Proteins: 21g

Salmon with Capers and Mashed Potatoes

The salmon with capers and mashed potatoes is a quick and easy meal to satisfy your guests.
Prep time and cooking time: 30 minutes|
Serves: 4

Ingredients To Use:

- 4 salmon fillets (skinless and boneless)
- 2 tsp. olive oil
- 1 tbsp. capers (drained)
- Juice from 1 lemon
- Salt and black pepper to taste

For the Potato Mash:

- 1/2 cup milk

- 2 tbsp. olive oil
- 1 lb. potatoes (peeled and chopped)
- 1 tbsp. dried dill

Step-by-Step Directions to Cook It:

1. Preheat the air fryer to 360°F.
2. Put potatoes in a pot, add water and salt, bring to a boil over medium heat for 15 minutes. Drain and transfer to a bowl and mash using a potato masher. Add 2 tbsp. oil, milk, dill, salt, and pepper. Whisk well and set aside.
3. Season the salmon with salt, pepper, and oil. Transfer to your air fryer basket, top with capers and cook for 8 minutes.
4. Serve and enjoy!

Nutritional value per serving:

Calories: 270kcal, Fat: 16g, Carb: 8g, Proteins: 16g

Lemony Saba Fish

This recipe creates a crusty and flaky fish; you are going to enjoy the subtle taste of this fish lingering on your palate.
Prep time and cooking time: 18 minutes|
Serves: 1

Ingredients To Use:

- 4 Saba fish fillets (boneless)
- 2 tbsp. lemon juice
- 2 tbsp. olive oil
- 3 red chili pepper, (chopped)
- 2 tbsp. garlic (minced)
- Salt and black pepper to taste

Step-by-Step Directions to Cook It:

1. Preheat the air fryer to 360°F.
2. Season the fish with salt, pepper, lemon juice, chili, garlic, and oil. Toss to coat, transfer to the air fryer and cook for 8 minutes, flipping halfway.
3. Serve and Enjoy!

Nutritional value per serving:

Calories: 290kcal, Fat: 4g, Carb: 6g, Proteins: 15g

Honey Sea Bass

The sea bass is a tasty and flavourful fish dish that is easy to prepare. The herbs and spices blended with the fish create a great flavor.

Prep time and cooking time: 20 minutes| Serves: 2

Ingredients To Use:

- 2 sea bass fillets
- 2 tbsp. mustard
- Zest from 1/2 orange, grated
- 1/2 lb. canned lentils, drained
- Juice from 1/2 orange
- 2 tbsp. olive oil
- 2 oz. watercress
- 2 tsp. honey
- A small bunch of parsley (chopped)
- A small bunch of dill (chopped)
- Salt and black pepper to taste

Step-by-Step Directions to Cook It:

1. Preheat the air fryer to 350⁰F.
2. In a bowl, add the orange zest, 1 tbsp of oil, juice, mustard, honey, and mix. Season the fillets with salt pepper. Rub the whole fillets with the honey mixture and transfer to the air fryer cooking basket. Close the lid and set the time for 10 minutes.
3. Meanwhile, place a pot over medium heat, add the lentils and boil for 1 minute. Add the rest of the oil, parsley, dill, watercress, and stir.
4. Serve with the fish and Enjoy!

Nutritional value per serving:

Calories: 160kcal, Fat: 3g, Carb: 2g, Proteins: 16g

Delicious French Cod

The combination of various herbs creates a creamy and tasty dish that's unforgettable.

Prep time and cooking time: 32 minutes| Serves: 4

Ingredients To Use:

- 2 lb. cod (boneless)
- 2 garlic cloves (minced)
- 2 tbsp. butter
- 3 tbsp. chopped Parsley
- 2 tbsp. olive oil
- 1/2 cup white wine
- 14 oz. canned tomatoes (stewed)
- Salt and black pepper to taste
- 1 yellow onion (chopped)

Step-by-Step Directions to Cook It:

1. Preheat the air fryer to 350⁰F.
2. Heat oil in a pan over medium heat, add onions and garlic and stir until it is fragrant and translucent. Add the wine and cook for another 1 minute; add the tomatoes and cook for another 2 minutes. Remove from heat and stir in the parsley.
3. Pour the mixture into a pan that fits into the air fryer, add the fish, and season with salt and pepper. Transfer to the air fryer ad closes the lid. Set the time for 14 minutes.
4. Serve the fish with the tomato sauce, enjoy!

Nutritional value per serving:

Calories: 215kcal, Fat: 5g, Carb: 16g, Proteins: 26g

Coconut Tilapia

This recipe is simple and easy to make; it is also creamy and infused with coconut flavor.

Prep time and cooking time: 20 minutes|

Serves: 4

- 4 medium tilapia fillets
- 1/2 jalapeno, chopped
- 1/2 cup of chopped cilantro
- 1/2 tsp. garam masala
- 2 garlic cloves, chopped
- 1 tsp. grated ginger
- 1/2 cup of coconut milk
- Salt and black pepper to taste
- Cooking spray

Step-by-Step Directions to Cook It:

1. Preheat the air fryer to 4000^{0}F.
2. In a food processor, add the coconut milk and other ingredients except for the fillets and pulse well. Spray the fish with cooking spray; add the fillets to the coconut mixture. Make sure that they are well coated, transfer to the air fryer cooking basket, and close the lid. Set the time for 10 minutes.
3. Serve hot and enjoy!

Nutritional value per serving:

Calories: 200kcal, Fat: 3g, Carb: 18g, Proteins: 26g

Special Catfish Fillets

This delicious delight is crispy on the outside, flaky on the inside. It can be enjoyed as a light lunch.
Prep time and cooking time: 22 minutes|
Serves: 4

Ingredients To Use:

- 2 catfish fillets
- 2 oz. butter
- 4 oz. Worcestershire sauce
- 3/4 cup ketchup
- 1 tsp. mustard
- 1/2 tsp. jerk seasoning
- 1 tbsp. Balsamic vinegar

- 1/2 tsp. minced garlic
- 1 tbsp. chopped parsley
- Salt and black pepper to taste

Step-by-Step Directions to Cook It:

1. Preheat the air fryer to 350^{0}F.
2. In a pan over medium heat, heat the butter and stir in Worcestershire sauce, vinegar, seasoning, ketchup, mustard, garlic, salt, and pepper. Remove from heat and add the fish fillets. Toss well and leave to marinate for 10 minutes, drain the fish.
3. Transfer them to the air fryer, set the time for 8minutes. Flip the fillets halfway through.
4. Serve garnished with parsley.

Nutritional value per serving:

Calories: 251kcal, Fat: 3g, Carb: 20g, Proteins: 21g

Oriental Fish

The oriental fish is a combination of different spices in one dish. Air frying the fish creates a unique but attractive flavor.
Prep time and cooking time: 22 minutes|
Serves: 4

Ingredients To Use:

- 2 lb. red snapper fillets (boneless)
- 1 tbsp. lemon juice
- 1 yellow onion
- 1 tbsp. oriental sesame oil
- 2 tbsp. water
- 1 tbsp. tamarind paste
- 1/2 tsp. ground cumin
- 3 tbsp. chopped mint leaves
- 1 tbsp. grated ginger
- 3 cloves garlic (minced)
- Salt and pepper to taste

Step-by-Step Directions to Cook It:

1. Preheat the air fryer to 320^{0}F.

2. In a food processor, add all the ingredients except the fish and lemon juice. Pulse until a smooth consistency is achieved. Coat the fish with the mixture.
3. Transfer the fish into the air fryer and close the lid. Cook the fish for 12 minutes, flip halfway through.
4. Drizzle with the lemon juice and serve.

Nutritional value per serving:

Calories: 241kcal, Fat: 8g, Carb: 15g, Proteins: 12g

Tasty Pollock

This is a nice recipe to prepare when you are bored with your regular meals. Your palate will feel comforted with this dish.
Prep time and cooking time: 25 minutes| Serves: 6

Ingredients To Use:

- 4 pollocks fillets (boneless)
- 2 tbsp. butter
- 1/2 cup sour cream
- 1/2 cup grated parmesan
- Salt and pepper to taste
- Cooking spray

Step-by-Step Directions to Cook It:

1. Preheat the air fryer to 320^0F.
2. In a bowl, mix all the ingredients except the pollock fillet and cooking spray. Spray the fillets with cooking spray and season with salt and pepper. Spread the sour cream mixture on the fillet and arrange in the air fryer. Close the lid and set the time for 15 minutes.
3. Serve and enjoy with salad.

Nutritional value per serving:

Calories: 290kcal, Fat: 13g, Carb: 12g, Proteins: 42g

Baked Shrimp Scampi

Baked shrimp scampi is a fancy dish that can be prepared for special occasions. The shrimps are tender and cooked to perfection.
Prep time and cooking time: 20 minutes| Serves: 4

Ingredients To Use:

- 1 lb. large shrimps
- 3/4 cup breadcrumbs
- 1/4 cup white wine
- 8 tbsp. butter (melted)
- 1/4 tsp. paprika
- 1/2 tsp. onion powder
- 1/4 tsp. cayenne pepper
- 1 tbsp. minced garlic
- 1/2 tsp. salt

Step-by-Step Directions to Cook It:

1. Preheat the Air fryer to 350^0F.
2. In a bowl, mix breadcrumbs, onion powder, paprika, cayenne pepper, salt, and set aside. In another bowl, mix the melted butter, garlic, and white wine. Stir in the shrimps and breadcrumbs mixture. Transfer to a casserole dish that fits into the air fryer.
3. Close the air fryer lid and set the time for 10 minutes.
4. Open the lid and serve. Enjoy!

Nutritional value per serving:

Calories: 322kcal, Fat: 21g, Carb: 15g, Proteins: 26g

Coconut Shrimp with Dip

This is a recipe you can easily get addicted to, which is crispy on the outside, juicy on the inside.
Prep time and cooking time: 20 minutes| Serves: 4

- 1 lb. raw shrimps (peeled and deveined)
- Oil for spraying
- 2 eggs beaten
- 1 tsp. salt
- 1/2 cup all-purpose flout
- 1/2 cup shredded coconut (unsweetened)
- 1/4 tsp. black pepper
- 1/4 cup panko breadcrumbs

Step-by-Step Directions to Cook It:

1. Preheat the air fryer to 390°F.
2. In a bowl, mix the coconut, breadcrumbs, black pepper, and salt, set aside. In another two bowls, add the flour to one bowl and beaten eggs to the other.
3. Dip the shrimps in the flour, followed by the eggs and finally the coconut mixture (ensure the shrimps are well coated with all the mixture).
4. Place the shrimp on a greased tray and transfer into the air fryer, spray with oil, and cover with the lid. Set the time for 4 minutes. Open the air fryer and flip the shrimps, respray with oil and cook for another 5 minutes.
5. Serve and enjoy with Thai sweet chili sauce.

Nutritional value per serving:

Calories: 279kcal, Fat: 11g, Carb: 17g, Proteins: 28g

Air Fryer White Fish

Crispy and crusty, this tasty air-fried fish is as tasty as it looks. From the ingredients to the preparation, it all creates a wonderful dish.
Prep time and cooking time: 30 minutes|
Serves: 4

Ingredients To Use:

- 4 white fish fillets (halved)
- 1 tsp. paprika

- 2 tbsp. olive oil
- Fish seasoning
- 1/2 tsp. black pepper
- 3/4 cup fine cornmeal
- 1/2 tsp. garlic powder
- 1/4 cup flour
- 1/2 tsp. black pepper
- 2 tsp. old bay

Step-by-Step Directions to Cook It:

1. Preheat the air fryer to 400°F.
2. Add all the ingredients except the olive oil to a ziploc bag and set aside. Rinse the fish and pat dry with a paper towel. Place the fish fillets in the ziploc bag and shake to coat or until totally covered with the seasoning.
3. Grease the air fryer basket tray and arrange the fish on it. Close the air fryer lid and set the time for 10 minutes. Open the air fryer lid and spray both sides of the fish with oil. Cook for an additional 7 minutes, flip halfway through.
4. Serve and enjoy!

Nutritional value per serving:

Calories: 193kcal, Fat: 1g, Carb: 21g, Proteins: 20g

Lobster Tail

The recipe is lovely for the holidays, and it is also quite easy to prepare.
Prep time and cooking time: 15 minutes|
Serves: 2

Ingredients To Use:

- 2 (6 oz.) lobster tail
- 1 tsp. lemon juice
- 2 tbsp. unsalted butter (melted)
- 1 tsp. salt
- 1 tsp. chopped chives
- 1 tbsp. minced garlic

1. Preheat the air fryer to 380°F.
2. To prepare the butter mixture, add the lemon juice, salt, chives, garlic in a bowl. Mix until well combined.
3. To prepare the lobster tail, cut through the shell, and remove the meat. Rest the meat on top of the shell. Transfer to an air fryer basket. Spread the butter mixture over the meat.
4. Transfer to the air fryer and close the lid, set the time for 4 minutes. Open the air fryer and spread more butter on the lobster; allow to cook for another 4 minutes or until done.
5. Serve and enjoy.

Nutritional value per serving:

Calories: 120kcal, Fat: 12g, Carb: 1g, Proteins: 10g

Air Fryer Marinated Salmon

You will be surprised at how crusty and flaky the salmon is, especially after being cooked to perfection.
Prep time and cooking time: 30 minutes| Serves: 4

Ingredients To Use:

- 4 salmon fillets
- 1/2 tbsp. minced garlic
- 6 tbsp. soy sauce
- 1 tbsp. brown sugar
- 1 green onion (finely chopped)
- 1/4 cup of Dijon mustard

Step-by-Step Directions to Cook It:

1. In a bowl, add all the ingredients and whisk until well combined. Pour the mixture over the salmon and refrigerate for 20 minutes.
2. Preheat the air fryer to 400°F, transfer the salmon into a greased pan that fits

into the air fryer. Place in the air fryer and close the lid, set the time for 12 minutes.
3. Remove from the air fryer, serve garnished with green onions, enjoy!

Nutritional value per serving:

Calories: 215kcal, Fat: 11g, Carb: 3g, Proteins: 34g

Hawaiian Salmon

The Hawaiian salmon recipe creates a colorful and vibrant dish that can be served as a romantic dinner.
Prep time and cooking time: 20 minutes| Serves: 2

Ingredients To Use:

- 2 salmon fillets
- 2o oz. canned pineapple pieces and juice
- 1 tbsp. Balsamic vinegar
- 1/2 tsp. grated ginger
- 1 tsp. onion powder
- 2 tsp. garlic powder
- Salt and pepper to taste

Step-by-Step Directions to Cook It:

1. Preheat the air fryer to 350°F.
2. Season the fillets with salt, pepper, onion powder, garlic powder, and rub well. Transfer to a pan that fits into the air fryer; add the pineapple pieces, juice, ginger, and mix gently. Drizzle with vinegar and transfer into your air fryer; set the time for 10 minutes.
3. Serve and enjoy!

Nutritional value per serving:

Calories: 200kcal, Fat: 8g, Carb: 12g, Proteins: 20g

Chinese Cod

The Asian cod is a nice and tasty recipe that

can be enjoyed with vegetable stir fry.
Prep time and cooking time: 20 minutes|
Serves: 2

Ingredients To Use:

- 2 cod fillets
- 1 tbsp. soy sauce
- 1 tsp. peanuts (crushed)
- 1/2 tsp. ginger (grated)
- 2 tsp. garlic powder

Step-by-Step Directions to Cook It:

1. Preheat the air fryer to 390^{0}F.
2. In a pan that fits into the air fryer, add all the ingredients, and toss gently. Transfer to the air fryer and close the lid. Set the time for 10 minutes.
3. Serve and enjoy!

Nutritional value per serving:

Calories: 234kcal, Fat: 10g, Carb: 12g, Proteins: 21g

Roasted Cod and Prosciutto

The roasted cod and prosciutto meal is creamy and fancy. Prepare on days when you wish to impress someone.
Prep time and cooking time: 20 minutes|
Serves: 4

Ingredients To Use:

- 4 cod fillets
- 3 tbsp. prosciutto (chopped)
- 1 tbsp. chopped parsley
- 1 shallot, chopped
- 2 tbsp. lemon juice
- 2 garlic (pressed)
- 1 tsp. Dijon mustard
- 1/4 cup melted butter
- Salt and black pepper to taste

Step-by-Step Directions to Cook It:

1. Preheat the air fryer to 390^{0}F.
2. In a bowl, mix all the ingredients except

the fillets, whisk thoroughly. Season the fillets with salt and pepper. Spread the prosciutto mixture all over the fillets, transfer to the air fryer basket. Close the lid and set the time for 10 minutes.
3. Serve and enjoy!

Nutritional value per serving:

Calories: 200kcal, Fat: 4g, Carb: 6g, Proteins: 13g

Salmon and Chives Vinaigrette

The salmon and chives vinaigrette recipe is a game-changer with simple but delectable ingredients that combines with the fish's flavor to create something unique.
Prep time and cooking time: 22 minutes|
Serves: 4

Ingredients To Use:

- 4 salmon fillets
- 3 tbsp. balsamic vinegar
- 2 tbsp. chopped dill
- 1/3 cup maple syrup
- 1 tbsp. olive oil
- 2 tbsp. chopped chives
- Salt and pepper to taste

Step-by-Step Directions to Cook It:

1. Preheat the air fryer to 350^{0}F.
2. Season the fish with salt, pepper, and oil. Transfer to the air fryer and close the lid. Set the time for 8 minutes, flip in between the cooking.
3. Meanwhile, place a pot over medium heat, add the vinegar, chives, maple syrup, and dill. Stir and cook for 3 minutes.
4. Serve the fish with chives vinaigrette on top, enjoy!

Nutritional value per serving:

Calories: 270kcal, Fat: 3g, Carb: 19g, Proteins: 21g

Prawn Wontons

The prawn wontons are crispy and crunchy and are better enjoyed with tomato ketchup.
Prep time and cooking time: 35 minutes|
Serves: 4

For Dough

- 5 tbsp. water
- 1-1/2 cup all-purpose flour
- 1/2 tsp. salt

For filling

- 2 cups minced prawns
- 2 tsp. soy sauce
- 2 tsp. vinegar
- 2 tsp. ginger-garlic paste
- 2 tbsp. oil

Step-by-Step Directions to Cook It:

1. Add all the dough ingredients to a bowl and mix. Knead the dough and cover with a plastic wrap. Place a saucepan over medium heat, add all the filling ingredients and cook for 10 minutes.
2. Preheat the air fryer to 200^0F.
3. Roll out doughs and place the filling in the center. Wrap the dough to cover the filling and pinch together at the edge.
4. Transfer the wontons to the air fryer basket and cover the lid. Set the time for 20 minutes.
5. Serve with ketchup or chili sauce.

Nutritional value per serving:

Calories: 281kcal, Fat: 6g, Carb: 18g, Proteins: 13g

Fish Fingers

Fish fingers are golden, super crispy, and crunchy on the outside but tender on the inside.
Prep time and cooking time: 1 hour 40

minutes| Serves: 2

Ingredients To Use:

- 1/2 lb. fish fillet cut into fingers
- 1 cup olive oil
- 1 tbsp. lemon juice
- 2 cups bread crumbs

For the marinade

- 3 tbsp. lemon juice
- 3 eggs
- 1-1/2 tbsp. ginger-garlic paste
- 2 tsp. ketchup
- 1-1/2 tsp. pepper powder
- 5 tbsp. cornflour
- 1 tsp. red chili flakes
- 2 tsp. salt

Step-by-Step Directions to Cook It:

1. Rub the lemon juice on the fingers and set aside. In a bowl, mix all the marinade ingredients. Wash the fingers after 1 hour and pat dry. Transfer into the marinade bowl and leave for 15 minutes.
2. Preheat the air fryer to 160^0F.
3. Dip the fingers in breadcrumbs and transfer to the air fryer, close the lid, and set the time for 25 minutes.
4. Serve with ketchup or chili sauce.

Nutritional value per serving:

Calories: 312kcal, Fat: 4g, Carb: 6g, Proteins: 17g

Halibut and Sun-Dried Tomatoes Mix

The halibut and sun-dried tomatoes are flavourful and easily to be prepared in 20 minutes.
Prep time and cooking time: 20 minutes|
Serves: 2

Ingredients To Use:

- 2 halibut fillets

- 6 sun-dried tomatoes (chopped)
- 1/2 tsp. red pepper flakes
- 2 tsp. olive oil
- 2 small red onions (sliced)
- 9 black olives (sliced and pitted)
- 4 rosemary sprigs (chopped)
- 1 fennel bulb (sliced)
- 2 garlic cloves
- Salt and black pepper to taste

Step-by-Step Directions to Cook It:

1. Preheat the air fryer to 390^{0}F.
2. Place the fillets in a pan that fits into the air fryer, season with salt, pepper, and oil. Add the onion, tomatoes, rosemary, olives, pepper flakes, and rosemary. Close the lid and set the time for 10 minutes.
3. Serve and enjoy!

Nutritional value per serving:

Calories: 280kcal, Fat: 11g, Carb: 16g, Proteins: 27g

Fish and Couscous

The fish and couscous recipe is a tasty and healthy meal that will have your taste bud salivating.
Prep time and cooking time: 25 minutes|
Serves: 4

Ingredients To Use:

- 2-1/2 lb. sea bass (gutted)
- 2 red onions (chopped)
- 5 tsp. fennel seeds
- 1/4 cup toasted almonds (sliced)
- 2 fennel bulb (cored and sliced)
- 3/4 cup whole wheat couscous (cooked)
- Cooking spray
- Salt and black pepper to taste

Step-by-Step Directions to Cook It:

1. Preheat the air fryer to 350^{0}F.
2. Season the fish with salt and pepper,

spray with cooking spray. Transfer to the air fryer cooking basket and close the lid. Set the time for 10 minutes.
3. Meanwhile, spray a saucepan with cooking oil and heat it over medium heat; add fennel seeds and cook for 1 minute. Add the fennel bulb, onion, almond, couscous, salt, and pepper. Cook for 2-3 minutes.
4. Serve the fish with the couscous.

Nutritional value per serving:

Calories: 321kcal, Fat: 7g, Carb: 17g, Proteins: 28g

Cod with Pearl Onions

The cod and pearl onion meal is rich creamy. The perfect comfort food on rainy days.
Prep time and cooking time: 25 minutes|
Serves: 2

Ingredients To Use:

- 2 cod fillets
- 1 tsp. dried thyme
- 8 oz. mushroom (sliced)
- 14 oz. pearl onion
- 1 tbsp. parsley
- Black pepper to taste

Step-by-Step Directions to Cook It:

1. Preheat the air fryer to 350^{0}F.
2. In a pan that fits into the air fryer, add all the ingredients, and toss gently. Transfer to the air fryer, close the lid, and set the time for 15 minutes.
3. Serve and enjoy!

Nutritional value per serving:

Calories: 270kcal, Fat: 10g, Carb: 12g, Proteins: 22g

Salmon and Avocado Salad

Salads are healthy and delicious, but when

they are combined with air-fried salmon, the taste upgrades to a high new level.
Prep time and cooking time: 30 minutes|
Serves: 4

Ingredients To Use:

- 2 salmon fillets
- 2 tbsp. white wine vinegar
- 2 tbsp. olive oil
- 1/4 cup melted butter
- 4 oz. mushroom (slices)
- 1 0z. crumbled feta cheese
- 8 oz. lettuce leaves (chopped)
- 12 cherry tomato (halved)
- 5 cilantro sprigs (chopped)
- 1 avocado (peeled and cubed)
- 1 jalapeno pepper (chopped)
- Salt and black pepper to taste

Step-by-Step Directions to Cook It:

1. Preheat the air fryer to 350^{0}F.
2. Place the salmon on a lined baking sheet, brush with olive oil. Season with salt and pepper, Transfer to the air fryer, and cook for 15 minutes. Remove and keep warm.
3. Meanwhile, heat the butter in a pan over medium heat, add the mushroom, and cook for 2 minutes. Remove and transfer to a salad bowl; add the jalapeno, mushroom, cilantro, avocado, tomatoes, oil, salt, pepper, and vinegar. Toss well and sprinkle with cheese.
4. Serve the fish with the salad. Enjoy!

Nutritional value per serving:

Calories: 230kcal, Fat: 6g, Carb: 15g, Proteins: 9g

Salmon Fries

This recipe provides you with a flaky and crispy delicious fish that's irresistible. The herbs are well infused with the fish to

created a flavored and tasty meal.
Prep time and cooking time: 20 minutes|
Serves: 4

Ingredients To Use:

- 1 lb. boneless salmon fillets
- 2 tsp. red chili flakes
- 2 cups breadcrumbs
- 2 tsp. oregano

For the marinade

- 4 tbsp. lemon juice
- 1-1/2 tbsp. ginger-garlic paste
- 4 eggs
- 1 tsp. red chili powder
- 2 tsp. salt
- 6 tbsp. cornflour
- 1 tsp. pepper powder

Step-by-Step Directions to Cook It:

1. In a bowl, mix all the marinade ingredients, add the salmon fillets and leave to marinate overnight.
2. Preheat the air fryer to 350^{0}F.
3. In a bowl, mix breadcrumbs, chili flakes and oregano, add the marinated fillets and mix. Transfer to the air fryer and cover with the lid, set the time for 15 minutes.
4. Serve and enjoy.

Nutritional value per serving:

Calories: 310kcal, Fat: 9g, Carb: 3g, Proteins: 17g

Salmon Fritters

Salmon fritter is a nice and delicious meal that can be enjoyed as lunch or dinner. It is crispy, delicious, and tasty.
Prep time and cooking time: 45 minutes|
Serves: 4

Ingredients To Use:

- 1 lb. fileted salmon
- 2 tbsp. freshly chopped coriander leaves

- 2 tbsp. garam masala
- 3 green chili (finely chopped)
- 2 tsp. freshly chopped ginger
- 1-1/2 tbsp. lemon juice
- Salt and pepper to taste

1. Preheat the air fryer to 160^{0}F.
2. In a food processor, add all the ingredients except the salmon. Pulse until it forms a smooth paste. Pour into a bowl and add the salmon, toss to coat.
3. Transfer to the air fryer, and close the lid. Set the time for 45 minutes.
4. Serve drizzled with lemon juice and enjoy!

Calories: 271kcal, Fat: 9g, Carb: 6g, Proteins: 14g

Prawn Galette

This recipe comes with readily available ingredients that make preparation and cooking easier and faster.
Prep time and cooking time: 45 minutes|
Serves: 4

- 1 lb. minced prawns
- 2 tbsp. freshly chopped coriander leaves
- 2 tbsp. garam masala
- 3 green chili (finely chopped)
- 2 tsp. freshly chopped ginger
- 1-1/2 tbsp. lemon juice
- Salt and pepper to taste

1. Preheat the air fryer to 160^{0}F.
2. Mix all the ingredients in a bowl, mold into a galette. Wet the galettes slightly with water and transfer to your air fryer basket. Close the lid and set the time for 25 minutes. Keep rolling to get evenly

cooked galettes.
3. Serve with ketchup or mint chutney.

Calories: 261kcal, Fat: 7g, Carb: 5g, Proteins: 14g

Clam Galette

Clam Galette is a nice and delicious meal for a lunch date. It is also highly nutritious and easy to prepare.
Prep time and cooking time: 45 minutes|
Serves: 4

- 1 lb. minced clams
- 2 tbsp. freshly chopped coriander leaves
- 2 tbsp. garam masala
- 3 green chili (finely chopped)
- 2 tsp. freshly chopped ginger
- 1-1/2 tbsp. lemon juice
- Salt and pepper to taste

1. Preheat the air fryer to 160^{0}F.
2. Mix all the ingredients in a bowl, mold into a galette. Wet the galettes slightly with water and transfer to your air fryer basket. Close the lid and set the time to 25 minutes. Keep rolling to get uniformly cooked galettes.
3. Serve with ketchup or mint chutney.

Calories: 268kcal, Fat: 5g, Carb: 7g, Proteins: 16g

Seafood Wontons

There is nothing as delightful as a plate of mouth-watering seafood. This recipe combines a lot of delicious, flavorful, and highly nutritious ingredients all in one plate.
Prep time and cooking time: 35 minutes|

Serves: 4

For Dough:
- 5 tbsp. water
- 1-1/2 cup all-purpose flour
- 1/2 tsp. salt

For filling:
- 2 cups minced seafood (shrimps, scallops, prawns, and oyster)
- 2 tsp. soy sauce
- 2 tsp. vinegar
- 2 tsp. ginger-garlic paste
- 2 tbsp. oil

Step-by-Step Directions to Cook It:

1. Add all the dough ingredients to a bowl and mix. Knead the dough and cover with a plastic wrap. Place a saucepan over medium heat, add all the filling ingredients and cook for 10 minutes.
2. Preheat the air fryer to 200^0F.
3. Roll out doughs and place the filling in the center. Wrap the dough to cover the filling and pinch together at the edge. Transfer the wontons to the air fryer basket and cover the lid. Set the time for 20 minutes.
4. Serve with ketchup or chili sauce.

Nutritional value per serving:

Calories: 280kcal, Fat: 5g, Carb: 16g, Proteins: 13g

Swordfish and Mango Salsa

One of the most attractive features of this dish is the vibrant, attractive color. Also, the taste is unforgettable.
Prep time and cooking time: 16 minutes|
Serves: 2

Ingredients To Use:

- 2 swordfish steaks
- A pinch of cumin
- 2 tsp. avocado oil
- 1 mango (chopped)
- A pinch of garlic powder
- 1 tbsp. chopped cilantro
- 1 avocado (pitted, peeled, and chopped)
- A pinch of ginger powder
- 1/2 tbsp. balsamic vinegar
- Salt and black pepper to taste
- 1 orange (peeled and sliced)

Step-by-Step Directions to Cook It:

1. Preheat the air fryer to 360^0F.
2. Season the fillets with onion powder, garlic powder, salt, pepper, cumin, and rub with half the oil. Transfer to the air fryer and cook for 6 minutes, flip in between the cooking.
3. Meanwhile, in a bowl, add the mango with cilantro, avocado, salt, pepper, vinegar, and oil. Mix well.
4. Serve fish with the mango salsa.

Nutritional value per serving:

Calories: 170kcal, Fat: 7g, Carb: 12g, Proteins: 16g

Crusted Salmon

This recipe creates a nice and flaky fish that melts in your mouth. Simply delicious!
Prep time and cooking time: 20 minutes|
Serves: 4

Ingredients To Use:

- 4 salmon fillets
- 1 tsp. chopped dill
- 1 cup pistachios (chopped)
- 1 tbsp. mustard
- 1/4 cup lemon juice
- Salt and black pepper to taste
- 2 tbsp. honey

Step-by-Step Directions to Cook It:

1. Preheat the air fryer to 350^0F.
2. In a bowl, add all the ingredients except

the salmon, whisk until well combined. Spread the mixture over the salmon and transfer it to the air fryer. Set the time for 10 minutes.
3. Serve and enjoy!

Nutritional value per serving:

Calories: 170kcal, Fat: 16g, Carb: 18g, Proteins: 20g

Chili Salmon

If you are on the search for something spicy, then this dish is perfect for you. Chili salmon is hot and delicious!
Prep time and cooking time: 25 minutes|
Serves: 12

Ingredients To Use:

- 1lb. wild salmon (cubed)
- 1/4 cup balsamic vinegar
- 1 egg
- 1/2 cup honey
- 2 tbsps. olive oil
- 1/3 cup flour
- 4 red chilies (chopped)
- 1/4 cup of water
- 3 garlic cloves (minced)
- 1 and 1/4 cups. Shredded coconut
- Salt and black pepper to taste

Step-by-Step Directions to Cook It:

1. Preheat the air fryer to 320°F.
2. To a bowl, add the flour, salt, and stir.
3. In a separate bowl, add the egg, black pepper, and whisk. Put the shredded coconut in a third bowl.
4. Dip the cubes in flour, egg, and coconut. Arrange in the air fryer basket and set the time for 8 minutes, shake the air fryer in between then cooking.
5. Boil water in a pan over medium heat; add chilies, vinegar, cloves, honey. Stir well and leave to simmer for 3-5 minutes.

6. Serve the salmon drizzled with the chili sauce, enjoy!

Nutritional value per serving:

Calories: 220kcal, Fat: 12g, Carb: 12g, Proteins: 13g

Mustard Salmon

The mustard salmon will only take about 20 minutes to air fry, and it is absolutely delicious.
Prep time and cooking time: 20 minutes|
Serves: 1

Ingredients To Use:

- 1 big salmon fillets
- 1 tbsp. coconut oil
- 1 tbsp. maple extract
- 2 tbsp. mustard
- Salt and pepper to taste
- Cooking spray

Step-by-Step Directions to Cook It:

1. Preheat the air fryer to 370°F.
2. In a bowl, add the maple and mustard, whisk well. Season the fillet with salt, pepper, and oil. Brush the salmon with the maple mixture, spray with cooking spray. Transfer the mixture to the air fryer and set the time for 10 minutes.
3. Serve and enjoy!

Nutritional value per serving:

Calories: 300kcal, Fat: 7g, Carb: 16g, Proteins: 20g

Carp Fritters

The carp fritters is a nice and tasty recipe that will leave you craving for more.
Prep time and cooking time: 35 minutes|
Serves: 4

- 10 carp fillets
- 3 eggs
- 3 onions chopped
- 1-1/2 tsp. salt
- 1-1/2 tbsp. ginger paste
- 1-1/2 tbsp. garlic paste
- 5 green chilies, freshly chopped
- 2 -1/2 tbsp. sesame seed
- 3 tsp. lemon juice
- 2 tsp. garam masala

Step-by-Step Directions to Cook It:

1. Preheat the air fryer to 160^{0}F.
2. In a food processor, add all the ingredients except the filets and the eggs. Pulse until it forms a smooth paste. Pour into a bowl and add the filets, toss to coat. Beat the egg in a bowl, add salt.
3. Dip the coated fish in the egg, then in the sesame seeds, transfer to the air fryer, and close the lid. Set the time for 25 minutes.
4. Serve and enjoy!

Nutritional value per serving:

Calories: 312kcal, Fat: 9g, Carb: 12g, Proteins: 13g

Squid and Guacamole

Squid and guacamole may seem like a weird combination at first, but you won't feel the same after trying this recipe. The meat is tasty and delicious.

Prep time and cooking time: 16 minutes|
Serves: 2

Ingredients To Use:

- 2 medium squid, tentacles separated and tubes scored lengthwise
- Juice from 1 lime
- 1 tbsp. olive oil
- Salt and pepper to taste

For the Guacamole:

- Juice from 2 lime
- 2 avocados (pitted, cored, and chopped)
- 2 red chilies, chopped
- 1 tomato, chopped
- 1 tbsp. chopped coriander
- 1 red onion, chopped

Step-by-Step Directions to Cook It:

1. Preheat the air fryer to 360^{0}F.
2. Season the squid with salt, pepper, and olive oil. Transfer to the air fryer basket and cook for 3 minutes per side. Remove and transfer to a bowl, drizzle with lime juice, and set aside.
3. Meanwhile, put the avocado in a bowl and mash, add the rest of the guacamole ingredients and mix well.
4. Serve the squid with the guacamole.

Nutritional value per serving:

Calories: 370kcal, Fat: 31g, Carb: 6g, Proteins: 20g

Chapter 4: Savory Beef

Beef Strip with Snow Pea and Mushrooms

Pea is a favorite ingredient in any meal. When combined with beef and mushroom, it results in an explosive taste.

Prep time and cooking time: 30 minutes| Serves: 2

Ingredients To Use:

- 2 beef steaks (cut into strips)
- 2 tbsp. soy sauce
- 7 oz. snow pea
- 1 medium yellow onion (cut into rings)
- 1 tbsp. olive oil
- 8 oz. white mushroom (cut into halves)
- Salt and black pepper to taste

Step-by-Step Directions to Cook It:

1. Preheat the air fryer to 350^{0}F.
2. In a bowl, mix the olive oil, soy sauce, and whisk. Toss in the beef strip to coat.
3. In a separate bowl, mix the mushroom, snow pea, onions, salt, and pepper. Transfer the contents in the bowl to a pan and fit it into the air fryer. Set the timer for 16 minutes and start cooking.
4. Turn up the air fryer's temperature to 400^{0}F, add the beef strip, and cook for another 6 minutes.
5. Serve.

Nutritional value per serving:

Calories: 231kcal, Fat: 7g, Carb:14 g, Proteins: 23g

Beef Fillet with Garlic Mayo

Beef fillet with garlic mayo is juicy, tender, and tastes wonderful. When complemented with mayo, it tastes heavenly.

Prep time and cooking time: 50 minutes| Serves: 8

Ingredients To Use:

- 3 lb. beef fillet
- 1 cup mayonnaise
- 4 tbsp. Dijon mustard
- 1/3 cup sour cream
- 1/4 cup chopped tarragon
- 2 tbsp. chopped chives
- 2 cloves garlic (minced)
- Salt and black pepper, to taste

Step-by-Step Directions to Cook It:

1. Preheat the air fryer to 370^{0}F.
2. Season the beef with salt and pepper, transfer to the air fryer, and cook for 20 minutes. Remove and set aside.
3. In a bowl, whisk the mustard and tarragon. Add the beef and toss, return to the air fryer and cook for 20 minutes.
4. In a separate bowl, mix the garlic, sour cream, mayonnaise, chives, salt, and pepper. Whisk and set aside.
5. Serve the beef with the garlic-mayo spread.

Nutritional value per serving:

Calories: 400kcal, Fat: 12g, Carb: 26g, Proteins: 19g

Mustard Marina Ted Beef

Mustard marina ted beef is a traditional American meal that has been served for generations. When air-fried, the taste of the bacon-wrapped beef roast is brought to a new level.

Prep time and cooking time: 55 minutes|

Serves: 6

- 3 lb. beef roast
- 6 bacon strips
- 1-3/4 beef stock
- 2 tbsp. butter
- 3/4 cup red wine
- 1 tbsp. horseradish
- 3 cloves garlic (minced)
- 1 tbsp. mustard
- Salt and pepper, to taste

Step-by-Step Directions to Cook It:

1. Preheat the air fryer to 400^{0}F.
2. In a bowl, add the butter, horseradish, mustard, garlic, salt, garlic, and mix. Rub the beef with the mixture.
3. Arrange the bacon on a cutting board, add the meat on top and wrap the beef with the bacon strips. Transfer to the air fryer and cook for 15 minutes. Remove the beef roast and transfer to a pan.
4. Add the stock and wine to the pan, lower the temperature to 360^{0}F and cook for 30minutes.
5. Carve the beef and serve.

Nutritional value per serving:

Calories: 350kcal, Fat: 9g, Carb: 27g, Proteins: 29g

Chinese Steak and Broccoli

Chinese beef and broccoli is a simple, healthy dish that is perfect for a ketogenic diet.
Prep time and cooking time: 30 minutes| Serves: 8

Ingredients To Use:

- 3/4 lb. steak cut into strips
- 1/3 cup oyster sauce
- 1/3 cup sherry
- 1 lb. broccoli florets
- 1 tsp. soy sauce
- 2 tsp. sesame oil
- 1 tsp. sugar
- 1 garlic clove (minced)
- 1 tbsp. olive oil

Step-by-Step Directions to Cook It:

1. Preheat the air fryer to 380^{0}F.
2. In a bowl, mix the oyster sauce, sesame oil, sherry, soy sauce, and sugar. Add the beef and mix; leave to marinate for 30 minutes.
3. Transfer the meat to a pan that fits into the air fryer, add the broccoli, garlic, oil, and toss together. Cook for 12 minutes.
4. Uncover the air fryer, serve, and enjoy.

Nutritional value per serving:

Calories: 330kcal, Fat: 12g, Carb: 17g, Proteins: 23g

Beef Brisket and Onion Sauce

This flavor-rich recipe is one of the tastiest briskets in this book. The onion sauce elevates the taste.
Prep time and cooking time: 2 hours 10 minutes| Serves: 6

Ingredients To Use:

- 4 lb. beef brisket
- 1 lb. yellow onion (chopped)
- 1/2 lb. chopped celery
- 1 lb. chopped carrot
- 4 cups of water
- 8 earl gray tea bags
- Salt and black pepper to taste

For the sauce:

- 1/2 lb. chopped celery
- 16 oz. canned tomatoes (chopped)
- 1 lb. chopped sweet onions
- 1 oz. minced garlic
- 1 cup brown sugar
- 1 cup white vinegar

- 4 oz. vegetable oil
- 8 earl grey teabags

1. Preheat the air fryer to 300°F.
2. Put water in a pan that fits into the air fryer. Add the onions, celery, carrots, salt, and pepper. Stir and allow to simmer over medium-high heat.
3. Add the beef brisket, 8 earl grey tea bags, and stir. Transfer to the air fryer and cook for 1 hour 30 minutes.
4. Meanwhile, place a pan over medium-high heat, add vegetable oil, and heat until shimmering. Add the sweet onion and sauté for 10 minutes. Add the remaining sauce ingredients and cook for 10 minutes. Remove and discard the teabags.
5. Cut and serve the beef brisket with the onion sauce.

Nutritional value per serving:

Calories: 400kcal, Fat: 12g, Carb: 26g, Proteins: 34g

Beef Curry

Curry is a unique ingredient in any dish, and its combination with the other spices in this recipe is just splendid.
Prep time and cooking time: 55 minutes| Serves: 4

Ingredients To Use:

- 2 lb. beef (cut into cubes)
- 2 tbsp. tomato sauce
- 3 medium potatoes (cut into cubes)
- 2 yellow onions chopped
- 2 tbsp. olive oil
- 1 tbsp. wine mustard
- 2 garlic cloves (minced)
- 2-1/2 tbsp. curry
- 10 oz. can coconut milk

- Salt and black pepper to taste

Step-by-Step Directions to Cook It:

1. Preheat the air fryer to 360°F.
2. Place a pan over medium heat (make sure the pan fits into your air fryer), add oil, and heat until shimmering. Add the onions and garlic, cook for 4 minutes or until translucent. Add the beef, curry powder, tomato sauce, coconut milk, salt, and pepper.
3. Stir and transfer to the air fryer; set the time for 40 minutes.
4. Serve and enjoy.

Nutritional value per serving:

Calories: 231kcal, Fat: 15g, Carb: 20g, Proteins: 27g

Garlic and Bell Pepper Beef

This savory beef recipe has a delightful aroma that is only superseded by its flavourful taste.
Prep time and cooking time: 1 hour | Serves: 4

Ingredients To Use:

- 11 oz. steak fillets (sliced)
- 1/2 cup beef stock
- 2 tbsp. olive oil
- 2 tbsp. fish sauce
- 4 cloves garlic (pressed)
- 1 red pepper (cut into thin strips)
- 4 green onions (sliced)
- 1 tbsp. sugar
- 2 tsp. cornflour
- Black pepper to taste

Step-by-Step Directions to Cook It:

1. In a pan, add beef, oil, garlic, black pepper, and bell pepper, stir, cover, and keep in the refrigerator for 30 minutes.
2. Preheat the air fryer to 360°F.
3. Transfer the pan to the air fryer and cook for 14 minutes. In a bowl, mix sugar and

fish sauce, pour over the beef and cook for an additional 7 minutes.

4. Serve and enjoy.

Calories: 243kcal, Fat: 3g, Carb: 24g, Proteins: 38g

Beef and Green Onion Marinade

A recipe to remember! The marinade infuses the beef with enough taste to have you drooling.

Prep time and cooking time: 30 minutes | Serves: 4

Ingredients To Use:

- 1 lb. lean beef
- 1 cup of soy sauce
- 5 garlic cloves (minced)
- 1/4 cup sesame seeds
- 1/2 cup of water
- 1 tsp. black pepper
- 1/4 cup brown sugar
- 1 cup green onion

Step-by-Step Directions to Cook It:

1. In a bowl, add soy sauce, onions, sugar, water, garlic, sesame seed, and pepper, whisk. Add the beef and toss to coat, leave for 10 minutes.
2. Preheat the air fryer to 390⁰F, drain the beef, and transfer to the air fryer. Cook for 20 minutes.
3. Serve with salad and enjoy.

Nutritional value per serving:

Calories: 329kcal, Fat: 8g, Carb: 24g, Proteins: 22g

Beef Roasted Wine Sauce

This savory recipe is perfect for entertaining guests. So yummy and tasty!

Prep time and cooking time: 55 minutes | Serves: 6

Ingredients To Use:

- 3 lb. beef roast
- 3 carrot (chopped)
- 3 oz. red wine
- 1/2 tsp. smoked paprika
- 5 potatoes chopped
- 1/2 tsp. salt
- 1 yellow onion (chopped)
- 4 garlic clove (pressed)
- 17 oz. beef stock
- 1/2 tsp. chicken salt

Step-by-Step Directions to Cook It:

1. Preheat the air fryer to 360⁰F.
2. In a bowl, add salt, paprika, and chicken salt, stir. Rub the beef with the mixture and transfer to a pan that will fit into the air dryer.
3. Add the remaining ingredients and cook for 45 minutes.
4. Enjoy and serve.

Nutritional value per serving:

Calories: 304kcal, Fat: 20g, Carb: 18g, Proteins: 32g

Short Ribs and Beer Sauce

The short rib in beer sauce is juicy and tender. And when paired with mashed potatoes, it creates a delicious taste that transcends regular beef dish. So satisfying!

Prep time and cooking time: 1 hour | Serves: 6

Ingredients To Use:

- 4 lb. short ribs (cut into small pieces)
- 1 dried Portobello mushroom
- 1 yellow onion (chopped)
- 1 cup chicken stock
- 6 thyme sprigs (chopped)
- 1/4 cup tomato paste
- 1 bay leaf
- 1 cup dark beer

- Salt and pepper to taste

1. Preheat the air fryer to 350⁰F.
2. In a pan that fits into your air fryer, heat oil over medium heat, add onion, stock, tomato paste, beer, mushroom, bay leaf, and thyme. Simmer for 3-5minutes.
3. Add the rib and transfer to the air fryer, cook for 40 minutes.
4. Bon appetite!

Nutritional value per serving:

Calories: 300kcal, Fat: 7g, Carb: 18g, Proteins: 23g

Beef and Cabbage Mix

Get your palate ready for a flavorful journey with this spice-rich beef combination. Bon Appetite!
Prep time and cooking time: 60 minutes | Serves: 6

Ingredients To Use:

- 2-1/2 lb. beef brisket
- 3 garlic cloves, preferably pressed
- 1 cup beef stock
- 1 cabbage cut into wedges
- 2 bay leaves
- 4 carrots, chopped
- 2 turnips (cut into smaller pieces)
- Salt and black pepper to taste

Step-by-Step Directions to Cook It:

1. Preheat the air fryer to 360⁰F.
2. Put the beef in a pan, add the stock, salt, pepper, carrots, cabbage, bay leaves, garlic, turnip, stir, transfer to the air fryer, and cover. Cook for 40 minutes.
3. Serve and enjoy.

Nutritional value per serving:

Calories: 355kcal, Fat: 16g, Carb: 18g, Proteins: 24g

Short Ribs and Special Sauce

In this recipe, the short ribs are air-fried until perfectly tender and juicy. Serve with the special sauce for a memorable taste.
Prep time and cooking time: 46 minutes| Serves: 4

Ingredients To Use:

- 4 lb. short ribs
- 1/2 cup of soy sauce
- 3 cloves garlic (pressed)
- 1/2 cup of water
- 2 tbsp. sesame oil
- 1/4 cup of rice wine
- 3 ginger slices
- 1/4 cup pear juice
- 1 tsp. vegetable oil
- 2 green onions chopped

Step-by-Step Directions to Cook It:

1. Preheat the air fryer to 350⁰F.
2. Heat oil in a pan over medium heat, add garlic, green onions, and ginger, stir and cook for 1 minute.
3. Add the rib and the remaining ingredients, transfer to the air fryer and cook for 35 minutes.
4. Serve and enjoy.

Nutritional value per serving:

Calories: 321kcal, Fat: 12g, Carb: 20g, Proteins: 14g

Beef Patty in Mushroom

The sauce used in this recipe completely elevated the taste of this recipe. Beef patty in mushroom is creamy, juicy, and tasty.
Prep time and cooking time: 35 minutes| Serves: 6

Ingredients To Use:

- 2 lb. ground beef
- 3/4 cup flour

- 1 tbsp. onion flakes
- 1/2 tsp. garlic powder
- 1/4 cup beef stock
- 1 tbsp. chopped parsley
- 1 tbsp. soy sauce
- Salt and pepper to taste

For the sauce:

- 1/2 cup beef stock
- 1/2 tsp. soy sauce
- 2 cups mushroom, sliced
- 2 tbsp. butter
- 1 cup yellow onion, chopped
- 2 tbsp. bacon fat
- 1/4 cup sour cream
- Salt and black pepper to taste

Step-by-Step Directions to Cook It:

1. Preheat the air fryer to 350^0F.
2. In a bowl, mix beef, pepper, salt, garlic powder, 1 tbsp soy sauce, ¼ cup beef stock, parsley, onions flakes, and flour. Stir and shape six patties. Transfer to the air fryer and cook for 14 minutes.
3. While the patties are still cooking, heat butter in a pan on medium heat, add the mushroom and cook for 4 minutes with constant stirring. Add onions and cook for another 4 minutes, add the soy sauce, sour cream, and simmer. Remove from heat.
4. Serve patties with mushroom sauce.

Nutritional value per serving:

Calories: 235kcal, Fat: 23g, Carb: 6g, Proteins: 32g

Greek Beef Meatballs Salad

This Greek beef meatball recipe will spice up your palate in a beautiful way. It's also simple and healthy.
Prep time and cooking time: 20 minutes|
Serves: 6

Ingredients To Use:

- 17 oz. ground beef
- 1 cup baby spinach
- 5 bread slice, cubed
- 1/4 cup parsley
- 1/4 cup milk
- 1/4 cup chopped mint
- 1 yellow onion (minced)
- 1 tbsp. olive oil
- 7 oz. cherry tomatoes (halved)
- 1 egg whisked
- 2 garlic cloves (minced)
- 2-1/2 tsp. dried oregano
- Cooking spray
- Salt and pepper to taste

Step-by-Step Directions to Cook It:

1. Preheat the air fryer to 370^0F.
2. In a bowl, add the bread and milk and allow to soak for 3 minutes. Squeeze and transfer to another bowl.
3. To the bread in the bowl, add egg, salt, pepper, mint, parsley, garlic, and onion. Stir and shaped into balls using ice-cream scooper.
4. Spray the meatballs with cooking spray, place in your air fryer and cook for 10 minutes.
5. In a bowl, mix spinach, cucumber, and tomatoes. Add the meatball, oil, pepper, salt, lemon juice, and yogurt. Toss, and serve.

Nutritional value per serving:

Calories: 200kcal, Fat: 4g, Carb: 13g, Proteins: 27g

Beef stuffed Squash

Are you searching for a perfect squash recipe? Then you are in luck because this beef stuffed squash sets the pace for others. It is easy to prepare and takes less than 1 hour. Cook in batches and you will enjoy this

delicious meal in no time.
Prep time and cooking time: 40 minutes|
Serves: 2

- 1 lb. ground beef
- 1 tsp. dried oregano
- 1 spaghetti squash (pricked)
- 3 garlic cloves (minced)
- 28 oz. canned tomatoes (chopped)
- 1 Portobello mushroom (sliced)
- 1/2 tsp. dried thyme
- 1 green bell pepper (chopped)
- 1/4 tsp. cayenne pepper
- 1 yellow onion (diced)
- Salt and pepper to taste

Step-by-Step Directions to Cook It:

1. Preheat the air fryer to 350^{0}F, transfer the spaghetti squash into the air fryer, and cook for 20 minutes. Remove and transfer to the cutting board and cut into halves. Remove and discard the seeds.
2. Heat a pan over medium heat, add the beef, garlic, onions, mushroom, stir and cook until the meat is golden brown. Add the remaining ingredients except for the squash and allow them to cook for 10 minutes.
3. Stuff the squash with the beef mix and transfer into the air fryer; cook for 10 minutes at 360^{0}F.
4. Serve and enjoy.

Nutritional value per serving:

Calories: 260kcal, Fat: 7g, Carb: 14g, Proteins: 10g

Beef Casserole

This traditional beef stew recipe is easy to prepare and works perfectly when entertaining guests. The beef is tasty and tender.

Prep time and cooking time: 1 hour 15 minutes| Serves: 12

Ingredients To Use:

- 2 lb. beef
- 2 tsp. mustard
- 2 cups of grated mozzarella
- 1 tbsp. olive oil
- 2 cups. chopped eggplant
- 28 oz. canned tomatoes (chopped)
- 1 tsp. dried oregano
- 2 tsp. Worcestershire sauce
- 2 tbsp. chopped parsley
- 16 oz. tomato sauce
- Salt and pepper to taste

Step-by-Step Directions to Cook It:

1. Preheat the air fryer to 360^{0}F.
2. In a bowl, add eggplant, salt, pepper, and oil, mix to coat.
3. In a separate bowl, add beef, mustard, salt, pepper, and Worcestershire sauce, stir well. Pour the mixture into a pan that fits into your air fryer and spread evenly; add the eggplant mix and tomato sauce. Sprinkle with parsley and oregano.
4. Transfer to the air fryer and cook 35 minutes.
5. Serve and enjoy.

Nutritional value per serving:

Calories: 200kcal, Fat: 12g, Carb: 16g, Proteins: 15g

Burgundy Beef Mix

The burgundy beef mix is easy to prepare and extremely tasty.
Prep time and cooking time: 1hour 10 minutes| Serves: 7

Ingredients To Use:

- 2 lb. beef chuck roast, cut into smaller cubes
- 4 carrots (chopped)

- 1 cup of water
- 1 cup. beef stock
- 3 tbsp. almond flour
- 2 yellow onions (chopped)
- 1 tbsp. chopped thyme
- 2 celery ribs (chopped)
- 1/2 lb. mushroom (sliced)
- 15 oz. canned tomatoes(chopped)
- 1/2 tsp. mustard powder
- Salt and black pepper to taste

1. Preheat the air fryer to 300°F.
2. Place a medium pot over high heat; add the meat and brown on all sides for 3-5 minutes. Add the tomato, carrot, onions, celery, mushroom, salt, pepper, mustard, stock, and thyme, stir.
3. In a bowl, add water and flour, stir. Add to the pot and transfer into the air fryer and cook for 1 hour.
4. Serve and enjoy.

Nutritional value per serving:

Calories: 275kcal, Fat: 13g, Carb: 17g, Proteins: 28g

Sirloin Steaks and Pico De Gallo

The steak is juicy and tender; moreover, the pico de gallo bumps up the taste.
Prep time and cooking time: 20 minutes| Serves: 4

Ingredients To Use:

- 4 medium sirloin steak
- 1 tsp. onion powder
- 1/2 tbsp. sweet paprika
- 1 tsp. garlic powder
- 2 tbsp. chili powder
- 1 tsp. ground cumin
- Salt and pepper to taste

For the Pico de Gallo:

- 2 tomatoes (chopped)

- 2 tbsp. lime juice
- 1 jalapeno (chopped)
- 1 small red onion (chopped)
- 1/4 cup chopped cilantro
- 1 small red onion (diced)
- 1/4 tsp. cumin
- 1 red onion (chopped)

Step-by-Step Directions to Cook It:

1. Preheat the air fryer to 360°F.
2. In a bowl, mix chili powder, onion powder, salt, pepper, garlic powder, paprika, and 1 tsp. cumin. Rub the steak on both sides with the mixture and transfer to your air fryer. Cook for 10 minutes.
3. Mix all the pico de gallo ingredients in a bowl and add pepper to taste.
4. Serve the steak with the pico de gallo at the side, enjoy.

Nutritional value per serving:

Calories: 200kcal, Fat: 12g, Carb: 15g, Proteins: 18g

Mexican Beef Mix

This recipe is like all traditional Mexican recipes; it's spicy and delicious.
Prep time and cooking time: 1hour 20 minutes| Serves: 8

Ingredients To Use:

- 2 lb. beef roast, cubes
- 2 green bell peppers (chopped)
- 6 garlic cloves (minced)
- 2 tbsp. olive oil
- 4 jalapenos (chopped)
- 2 yellow onions (diced)
- 1/2 cup of water
- 1 tsp. dried oregano
- 1 Habanero pepper (chopped)
- 2 tbsp. cilantro (chopped)
- 14 oz. canned tomatoes (chopped)

- 1/2 cup of black olive (pitted and chopped)
- 1 and 1/2 tsp. ground cumin
- Salt and pepper to taste

Step-by-Step Directions to Cook It:

1. Preheat the air fryer to 300^0F.
2. In a pan, add all the ingredients and stir, transfer to the air fryer and cook for 1 hour 10 minutes.
3. Serve garnished with olives.

Nutritional value per serving:

Calories: 305kcal, Fat: 14g, Carb: 1825g, Proteins: g

Coffee Flavoured Steak

A defining feature of this dish is the ground coffee added to improve the flavor and aroma.
Prep time and cooking time: 25 minutes| Serves: 4

Ingredients To Use:

- 4 rib-eye steak
- 2 tbsp. garlic powder
- 2 tbsp. chili powder
- 1-1/2 tbsp. ground coffee
- 2 tbsp. onion powder
- 1/2 tbsp. sweet paprika
- Pinch of cayenne pepper
- 1/4 tsp. ground ginger
- Black pepper to taste
- 1/4 tsp. ground coriander

Step-by-Step Directions to Cook It:

1. Preheat the air fryer to 360^0F.
2. In a bowl, mix all the ingredients except the steak and stir. Rub the steak thoroughly with the mixture.
3. Transfer to the air fryer and cook for 15 minutes.
4. Serve and enjoy.

Nutritional value per serving:

Calories: 160kcal, Fat: 10g, Carb: 14g, Proteins: 12g

Balsamic Beef

Balsamic beef is the perfect comfort food. It is always there to pick you up on rainy days and sunny ones.
Prep time and cooking time: 1hour 10 minutes| Serves: 6

Ingredients To Use:

- 1 medium beef roast
- 4 garlic cloves (pressed)
- 1 cup beef stock
- 1 tbsp. Worcestershire sauce
- 1 tbsp. soy sauce
- 1/2 cup balsamic vinegar
- 1 tbsp. honey

Step-by-Step Directions to Cook It:

1. Preheat the air fryer to 360^0F.
2. In a pan, mix beef roast with vinegar, Worcestershire sauce, honey, garlic, stock, and soy sauce. Transfer into the air fryer and cook for 1 hour.
3. Serve and enjoy!

Nutritional value per serving:

Calories: 311kcal, Fat: 12g, Carb: 20g, Proteins: 16g

Beef Medallion Mix

The beef mix is tender and juicy and can be prepared in no time—the perfect meal for a weeknight.
Prep time and cooking time: 2hours 10 minutes| Serves: 4

Ingredients To Use:

- 4 beef medallion
- 2 tbsp. lime juice
- 1 cup tomatoes (crushed)

- 2 tbsp. soy sauce
- 1 tsp. chili powder
- 1 tbsp. hot pepper
- 2 tsp. onion powder
- 2 tsp. onion powder
- Salt and black pepper to taste

Step-by-Step Directions to Cook It:

1. In a bowl, mix all the ingredients except the beef and whisk well. Arrange the beef in a pan, pour the sauce over the beef. Set aside for 2 hours.
2. Preheat the air fryer to 360^0F.
3. Discard the tomato marinade, and transfer to the air fryer. Cook for 10 minutes.
4. Serve and enjoy!

Nutritional value per serving:

Calories: 230kcal, Fat: 4g, Carb: 13g, Proteins: 14g

Beef Kabobs

Beef kabobs are the perfect meal for a summer gathering; the flavors and taste will leave your guest craving for more.
Prep time and cooking time: 20 minutes|
Serves: 4

Ingredients To Use:

- 2 lb. sirloin steak (cut into medium sizes)
- 2 tbsp. chili powder
- 1 red onion (chopped)
- 1/4 cup olive oil
- 2 red peppers (chopped)
- 1/2 tbsp. ground cumin
- 2 tbsp. hot sauce
- Juice from 1 lime
- 1 zucchini (sliced)
- 1/4 cup of salsa
- Salt and pepper to taste

Step-by-Step Directions to Cook It:

1. Preheat the air fryer to 370^0F.

2. In a bowl, mix oil, salsa, hot sauce, cumin, lime juice, black pepper, and salt. Whisk thoroughly.
3. Arrange the meat, bell pepper, onions, and zucchini on a skewer, brush with salsa mix. Arrange in your air fryer and cook for 10 minutes.
4. Better enjoyed with salad at the side.

Nutritional value per serving:

Calories: 170kcal, Fat: 5g, Carb: 13g, Proteins: 16g

Mediterranean Steak Scallops

The flavored steak is served with the scallion, which serves as an excellent additive to the dish. A perfect meal to cook for a large crowd.
Prep time and cooking time: 25 minutes|
Serves: 2

Ingredients To Use:

- 2 beef steaks
- 1/4 cup butter
- 1 tsp. lemon zest
- 4 garlic cloves, pressed
- 1 shallot, chopped
- 10 sea scallops
- 2 tbsp. chopped parsley
- 1/4 cup vegetable stock
- 2 tbsp. chopped basil
- 2 tbsp. lemon juice
- Salt and pepper to taste

Step-by-Step Directions to Cook It:

1. In a bowl, mix all the ingredients except the beef. Arrange the beef in a dish and pour the sauce over it. Leave to marinate for 2 hours.
2. Preheat the air fryer to 360^0F.
3. Discard the marinade and transfer beef to the air fryer, cook for 10 minutes.
4. Serve and enjoy with salad on the side.

Nutritional value per serving:
Calories: 150kcal, Fat: 2g, Carb: 14g, Proteins: 17g

Air Fryer Beef Steak

Air fryer beef steak is easy to prepare, and the final taste will leave you wanting for more. Juicy and delicious, enjoy with salad as a side.
Prep time and cooking time: 20 minutes| Serves: 4

Ingredients To Use:

- 2 lb. rib-eye steak
- 1 tbsp. olive oil
- Pepper and salt to taste

Step-by-Step Directions to Cook It:

1. Preheat the air fryer to 356^{0}F.
2. Season the beef on both sides with salt and pepper, rub with olive oil. Transfer into the air fryer and cook for 15 minutes (flip after 7 minutes).
3. Remove and allow the meat to rest for 3 minutes, carve, and serve. Enjoy!

Nutritional value per serving:

Calories: 233kcal, Fat: 19g, Carb: 2g, Proteins: 16g

Mushroom Meatloaf

This is the right recipe for recreating a juicy and tender meatloaf. It also tastes better when served with sauce.
Prep time and cooking time: 30 minutes| Serves: 4

Ingredients To Use:

- 14 oz. lean ground beef
- 3 tbsp. breadcrumbs
- 1 chorizo sausage (finely chopped)
- 1 garlic clove (minced)
- 2 tbsp. freshly chopped cilantro
- 1 small onion (chopped)
- 1 egg
- 3 tbsp. olive oil
- 2 tbsp. freshly sliced mushroom
- Salt and pepper to taste

Step-by-Step Directions to Cook It:

1. Preheat the air fryer to 390^{0}F.
2. In a bowl, add all the ingredients except mushroom, mix until well combined. Pour the mixture into a bowl and level the surface with a spatula.
3. Arrange the mushroom on top and drizzle with oil. Transfer to the air fryer basket, close the lid of the air fryer. Set time to 25 minutes, open the air fryer, and remove the meatloaf. Allow to rest and serve.

Nutritional value per serving:

Calories: 284kcal, Fat: 7.9g, Carb: 46g, Proteins: 17.9g

Air Fried Steak Sandwich

One salient advantage of this recipe is that it can be prepared in less than 30 minutes; perfect for the morning rush.
Prep time and cooking time: 22 minutes| Serves: 4

Ingredients To Use:

- 6 oz. sirloin steak cut into smaller pieces
- 8 medium-size cherry tomatoes (sliced)
- 1/2 tbsp. soy sauce
- 1 cup arugula, rinsed and dried
- 1/2 tbsp. of mustard powder
- 1 tbsp. bleu cheese (crumbled)
- 1 hoagie bun (sliced in half)

Step-by-Step Directions to Cook It:

1. Preheat the air fryer to 320^{0}F.
2. In a bowl, mix onion powder and soy sauce until thoroughly combined. Immerse the steak in the mixture for 1-2

minutes. Arrange the steak on a tin foil and transfer to the air fryer basket. Lay the hoagie-bun halves in the air fryer (crusty side up, soft-side down).

3. Close the air fryer lid and set time to 10 minutes; open the lid and flip the hoagie-buns (crusty side down, soft-side up). Sprinkle bleu cheese on the buns, close the air fryer and cook additional 6 minutes.

4. Open the air fryer lid, Remove the hoagie buns, arrange the steak, tomatoes, and arugula on the halved bun. Close with the other half, enjoy.

Calories: 284kcal, Fat: 7.9g, Carb: 5.5g, Proteins: 17.9g

Carrot and Beef Cocktail Balls

This Carrot and Beef cocktail balls recipe is fragrant and flavor-packed.
Prep time and cooking time: 25 minutes| Serves: 10

Ingredients To Use:
- 1 lb. ground beef
- 1 egg
- 1 red onion (chopped)
- 2 cloves garlic
- 1/2 tsp. dried oregano
- 1/2 tsp. Salt
- 1/2 tsp. dried rosemary (crushed)
- 1/2 tsp. dried basil
- 3/4 breadcrumbs
- 2 carrots (diced)
- 1/2 tsp. black pepper
- 1 cup plain flour

Step-by-Step Directions to Cook It:
1. Preheat the air fryer to 350^0F.
2. Place the ground beef in a bowl, add onion, carrot, and garlic in a food processor. Pulse until smooth. Pour the

mixture into the bowl containing the meat, add the remaining ingredient, and mix.

3. Shape the mixture into a ball and refrigerate for 30 minutes, remove and roll into the flour. Arrange in the air fryer and close the lid. Set time to 20 minutes, turning occasionally.

4. Serve and enjoy.

Calories: 284kcal, Fat: 7.9g, Carb: 4.5g, Proteins: 23g

Beef Steak with Beans

This delicious and spicy recipe is best served and enjoyed with rice for maximum taste and aroma.
Prep time and cooking time: 15 minutes| Serves: 4

Ingredients To Use:
- 4 beef steak cut into strips
- 3/4 cup beef broth
- 1 cup green onions (chopped)
- 1/4 tsp. dried basil
- 1 can tomatoes (crushed)
- 1 red bell pepper (seed removed and thinly sliced)
- 1 can of cannellini beans
- 2 garlic cloves (minced)
- 1/2 tsp. sea salt
- 1/2 tsp. cayenne pepper
- Black pepper to taste

Step-by-Step Directions to Cook It:
1. Preheat the air fryer to 3900F.
2. In a pan that fits into the air fryer, add garlic, onions, steak. Close the air fryer and set the time to 10 minutes. Open the lid and stir in the remaining ingredients.
3. Cover and set time to 5 minutes, open the lid, and serve.
4. Enjoy!

Calories: 275kcal, Fat: 7.5g, Carb: 4.3g, Proteins: 25g

Flavoured Rib Eye Steak

The name of the recipe says it all. You get a juicy and tender steak that just melts on your palate.
Prep time and cooking time: 30 minutes|
Serves: 4

Ingredients To Use:

- 2lb. rib-eye steak
- 1 tbsp. olive oil
- Salt and black pepper to taste

Rub

- 2 tbsp. onion powder
- 1 tbsp. brown sugar
- 3 tbsp. sweet paprika
- 1 tbsp. grounded cumin
- 2 tbsp. garlic powder
- 1 tbsp. dried rosemary
- 2 tbsp. dried oregano

Step-by-Step Directions to Cook It:

1. Preheat the air fryer to 400^0 F.
2. In a bowl, mix all the rub ingredients. Rub the steak on both sides with the mixture.
3. Season the steak with salt and pepper, and rub with olive oil.
4. Put in your air fryer and cook for 20 minutes (flip after 10minutes).
5. Remove the steak and allow it to sit for 5 minutes. Slice and enjoy with salad.

Nutritional value per serving:

Calories: 320kcal, Fat: 8g, Carb: 22g, Proteins: 21g

Chinese-Style Spicy and Herby Beef

The herbs and spices in this delightful Chinese recipe infuse the beef with great taste.
Prep time and cooking time: 45 minutes|
Serves: 4

Ingredients To Use:

- 1 lb. flank steak (cut into smaller)
- 3 tbsp. Shaoxing wine
- 1 tsp. fresh sage leaves (minced)
- 1/3 cup olive oil
- 3 cloves garlic (minced)
- 3 tsp. sesame oil
- 2 tbsp. tamari
- 1/8 tsp. xanthium
- 1 tsp. fresh rosemary, freshly minced
- 1 tsp. hot sauce
- 1/2 tsp. freshly cracked pepper

Step-by-Step Directions to Cook It:

1. Preheat the air fryer to 345^0 F.
2. Warm oil in a pan over medium heat, add garlic, and sauté until fragrant. Add the remaining ingredient and stir.
3. Transfer to the air fryer and set time to 18 minutes.
4. Serve and enjoy!

Nutritional value per serving:

Calories: 254kcal, Fat: 24g, Carb: 8g, Proteins: 21g

Filet Mignon Steak

With this recipe, you don't have to go to a restaurant to get your premium filet mignon.
Prep time and cooking time: 45 minutes|
Serves: 6

Ingredients To Use:

- 6 filet mignon steaks
- 1/2 cup heavy cream
- 2 tsp. freshly cracked peppercorn (mixed)
- 1/2 medium-size garlic bulb (peeled and pressed)
- 1-1/2 tbsp. apple cider

- 1-1/2 tsp. sea salt flakes
- A dash of hot sauce

Step-by-Step Directions to Cook It:

1. Preheat the air fryer to 385⁰ F.
2. Season the steak with peppercorn and salt flakes. Transfer to the air fryer basket. Cook for 24 minutes, turning halfway through the cooking time. Remove and set aside.
3. Place a saucepan over medium heat, add all the ingredients and whisk until it assumes a uniform consistency.
4. Serve the steak with the sauce.

Nutritional value per serving:

Calories: 452kcal, Fat: 32g, Carb: 8g, Proteins: 26g

Marinated Cajun Beef

The marinated beef is air-fried until it is tender and succulent; the result is absolutely delicious.

Prep time and cooking time: 1hour 25 minutes| Serves: 2

Ingredients To Use:

- 3/4 lb. beef tenderloins
- 1/2 tsp. freshly ground pepper
- 1-1/2 tsp. olive oil
- 1/2 tsp. garlic powder
- 1/3 tsp. pear cider vinegar
- 1/3 tsp. cayenne pepper
- 2 tbsp. Cajun seasoning
- 1/3 cup beef broth
- 1/2 tsp. freshly ground pepper
- 1 tsp. salt

Step-by-Step Directions to Cook It:

1. Preheat the air fryer to 385⁰ F.
2. Season the beef with black pepper, cayenne, and salt. Set aside. In a bowl, mix the remaining ingredients and add the meat. Leave to marinate for 40 minutes.
3. Transfer the beef to the air fryer basket, cook for 22 minutes, flipping halfway through.
4. Serve and enjoy!

Nutritional value per serving:

Calories: 283kcal, Fat: 23g, Carb: 5g, Proteins: 53g

Meatball with Spicy Sauce

Spicy and full of flavors, the combination of various ingredients in this recipe makes it an absolute delight.

Prep time and cooking time: 40 minutes| Serves: 4

Ingredients To Use:

- 1 lb. beef sausage meat
- 4 tbsp. pork rind
- 1/3 tsp. ground black pepper
- 3 garlic cloves preferably pressed
- 1/3 cup green onions
- Salt to taste

For the sauce:

- 1/3 cup tomato paste
- 1/3 yellow onion, minced
- 2 tbsp. Worcestershire sauce
- 1/2 balsamic vinegar
- 1 tsp. cumin powder
- Dash of tobacco sauce

Step-by-Step Directions to Cook It:

1. Preheat the air fryer to 365⁰F.
2. Add all the ingredients to a bowl and mix until well combined. Roll into a ball and transfer into the air fryer. Cook for 13 minutes.
3. Place a saucepan over medium heat, add all the sauce ingredients and cook for 10 minutes.
4. Serve the meatball with the sauce, enjoy!

Calories: 360kcal, Fat: 23g, Carb: 6g, Proteins: 23g

Steak with Cascabel- Garlic Sauce

The cascabel sauce is the secret ingredient that defines this recipe. It creates a wonderful taste with wild rice.
Prep time and cooking time: 40 minutes| Serves: 4

Ingredients To Use:

- 1-1/2 lb. steak, trimmed and cubed
- 2 tsp. brown mustard
- 1/2 cup of finely chopped scallion
- 2 tbsp. mayonnaise
- 3 cloves garlic, pressed
- 2 tsp. minced cascabel
- 1/3 cup crème Fraiche
- 2 tsp. cumin seeds
- Freshly cracked peppercorn to taste
- Freshly ground black pepper to taste
- 1 tsp. salt

Step-by-Step Directions to Cook It:

1. Preheat the air fryer to 390^0 F.
2. Place a pan over medium heat, add the cumin seed and fry until they pop. Season the beef with salt, pepper, and fried cumin seed. Arrange the beef in a baking dish that fits into the air fryer, add the cascabel, scallion, and garlic. Close the lid and set the time to 8 minutes.
3. Open and add the crème fraiche, peppercorn, mayonnaise, mustard and cook for additional 7 minutes.
4. Serve with hot wild rice.

Nutritional value per serving:

Calories: 229kcal, Fat: 16g, Carb: 8g, Proteins: 37g

Spicy Paprika Steak

An easy dish to prepare following the instruction, and you will have a juicy and wonderfully spiced steak in no time.
Prep time and cooking time: 40 minutes| Serves: 2

Ingredients To Use:

- 2 beef steak
- 1 tbsp. brandy
- 1-1/2 tbsp. olive oil
- 1 tbsp. brandy
- 3 cloves garlic, sliced
- 1/2 ancho chili pepper (soaked in hot water)
- 2 tsp. smoked paprika
- 1 tsp. ground allspice

Step-by-Step Directions to Cook It:

1. Preheat the air fryer to 385^0 F.
2. Season the steak with paprika, salt, and allspice, transfer to a baking pan that fits your air fryer. Sprinkle the garlic and minced ancho chili on top. Drizzle with brandy and olive oil.
3. Transfer to the air fryer, close the lid. Set the time for 14 minutes, turning halfway through.
4. Serve warm.

Nutritional value per serving:

Calories: 450kcal, Fat: 26g, Carb: 4g, Proteins: 58g

Meatloaf with Mustard and Pepper

This meatloaf with mustard and pepper recipe is yummy and packed full of flavors. Enjoy it on a good weekend.
Prep time and cooking time: 55 minutes| Serves: 5

- 1 lb. ground beef
- 1/2 lb. ground veal
- 2 garlic cloves (pressed)
- 2 tbsp. soy sauce
- 1 egg
- 1/2 cup pork rinds
- 1 onion, chopped
- 1 tbsp. Dijon mustard
- 7 oz. tomato puree
- 4 tbsp. vegetable juice
- 1 (1-ounce) package ranch dressing mix
- 2 bell pepper, chopped
- Salt and pepper to taste

Step-by-Step Directions to Cook It:

1. Preheat the air fryer to 330^0 F.
2. In a bowl, add all the beef, veal, pork rinds, garlic, vegetable juice, tomato paste, soy sauce, bell pepper, onion, ranch dressing mix, egg, tomato paste, ground pepper; mix until well combined.
3. Pour into a greased meatloaf pan, transfer to the air fryer. Set time to 25 minutes. Meanwhile, whisk tomato puree and mustard. Spread the topping on the meatloaf and cook for additional 2 minutes.
4. Allow to rest for 3-5 minutes, serve, and enjoy!

Nutritional value per serving:

Calories: 298kcal, Fat: 24g, Carb: 9g, Proteins: 32g

Korean Beef Bowl

Koreans are known for their spicy dishes and flavourful taste, and this is no different. Enjoy the best of Korean delicacy with this meal.
Prep time and cooking time: 35 minutes| Serves: 4

Ingredients To Use:

- 1 lb. ground beef
- 4 tbsp. chicken stock
- 2 tsp. olive oil
- 1 tbsp. minced garlic
- 4 oz. chopped chives stem
- 1 tsp. ground ginger
- 2 tbsp. apple cider vinegar
- 1 tbsp. flax seeds
- 1 tsp. stevia extract

Step-by-Step Directions to Cook It:

1. Preheat the air fryer to 370^0 F.
2. In a bowl, add the beef, vinegar, garlic, olive oil, and mix. Transfer to air fryer basket tray and set time to 8 minutes, close the air fryer lid.
3. Open the lid and stir in the remaining ingredients; close the air fryer lid. Set time to 10 minutes.
4. Open the lid and stir the dish, serve, and enjoy!

Nutritional value per serving:

Calories: 258kcal, Fat: 10.1g, Carb: 4.2g, Proteins: g

Carrots Beefcake

This carrot beefcake recipe is delicious and can also be served as a dessert. Amazing right?
Prep time and cooking time: 1 hour 10 minutes| Serves: 10

Ingredients To Use:

- 2 lb. lean ground beef
- 3 eggs, beaten
- 2 cups of shredded carrot
- 1/2 lb. ground pork
- 1 cup dried breadcrumbs
- 1/3 cup almond milk
- 1 oz. onion soup mix

1. Preheat the air fryer to 360⁰ F.
2. In a bowl, mix all the ingredients until well combined. Grease a meatloaf pan and pour the mixture in the meatloaf pan. Place the pan in the hair fryer and close the lid.
3. Select bake on the air fryer and set time to 60 minutes.
4. Open the air fryer, serve and enjoy your meal.

Nutritional value per serving:

Calories: 212kcal, Fat: 24.8g, Carb: 43.8g, Proteins: 19g

Beef Stroganoff

Beef stroganoff is a creamy and juicy delicacy that can make any bad day better. An ideal comfort food!
Prep time and cooking time: 50 minutes| Serves: 3

Ingredients To Use:

- 1 lb. thin steak
- 1 cup sour cream
- 4 cups beef broth
- 4 tbsp. butter
- 16 oz. egg noodles, cooked
- 8 oz. mushroom
- 1 onion (chopped)

Step-by-Step Directions to Cook It:

1. Preheat the air fryer to 400⁰F.
2. Melt butter in a pan over medium heat, and transfer to a bowl. Add sour cream, beef broth, onion, mushroom, and mix. Pour the mixture over the beef and set aside for 10 minutes.
3. Transfer the beef to the air fryer basket, close the lid, and set time to 10 minutes.
4. Open and serve with the cooked egg noodles, enjoy!

Nutritional value per serving:

Calories: 458kcal, Fat: 37g, Carb: 1g, Proteins: 21g

Beef with Apple and Plum

The blend of apple and plum in this recipe creates a sweet and creamy taste that will have you craving for more.
Prep time and cooking time: 40 minutes| Serves: 4

Ingredients To Use:

- 2 lb. beef (cubed)
- 2 tbsp. melted butter
- 1 cup plums (pitted and halved)
- 1 cup apple (pitted and halved)
- Salt and pepper to taste

Step-by-Step Directions to Cook It:

1. Preheat the air fryer to 390⁰ F.
2. In the air fryer pan, mix all the ingredients. Transfer to the air fryer and set the time for 30 minutes.
3. Serve and enjoy!

Nutritional value per serving:

Calories: 290kcal, Fat: 12g, Carb: 19g, Proteins: 27g

Flanked Steak Beef

This recipe is spicy, tasty, and a lovely way to enjoy your beef.
Prep time and cooking time: 30 minutes| Serves: 4

Ingredients To Use:

- 1 lb. flank steak (sliced)
- 1/2 cup soy sauce
- 1/2 cup water
- 1/4 cup xanthum gum
- 3/4 cup swerve, packed
- 2 tsp. vegetable oil
- 1/2 tsp. minced garlic

- 1/2 cup soy sauce

Step-by-Step Directions to Cook It:

1. Preheat the air fryer to 390^0 F, grease the air fryer basket.
2. Coat the steak on both sides with xanthum, transfer to the greased air fryer basket.
3. Set the time for 10 minutes, open the air fryer, place a saucepan over medium heat, stir in the rest of the ingredients, bring to boil.
4. Serve the steak with sauce.

Nutritional value per serving:

Calories: 312kcal, Fat: 11.8g, Carb: 1.8g, Proteins: 34g

Beef Roast

This beef roast dish is simple and can be prepared in no time.
Prep time and cooking time: 65 minutes| Serves: 4

Ingredients To Use:

- 2 lb. beef roast
- 3 tbsp. garlic
- 1 tbsp. smoked paprika
- 3 tbsp. minced garlic
- Salt and pepper to taste

Step-by-Step Directions to Cook It:

1. Preheat the air fryer to 390^{0}F.
2. In a bowl, combine all the ingredients and mix to coat the roast. place the roast in the air fryer and set the time for 55 minutes.
3. Serve and enjoy!

Nutritional value per serving:

Calories: 254kcal, Fat: 12g, Carb: 2g, Proteins: 23 g

French Beef Toast

The French beef toast is a simple recipe with easy-to-access ingredients. It can be prepared for breakfast or a light lunch.
Prep time and cooking time: 25 minutes| Serves: 2

Ingredients To Use:

- 1/2 lb. slice of beef
- 4 slices of bread
- 1 egg white for every two-slice
- 1 tsp. sugar for every two slices

Step-by-Step Directions to Cook It:

1. Preheat the air fryer to 180^{0}F.
2. On a cutting board, put two slices together and cut diagonally, set aside. In a bowl, add egg white and sugar. Whisk until foamy. Dip the bread in the mixture.
3. Place a pan over medium heat and cook the beef for 5-10 minutes. Place your coated bread in the air fryer basket, set the time for 20 minutes, turning at halfway.
4. Remove and top with the beef, serve and enjoy!

Nutritional value per serving:

Calories: 183kcal, Fat: 5g, Carb: 16g, Proteins: 10g

Sage Beef

Sage is often ignored and overlooked, but this delicacy explores the flavor and aroma of sage. It creates a wonderful recipe.
Prep time and cooking time: 40 minutes| Serves: 4

Ingredients To Use:

- 2 lb. beef (cubed)
- 1 tsp. Italian seasoning
- 1/2 tsp. grounded coriander
- 1 tbsp. freshly chopped sage
- 1/2 tbsp. garlic powder
- 2 tbsp. butter (melted)
- Salt and black pepper

1. Preheat the air fryer to 390⁰ F.
2. in an air fryer pan, mix all the ingredients, transfer into the air fryer, and set time to 30 minutes.
3. Serve and enjoy.

Calories: 290kcal, Fat: 11g, Carb: 20g, Proteins: 29g

Beef, Olives, and Tomatoes

Beef with olives and tomatoes is a rich and creamy delicacy that will set your taste buds on a wild, beautiful dance. It is spicy and delicious with nice aroma.
Prep time and cooking time: 45 minutes| Serves: 4

- 2 lb. beef (cubed)
- 1 tbsp. smoked paprika
- 1 cup black olives (pitted and halved)
- 3 tbsp. olive oil
- 1 cup cherry tomatoes (halved)
- 1 tsp. ground coriander
- Salt and black pepper to taste

1. Preheat the air fryer to 390⁰ F.
2. In a pan that fits, mix all the ingredients, and transfer to the air fryer. Set time to 35 minutes.
3. Serve and enjoy!

Calories: 291kcal, Fat: 12g, Carb: 19g, Proteins: 26g

Beef Schnitzel

The amazing recipe is tangy and delicious.
Prep time and cooking time: 55 minutes| Serves: 2

- 1 beef schnitzel cut into strips
- 2 tbsp. vegetable oil
- 1 whole lemon
- 2 oz. breadcrumbs
- 1 whole egg, whisked

1. Preheat the air fryer to 356⁰ F.
2. In a bowl, add breadcrumbs, vegetable oil, and mix. Dip the schnitzel into the egg, then into the breadcrumb mixture to coat. Transfer to the air fryer cooking basket and set time for 12 minutes.
3. Drizzle with lemon juice and serve.

Calories: 346kcal, Fat: 11g, Carb: 3g, Proteins: 33g

Beef Roast with Red Potatoes

Beef roast with red potatoes is a classic recipe that can be prepared for lunch or dinner.
Prep time and cooking time: 55 minutes| Serves: 3

- 4 lb. roast beef
- 3 lb. red potatoes halved
- 2 tbsp. olive oil
- 1/2 tsp. freshly chopped rosemary
- 1 tsp. dried thyme
- 1 tsp. salt
- 1/4 tsp. freshly ground black pepper
- Black pepper, olive oil, and salt for garnish.

1. Preheat the air fryer to 360⁰ F.
2. In a bowl, mix all the spices and set aside. Rub oil onto the beef and season with the spice mixture.

3. Transfer the beef to the air fryer cooking basket and set time to 20 minutes. Open the air fryer and flip the meats, add the potatoes, and season with pepper and oil. Cook for another 20 minutes.
4. Remove the steak and allow to rest; cook the potatoes for an additional 10 minutes at 400°F.
5. Serve with the steak.

Nutritional value per serving:

Calories: 346kcal, Fat: 11g, Carb: 4g, Proteins: 32g

Sirloin steak with Cremini Mushroom Sauce

The sirloin steak is succulent and tender when coupled with the creamy and tasty cremini mushroom sauce. It has a taste you will never forget!
Prep time and cooking time: 40 minutes| Serves: 5

Ingredients To Use:
- 2 lb. sirloin steak cut into 5 pieces
- 1 lb. cremini mushroom sliced
- 1/2 tsp3 dried rosemary
- 1 tsp3 mustard
- 1/4 tsp. dried thyme
- 1 cup sour cream
- 2 tbsp. butter
- 1/2 tsp. curry powder
- 1 tsp. cayenne pepper
- 1/2 tsp3 dried dill
- Salt and black pepper to taste

Step-by-Step Directions to Cook It:
1. Preheat the air fryer to 396° F.
2. Grease a baking pan with butter, add the steak, cayenne pepper, black pepper, salt, dill, rosemary, and thyme. Stir and

transfer to the air fryer. Set time to 9 minutes.
3. Open the air fryer, stir in the remaining ingredients and cook for another 5-7 minutes.
4. Serve and enjoy!

Nutritional value per serving:

Calories: 349kcal, Fat: 12g, Carb: 4g, Proteins: 49g

Irish Whisky Steak

Try something new with this great recipe; the result will be the most unlike taste you've ever experienced.
Prep time and cooking time: 2hours 45 minutes | Serves: 6

Ingredients To Use:
- 2 lb. sirloin steak
- 2 tbsp. olive oil
- 1-1/2 tbsp. tamari sauce
- 2 tbsp. Irish whiskey
- 1/3 tsp. ground ginger
- 2 garlic cloves (minced)
- 1/3 tsp. cayenne pepper
- Fine sea salt to taste

Step-by-Step Directions to Cook It:
1. Preheat the air fryer to 395° F.
2. In a bowl, add all the ingredient except olive oil in a bowl, pour into a ziploc bag, and leave to marinate for 2 hours.
3. Remove and drizzle with olive oil, transfer to the air fryer basket and cook for 22 minutes, turning halfway through.
4. Serve and enjoy.

Nutritional value per serving:

Calories: 260kcal, Fat: 17g, Carb: 8g, Proteins: 35g

Chapter 5: Flavourful Lamb and Goat Recipes

Lamb Curry

Curry dish is always a favorite, and spicy is the best word to describe this irresistible delicacy. Dinner can never get boring with lamb curry.

Prep time and cooking time: 55 minutes|
Serves: 4

Ingredients To Use:

- 2 lb. lamb (cut into cubes)
- 3 medium potatoes (cut into cubes)
- 2 tbsp. olive oil
- 2 garlic cloves (minced)
- 2 tbsp. tomato sauce
- 2-1/2 tbsp. curry
- 2 yellow onions chopped
- 10 oz. can coconut milk
- 1 tbsp. wine mustard
- Salt and black pepper to taste

Step-by-Step Directions to Cook It:

1. Preheat the air fryer to 360°F.
2. Place a pan over medium heat (make sure the pan fits into your air fryer), add oil, and heat until shimmering. Add the onions and garlic, cook for 4 minutes or until translucent. Add the lamb, curry powder, tomato sauce, coconut milk, salt, and pepper.
3. Stir and transfer to the air fryer, set time for 40 minutes.
4. Serve and enjoy.

Nutritional value per serving:

Calories: 218kcal, Fat: 9g, Carb: 12g, Proteins: 26g

Lamb Meatballs

Lamb meatballs are herby, spicy and would soon become your daily favorite, especially when served with the green goddess sauce.
Prep time and cooking time: 50 minutes|
Serves: 4

Ingredients To Use:

- 1 lb. ground lamb
- 1 tsp. cumin
- 3 tbsp. extra-virgin olive oil
- 3 cloves garlic, minced
- 2 tbsp. freshly chopped parsley
- 1 egg, whisked
- 1/4 tsp. crushed red pepper flakes
- 2 tsp. freshly chopped oregano
- Salt and black

For the Green Goddess Sauce:

- 1-1/2 cup Greek yogurt
- 1-1/2 cup basil leaves
- 1/2 cup mayonnaise
- Juice of 1 lemon
- 1/2 cup parsley leaves
- 2 cloves garlic
- 1/4 cup freshly chopped chives
- 1/4 cup fresh oregano leaves
- Kosher salt

Step-by-Step Directions to Cook It:

1. Preheat the air fryer to 370°F.
2. In a bowl, combine egg, red pepper, garlic, salt, oregano, parsley, ground lamb, cumin, and pepper. Using an ice-cream scooper, form into 16 meatballs. Line a baking pan that fits into the air

fryer with parchment paper.

3. Arrange the meatball in the baking pan and drizzle with oil. Transfer to the air fryer and set time for 20 minutes.
4. To prepare the sauce, add all ingredients in a food processor and pulse. Season with kosher salt and pepper.
5. Serve the meatballs with the dip.
6. Enjoy.

Nutritional value per serving:

Calories: 205kcal, Fat: 9g, Carb: 10g, Proteins: 23g

Lamb and Snow Pea

The lamb and snow pea stir-fry is an aroma filled dish that can be get ready in 25 minutes. Moreover, you can get juicy and tasty meat too!
Prep time and cooking time: 25 minutes| Serves: 4

Ingredients To Use:

- 1 lb. lean lamb backstrap (sliced)
- 17 0z. trimmed snow pea
- 1 garlic clove, crushed
- 1 lemongrass stem (chopped)
- 1/3 cup rice wine
- 1-1/2 tsp. peanut oil
- 1/3 cup soy sauce
- 1 small white onion (sliced)
- Steamed jasmine rice to serve

Step-by-Step Directions to Cook It:

1. Preheat the air fryer to 350^{0}F.
2. In a bowl, mix peanut oil, soy sauce, and whisk. Toss in the lamb strip to coat. In another bowl, mix snow pea, onions, salt, lemongrass stem, rice wine, garlic, and pepper. Transfer to a pan and fit into the air fryer, set time to 16 minutes.
3. Increase the air fryer's temperature to 400^{0}F, add the lamb strip, and cook for

another 6 minutes.
4. Serve and enjoy!

Nutritional value per serving:

Calories: 259kcal, Fat: 7g, Carb: 2g, Proteins: 21g

Garlic Mutton

Garlic mutton is a versatile side dish that is spicy as well as tasteful. You can also enjoy it as a main meal.
Prep time and cooking time: 1 hour | Serves: 4

Ingredients To Use:

- 1 lb. boneless lamb (cut into cubes)
- 1 medium onion, thinly sliced
- 3 tbsp. mustard seed
- 1 sprig of curry leaves
- 3 tbsp. chopped garlic
- 2 tsp. chili powder
- 4 green chili, diced
- 1/4 cup vinegar
- 1 lime
- 2 tbsp. chopped mint leaves
- 2 tbsp. chopped coriander leaves
- Salt and black pepper to taste

Step-by-Step Directions to Cook It:

1. In a food processor, add all the ingredients except the mutton and pulse until it forms a smooth paste. Season the mutton with salt and pepper, transfer to the marinade and leave to rest overnight.
2. Preheat the air fryer to 250^{0}F.
3. Transfer the mutton to the air fryer and cook for 1o minutes. Uncover and add the marinade, cook for an additional 5 minutes.
4. Serve and enjoy!

Nutritional value per serving:

Calories: 249kcal, Fat: 9g, Carb: 10g, Proteins: 19g

Garlic Lamb Chops

The delicious garlic lamb chops are easy to prepare and can be ready in 20 minutes. The garlic blends with the richness of the lamb to create a great dish.

Prep time and cooking time: 20 minutes| Serves: 4

Ingredients To Use:

- 8 lamb chops
- 4 garlic cloves (minced)
- 1 tbsp. chopped oregano
- 3 tbsp. olive oil
- 1 tbsp. chopped coriander
- Salt and pepper to taste

Step-by-Step Directions to Cook It:

1. Preheat the air fryer to 350^0F.
2. In a bowl, mix all the ingredients. Add the lamb chops and toss to coat.
3. Transfer to the air fryer and cook for 10 minutes.
4. Serve and enjoy!

Nutritional value per serving:

Calories: 231kcal, Fat: 7g, Carb: 6g, Proteins: 23g

Oriental Air Fried Lamb

Oriental fried lamb is the ultimate meal for any season. The spice and herbs' flavors, coupled with the meat's delicious taste creates a hearty meal.

Prep time and cooking time: 52 minutes| Serves: 8

Ingredients To Use:

- 2-1/2 lb. lamb shoulder (chopped)
- 9 oz. plumps (pitted)
- 3 tbsp. honey
- 3 oz. almond (peeled and chopped)
- 8 oz. veggie stock
- 3 tbsp. olive oil

- 2 yellow onions (chopped)
- 1 tsp. turmeric powder
- 1 tsp. cinnamon powder
- 2 cloves garlic (minced)
- 1 tsp. ginger powder
- 1 tsp. cumin powder
- Salt and black pepper to taste

Step-by-Step Directions to Cook It:

1. Preheat the air fryer to 350^0F.
2. In a bowl, add ginger, cinnamon, turmeric, olive oil, cumin, garlic, and lamb. Mix well and transfer to the air fryer basket, close the lid and cook for 8 minutes.
3. Open the lid and add honey, plums, stock, and onions. Cook for 35 minutes.
4. Serve and enjoy!

Nutritional value per serving:

Calories: 324kcal, Fat: 13g, Carb: 23g, Proteins: 20g

Marinated Lamb and Veggies

The marinated lamb and veggies is a perfect blend of sweet and savory flavors. The dish is pretty easy to prepare and comes with bright flavors.

Prep time and cooking time: 40 minutes| Serves: 4

Ingredients To Use:

- 8 oz. lamb loin (sliced)
- 1 onion (sliced)
- 1 carrot (chopped)
- 3 oz. beans sprouts
- 1/2 tbsp. olive oil

Marinade:

- 1/2 apple, grated
- 1 tbsp. sugar
- 1 garlic clove, minced
- 5 tbsp. soy sauce
- 1 tbsp. grated ginger

- 2 tbsp. orange juice
- 1 onion (grated)
- Salt and pepper to taste

Step-by-Step Directions to Cook It:

1. Preheat the air fryer to 350^{0}F.
2. In a bowl, add all the marinade ingredients, whisk and set aside. In a pan that fits into the air fryer, heat oil, add onions, and beans sprout. Cook for 3 minutes; add the lamb and the marinade.
3. Transfer into the air fryer, close the lid and cook for 25 minutes.
4. Serve and enjoy!

Nutritional value per serving:

Calories: 265kcal, Fat: 3g, Carb: 18g, Proteins: 22g

Lamb and Cabbage Mix

This super versatile dish is loaded with Greek flavors that you are going to love. The cabbage makes it a vegetable-rich meal. Prep time and cooking time: 30 minutes| Serves: 4

Ingredients To Use:

- 2 lb. lamb
- 3 garlic cloves, preferably pressed
- 1 cup beef stock
- 2 tsp. coriander
- 2 tsp. nutmeg
- 1 cabbage cut into wedges
- 2 bay leaves
- 4 carrots, chopped
- 2 turnips (cut into smaller pieces)
- Salt and black pepper to taste

Step-by-Step Directions to Cook It:

1. Preheat the air fryer to 360^{0}F.
2. Put the beef in a pan, add the stock, coriander, nutmeg, salt, pepper, carrots, cabbage, bay leaves, garlic, turnip, stir, transfer to the air fryer, and cover. Cook

for 20 minutes.
3. Serve and enjoy.

Nutritional value per serving:

Calories: 250kcal, Fat: 14g, Carb: 18g, Proteins: 24g

Lemony Lamb Leg

The lemony lamb leg can be prepared for celebration or special occasion. The spices imbue the lamb with a deep and earthy flavor. Prep time and cooking time: 1hour 10 minutes| Serves: 6

Ingredients To Use:

- 4 lb. lamb leg
- 2 tbsp. chopped parsley
- 2 lb. baby potatoes
- 1 tbsp. lemon rind, grated
- 2 springs rosemary, chopped
- 2 tbsp. oregano, chopped
- 2 tbsp. olive oil
- 2 tbsp. lemon juice
- 1 cup beef stock
- 3 garlic cloves, minced
- Salt and black pepper to taste

Step-by-Step Directions to Cook It:

1. Make small cuts all over the lamb and insert rosemary, season with salt and pepper. In a bowl, mix 1 tbsp. Oil with oregano, lemon juice, rind, parsley, and garlic. Stir and rub the lamb with the mix.
2. Preheat the air fryer to 360^{0}F.
3. In a pan that fits Into the air fryer, heats the remaining oil. Add the potatoes and cook for 3 minutes. Add the lamb and stock, stir and transfer into the air fryer. Set time to 1hour.
4. Serve and enjoy!

Nutritional value per serving:

Calories: 264kcal, Fat: 4g, Carb: 24g, Proteins: 32g

Mutton Momos

The mutton momos is a heart-warming dish that is popular in Nepal. Although similar to Chinese dumplings, this dish is still rich taste and flavor.

Prep time and cooking time: 3o minutes| Serves: 4

Ingredients To Use:

For dough:
- 1-1/2 cup all-purpose flour
- 5 tbsp. water
- 1/2 tsp. salt

For filling:
- 2 tsp. vinegar
- 2 tbsp. coriander leaves
- 1 tsp. ground cumin
- 1 onion, chopped
- 2 tsp. soy-sauce
- 2 cup minced mutton
- 2 tsp. ginger-garlic paste
- 2 tbsp. oil

Step-by-Step Directions to Cook It:

1. In a bowl, add the dough ingredients and mix. Knead the dough and cover with a plastic wrap, set aside.
2. Preheat the air fryer to 200^0F.
3. For the filling, add all the ingredients in a bowl and mix thoroughly. Roll out the dough and cut into small squares. Place the dough's middle fillings, wrap the dough to cover the fillings, and pinch the edges together.
4. Transfer to the air fryer and close the lid. Set time to 20 minutes.
5. Serve and enjoy with sauce or ketchup.

Nutritional value per serving:

Calories: 471kcal, Fat: 14g, Carb: 15g, Proteins: 31g

Lamb and Creamy Brussels Sprouts

Lamb and creamy brussel sprouts may easily overtake the Sunday specials. It is delicious, tasty, and full of flavors.

Prep time and cooking time: 1 hour 20 minutes| Serves: 4

Ingredients To Use:

- 2 lb. lamb leg, scored
- 1 tbsp. melted butter
- 2 tbsp. olive oil
- 1/2 cup sour cream
- 1 tbsp. thyme
- 1-1/2 lb. brussels sprouts (trimmed)
- 1 garlic clove (minced)
- 1 tbsp. rosemary
- Salt and black pepper to taste

Step-by-Step Directions to Cook It:

1. Preheat the air fryer to 375^0F.
2. Season the lamb with salt, rosemary, thyme, and pepper. Brush with oil and transfer to the air fryer basket. Close the lid and cook for 1 hour, remove and set aside.
3. In a pan that fits into the air fryer, mix Brussel sprouts with salt, pepper, garlic, sour cream. Transfer into the air fryer and cook for 10 minutes at 400^0F.
4. Serve and enjoy!

Nutritional value per serving:

Calories: 440kcal, Fat: 19g, Carb: 2g, Proteins: 43g

Lamb Shanks

The lamb shank is tender, moist, and juicy when cooked to perfection. It also brings out your inner creative chef talent.

Prep time and cooking time: 55 minutes| Serves: 4

- 4 lamb shanks
- 2 tsp. honey
- 4 tsp. crushed coriander seeds
- 1 yellow onion, chopped
- 5 oz. dry sherry
- 1 tbsp. olive oil
- 2-1/2 cups chicken stock
- 2 tbsp. white flour
- Salt and pepper to taste
- 4 bay leaves

Step-by-Step Directions to Cook It:

1. Preheat the air fryer to 360^{0}F.
2. Season the lamb shank with salt, pepper, and rub with oil. Transfer to the air fryer and cook for 10 minutes.
3. In a pan that fits into your air fryer, heat oil on medium heat. Add onions, coriander seed, and cook for 5 minutes or until translucent. Add the remaining ingredients and allow to simmer for 3 minutes. Add the lamb and transfer into the air fryer, close the lid, and cook for 5 minutes.
4. Serve and enjoy!

Nutritional value per serving:

Calories: 283kcal, Fat: 4g, Carb: 17g, Proteins: 26g

Creamy Lamb

Creamy lamb is a tasty dish, and the perfect recipe as a comfort food. It can be served as lunch or dinner.
Prep time and cooking time: 1 hour 15 minutes| Serves: 4

Ingredients To Use:

- 5 lb. leg of lamb
- 1 cup white wine
- 1/2 cup butter
- 2 garlic cloves, minced

- 2 cups low fat buttermilk
- 2 tbsp. basil, chopped
- 2 tbsp. mustard
- 2 tbsp. tomato paste
- 1 tbsp. cornstarch mixed with 1 tbsp. water
- Salt and black pepper to taste
- 1/2 cup sour cream

Step-by-Step Directions to Cook It:

1. In a large bowl, add the lamb and buttermilk. Mix well and refrigerate for 24 hours.
2. Preheat the air fryer to 300^{0}F.
3. Pat dry the lamb and transfer to a pan that fits into the air fryer, set aside. In a bowl, add mustard, tomato paste, basil, rosemary, salt, pepper, and garlic. Whisk and spread over the lamb. Close the lid and set the time to 60 minutes.
4. Remove the lamb, heat the juice, add cornstarch, sour cream, salt, and pepper. Stir well and remove from heat.
5. Serve and enjoy with the sauce.

Nutritional value per serving:

Calories: 287kcal, Fat: 4g, Carb: 19g, Proteins: 25g

Lamb Ragu

Lamb ragu is a tasty and flavourful dish that comes together within 1 hour. It can easily take the place of your favorite dinner.
Prep time and cooking time: 1 hour | Serves: 4

Ingredients To Use:

- 2 tbsp. olive oil
- 1 lb. ground lamb
- 1 yellow onion, chopped
- 1 (28-ounce) can crushed tomatoes
- 4 garlic cloves, chopped
- Pinch of red pepper flakes
- 2 tbsp. tomato paste

- 2 tsp. oregano
- A handful of parmesan cheese for serving
- Salt and black pepper to taste
- 12 oz. cooked pasta

1. Preheat the air fryer to 350^{0}F.
2. In a pan that fits into the air fryer, heat oil until shimmering. Add onions, garlic and cook until translucent. Add the red pepper flakes, tomato paste, crushed tomato, salt, pepper, and lamb.
3. Transfer into the air fryer, and cook for 30 minutes.
4. Serve garnish with cheese and oregano; enjoy with the cooked pasta.

Calories: 312kcal, Fat: 23g, Carb: 13g, Proteins: 15g

Moroccan Lamb Stuffed Squash

This irresistible dish is the ultimate main course meal. It is flavourful, sweet, and a good weeknight special.
Prep time and cooking time: 50 minutes | Serves: 2

- 1 lb. ground lamb
- 1 tsp. dried oregano
- 1 spaghetti squash (pricked)
- 3 garlic cloves (minced)
- 28 oz. canned tomatoes (chopped)
- 1 Portobello mushroom (sliced)
- 1/2 tsp. dried thyme
- 1 green bell pepper (chopped)
- 1/4 tsp. cayenne pepper
- 1 yellow onion (diced)
- Salt and pepper to taste

- 1/3 cup crumbled feta cheese
- 1 tbsp. unsalted butter
- 1/3 cup breadcrumbs

1. Preheat the air fryer to 350^{0}F, put the spaghetti squash into the air fryer, and cook for 20 minutes. Remove and transfer to the cutting board and cut into halves. Remove and discard the seeds.
2. Heat a pan over medium heat, add the lamb, garlic, onions, mushroom, stir and cook until the meat is golden brown. Add the remaining ingredients except for the Squash and allow them to cook for 10 minutes.
3. Stuff the Squash with the beef mix and transfer into the air fryer; cook for 10 minutes at 360^{0}F.
4. Meanwhile, place a saucepan over medium heat, add butter, and heat until shimmering. Pour the butter over the breadcrumb mixture and toss to combine. Season with salt and black pepper, add the cheese and mix gently.
5. Serve with the toppings and enjoy!

Calories: 260kcal, Fat: 10g, Carb: 18g, Proteins: 13g

Crispy Lamb

This recipe creates a juicy, crispy, and tender lamb that gives you pleasure as you chew. This wonderful dish can be ready in 40 minutes.
Prep time and cooking time: 40 minutes| Serves: 4

- 28 oz. rack of lamb
- 2 tbsp. macadamia nuts (toasted and crushed)

- 1 garlic clove (minced)
- 1 egg
- 1 tbsp. breadcrumbs
- 1 tbsp. olive oil
- 1 tbsp. chopped
- Salt and black pepper to taste

1. Preheat the air fryer to 350°F.
2. In a bowl, mix oil with garlic and stir well, set aside. In another bowl, mix rosemary with nuts and breadcrumbs. Season the meat with salt, pepper, and oil mixture.
3. Whisk egg in a bowl, dip the meat in the egg and then the breadcrumb mixture. Transfer to the air fryer and cook for 25 minutes. Increase the temperature to 400°F and cook for an additional 5 minutes.
4. Serve and Enjoy!

Nutritional value per serving:

Calories: 230kcal, Fat: 2g, Carb: 10g, Proteins: 12g

Lamb Chili

Lamb chili is the perfect spicy dish for those who love spicy and tasty food. It is simply delicious.
Prep time and cooking time: 30 minutes | Serves: 4

Ingredients To Use:

- 1 lb. lamb (cut into cubes)
- 2-1/2 tsp. ginger-garlic paste
- 1/4 tsp. salt
- 1 tsp. red chili sauce
- 1/4 tsp. black pepper

For the marinade:

- 2 tsp. soy sauce
- 1/2 tbsp. red chili sauce
- 1/4 tsp. ajinomoto
- 1-2 tbsp. honey

- 2 tbsp. olive oil
- 2 tsp. red pepper flakes
- 1-1/2 tsp. ginger-garlic paste
- 2 tbsp. tomato ketchup

Step-by-Step Directions to Cook It:

1. In a bowl, add all the marinade ingredients and mix. Add the lamb fingers and leave to marinate overnight.
2. Preheat the air fryer to 160°F.
3. In a bowl, mix oregano with breadcrumbs and red chili flakes. Dip the fingers in the breadcrumb mixture and transfer to the air fryer. Close the lid and cook for 15 minutes.
4. Place a saucepan over medium heat, transfer the marinade and cook for 5 minutes.
5. Serve with the sauce and enjoy.

Nutritional value per serving:

Calories: 246kcal, Fat: 10g, Carb: 11g, Proteins: 23g

Lamb Fries

Lamb fries is a tasty delight, crispy on the outside, soft and juicy on the inside. It can be prepared with off-the-rack ingredients.
Prep time and cooking time: 20 minutes| Serves: 4

Ingredients To Use:

- 1 lb. boneless lamb (cut into fingers)
- 2 tsp. red chili flakes
- 2 tsp. oregano
- 2 cups dry breadcrumbs

For the Marinade:

- 4 tbsp. lemon juice
- 6 tbsp. cornflour
- 1-1/2 tbsp. ginger-garlic paste
- 1 tsp. red chili powder
- 4 eggs
- 2 tsp. salt

- 1 tsp. pepper powder

1. In a bowl, add all the marinade ingredients and mix. Add the lamb fingers and leave to marinate overnight.
2. Preheat the air fryer to 160^0F.
3. In a bowl, mix oregano with breadcrumbs and red chili flakes. Dip the fingers in the breadcrumb mixture and transfer to the air fryer. Close the lid and cook for 15 minutes.
4. Serve and enjoy!

Nutritional value per serving:

Calories: 341kcal, Fat: 7g, Carb: 9g, Proteins: 27g

Lamb momos

The delicious lamb momos is a steaming delight and can be served with dippings, sauce, or broth.
Prep time and cooking time: 30 minutes|
Serves: 4

Ingredients To Use:

For dough:
- 1-1/2 cup all-purpose flour
- 5 tbsp. water
- 1/2 tsp. salt

For filling
- 2 tsp. vinegar
- 2 tbsp. coriander leaves
- 1 tsp. ground cumin
- 1 onion, chopped
- 2 tsp. soy-sauce
- 2 cup minced mutton
- 2 tsp. ginger-garlic paste
- 2 tbsp. oil

Step-by-Step Directions to Cook It:

1. In a bowl, add the dough ingredients and mix. Knead the dough and cover with a plastic wrap, set aside.

2. Preheat the air fryer to 200^0F.
3. For the filling, add all the ingredients in a bowl and mix thoroughly. Roll out the dough and cut into small squares. Place the dough's middle fillings, wrap the dough to cover the fillings, and pinch the edges together.
4. Transfer to the air fryer and close the lid. Set time to 20 minutes.
5. Serve and enjoy with sauce or ketchup.

Nutritional value per serving:

Calories: 305kcal, Fat: 9g, Carb: 18g, Proteins: 12g

Lamb Burger Cutlets

Lamb burger cutlets are nice; they can be eaten with sauce or arranged to make breakfast burgers.
Prep time and cooking time: 2o minutes|
Serves: 4

Ingredients To Use:

- 1/2 lb. minced lamb
- 1/4 tsp. dried mango powder
- 1 tsp. lemon juice
- 1 green chili (finely chopped)
- 1/2 cup boiled peas
- 1/4 tsp. finely chopped ginger
- 1/4 tsp. cumin
- 1 tbsp. freshly chopped coriander
- 1/2 cup breadcrumbs
- 1/4 tsp. red chili powder
- Salt to taste

Step-by-Step Directions to Cook It:

1. Preheat the air fryer to 250^0F.
2. In a bowl, add all the ingredients and mix well. Mold the mixture into round cutlets and roll them out on a flat surface.
3. Arrange in the air fryer basket and close the lid. Set time to 15 minutes, flip halfway.

4. Serve with sauce and enjoy!

Nutritional value per serving:

Calories: 391kcal, Fat: 8g, Carb: 3g, Proteins: 38g

Lamb Shanks and Carrots

This meal is tasty and delicious and can be prepared with readily available ingredients in your kitchen.

Prep time and cooking time: 55 minutes| Serves: 4

Ingredients To Use:

- 4 lamb shanks
- 2 tbsp. water
- 2 tbsp. paste
- 2 tbsp. olive oil
- 4 oz. red wine
- 6 carrots, chopped
- 1 tsp. oregano
- 1 tomato, chopped
- Salt and black pepper to taste

Step-by-Step Directions to Cook It:

1. Preheat the air fryer to 360^0F.
2. Season the lamb shank with salt, pepper, and rub with oil. Transfer to the air fryer and cook for 10 minutes.
3. In a pan that fits into your air fryer, add carrot and the remaining ingredients. Add the lamb. Stir and transfer into the air fryer, close the lid, and cook for 35 minutes.
4. Serve and enjoy!

Nutritional value per serving:

Calories: 321kcal, Fat: 16g, Carb: 14g, Proteins: 26g

Tasty Lamb Ribs

Tasty lamb ribs are a treat you will want to enjoy with friends and family. All the ingredients are well blended to create a flavourful dish.

Prep time and cooking time: 55 minutes| Serves: 8

Ingredients To Use:

- 8 lamb ribs
- 1 tbsp. chopped rosemary
- 2 carrots, chopped
- 3 tbsp. white flour
- 4 garlic cloves, minced
- 2 tbsp. olive oil
- 2 cups veggie stock
- Salt and black pepper to taste

Step-by-Step Directions to Cook It:

1. Preheat the air fryer to 360^0F.
2. Season the lamb ribs with salt, pepper, rub with olive oil and garlic. Transfer to the air fryer and cook 10 minutes.
3. In a dish that fits into your air fryer, mix stock with flour and whisk. Add rosemary, lamb ribs, and carrots. Transfer into the air fryer and cook for 30 minutes.
4. Serve and enjoy!

Nutritional value per serving:

Calories: 302kcal, Fat: 7g, Carb: 22g, Proteins: 25g

Provencal lamb

The Provencal lamb is a rich and delicious dish that can be prepared in no time at all. The potatoes enliven the rich taste of the meal.

Prep time and cooking time: 50 minutes | Serves: 2

Ingredients To Use:

- 1 lb. lamb rack
- 3 tbsp. olive oil, divided
- 2 medium boiled potatoes
- 2 garlic cloves, minced
- 2 tsp. chopped thyme

- 2 medium tomatoes, halved
- 1 tsp. chopped rosemary
- 1/3 cup. sliced shallots
- 2 tbsp. water
- Salt and pepper to taste

Step-by-Step Directions to Cook It:

1. Preheat the air fryer to 360^{0}F.
2. In a bowl, add garlic, salt, thyme, rosemary, and pepper, mix until it forms a paste. Season the lamb with salt, pepper, and the paste. Heat oil in a pan that fits into your air fryer brown the lamb for 2 minutes. Remove and set aside, add the shallots and potatoes, cook for 5 minutes. Add the remaining ingredients with the lamb.
3. Transfer into the air fryer, cover the lid and cook for 25 minutes.
4. Serve and enjoy!

Nutritional value per serving:

Calories: 261kcal, Fat: 10g, Carb: 17g, Proteins: 16g

Lamb Casserole

Lamb casserole is one of the best comfort foods you will ever taste. Nothing can be compared to the aroma and the tender taste of the lamb.
Prep time and cooking time: 1 hour 15 minutes | Serves:8

Ingredients To Use:

- 2 lb. lamb
- 2 tsp. mustard
- 2 cups of grated mozzarella
- 1 tbsp. olive oil
- 2 cups. chopped eggplant
- 28 oz. canned tomatoes (chopped)
- 1 tsp. dried oregano
- 2 tsp. Worcestershire sauce
- 2 tbsp. chopped parsley

- 16 oz. tomato sauce
- Salt and pepper to taste

Step-by-Step Directions to Cook It:

1. Preheat the air fryer to 360^{0}F.
2. In a bowl, add eggplant, salt, pepper, and oil, mix to coat.
3. In another bowl, add lamb, mustard, salt, pepper, and Worcestershire sauce, stir well. Pour the mixture into a pan that fits into your air fryer and spread evenly; add the eggplant mix and tomato sauce. Sprinkle with parsley and oregano.
4. Transfer to the air fryer and cook 35 minutes.
5. Serve and enjoy!

Nutritional value per serving:

Calories: 210kcal, Fat: 10g, Carb: 14g, Proteins: 18g

Mediterranean Lamb Meatballs

Mediterranean dishes are always a delight, but these juicy and succulent meatballs have it all. It can be served as a main course meal or side dish.
Prep time and cooking time: 1 hour | Serves: 4

Ingredients To Use:

- 1 lb. ground lamb
- 3/4 cup breadcrumbs
- 1-1/2 tbsp. kosher salt
- 1-1/2 tbsp. Italian seasoning

For the tomato sauce:

- 5 cloves garlic
- 4 cups. water
- 1 onion, minced
- 1 tsp. cumin
- 5 cloves garlic, minced
- 3 red chilies, chopped
- 28 oz. can of crushed tomatoes
- 1 tbsp. dried parsley
- Salt and black pepper to taste

- Greek yogurt for toppings

1. Preheat the air fryer to 360℉.
2. In a bowl, add all the meatball ingredients and mix thoroughly. Scoop into a ball. In a pan that fits into the air fryer, heat oil on medium heat. Add the meatballs and brown for 5 minutes.
3. In a bowl, mix all the sauce ingredients, pour over the meatballs, and transfer into your air fryer. Close the lid and set time to 30 minutes.
4. Serve and enjoy!

Nutritional value per serving:

Calories: 185kcal, Fat: 11g, Carb: 8g, Proteins: 14g

Greek Lamb Chop

The super tender and flavourful Greek lamb chop comes together in no time at all. The herbs and spice are well infused in the lamb to create a juicy taste.
Prep time and cooking time: 35 minutes|
Serves: 4

Ingredients To Use:
- 8 loin lamb chops
- 2 tbsp. olive oil
- 1 tsp. oregano
- 4 tbsp. grainy mustard
- 1 tsp. thyme
- Salt and pepper

Step-by-Step Directions to Cook It:
1. Preheat the air fryer to 360℉.
2. In a bowl, mix oil with oregano, mustard, and thyme. Season the lamb chops with salt and pepper, brush with the mustard mixture. Allow to rest for a few minutes, transfer to the air fryer, and cook for 20 minutes.
3. Serve and enjoy with sauce or dip.

Nutritional value per serving:

Calories: 324kcal, Fat: 7g, Carb: 1g, Proteins: 35g

Lamb Chops with Balsamic Glaze

Your tongue will appreciate the tender and juicy lamb chops coupled with the sweet taste of the balsamic glaze. Easy to prepare for everyday cooking.
Prep time and cooking time: 40 minutes |
Serves: 4

Ingredients To Use:
- 8 loin lamb chops
- 2 tbsp. olive oil
- 1 tsp. pepper
- 2 tbsp. minced garlic
- 1/4 cup bourbon
- 1/2 cup brown sugar
- 1 tsp. salt
- 1/4 tsp. cayenne pepper
- 1/2 cup balsamic vinegar
- 1 tbsp. melted butter

Step-by-Step Directions to Cook It:
1. Preheat the air fryer to 360℉.
2. Season the lamb chops with salt, pepper, and rub with oil. Transfer to the air fryer and cook for 5 minutes. Remove and set aside.
3. In a pan that fits into the air fryer, heat oil on medium heat. Add garlic and cook until fragrant. Add the remaining ingredients with the lamb and cook for 20 minutes.
4. Serve and enjoy!

Nutritional value per serving:

Calories: 301kcal, Fat: 10g, Carb: 21g, Proteins: 12g

Air fryer Lamb rack

The air fryer lamb rack is a super tender and

delicious dish that couldn't be any easier. It can be prepared in 30 minutes and is perfect for the ideal dinner.

Prep time and cooking time: 30 minutes | Serves: 4

Ingredients To Use:

- 2 rack of lamb
- 1 tbsp. minced rosemary
- 2 garlic cloves, pressed
- 1/2 cup Dijon mustard
- Salt and pepper to taste

Step-by-Step Directions to Cook It:

1. Preheat the air fryer to 360^{0}F.
2. Rinse the lamb rack and pat dry, season with salt and pepper, set aside. In a bowl, add garlic, rosemary, and mustard, mix well. Rub the lamb with the mixture and transfer to the air fryer basket. set time to 10 minutes.
3. Serve and enjoy!

Nutritional value per serving:

Calories: 321kcal, Fat: 12g, Carb: 1g, Proteins: 21g

Lamb Chops with Horseradish Sauce

Lamb chops with horseradish sauce are the perfect meal to entertain a special visitor. It is easy to prepare, flavourful, and tasty with the sauce.

Prep time and cooking time: 55 minutes | Serves: 2

Ingredients To Use:

- 8 loins lamb chops
- 1 tsp. black pepper
- 2 tbsp. vegetable oil
- 2 cloves garlic, minced
- 1 tsp. salt

Horseradish sauce:

- 1-1/2 tbsp. prepared horseradish
- 1/2 cup. mayonnaise
- 1 tbsp. Dijon mustard
- 2 tsp. sugar

Step-by-Step Directions to Cook It:

1. Preheat the air fryer to 360^{0}F.
2. season the lamb with salt, pepper, and rub with oil. Leave to marinate for 15 minutes. In a bowl, add horseradish, mayonnaise, sugar, and mustard. Stir well and half the sauce. Dip the lamb chops in the sauce, transfer to the air fryer, and set time to 15 minutes. Increase the temperature to 390^{0}F, cook for additional 5 minutes, flipping halfway.
3. Serve and enjoy with the sauce!

Nutritional value per serving:

Calories: 321kcal, Fat: 24g, Carb: 4g, Proteins: 21g

Lamb Roast and potatoes

Lamb roast and potatoes are a meal you will always like to prepare. The meat is tender and juicy combined with potatoes and spice , simply delicious.

Prep time and cooking time: 55 minutes | Serves: 6

Ingredients To Use:

- 4 lb. lamb roast
- 6 potatoes, halved
- 1 spring rosemary
- 4 bay leaves
- 1/2 cup lamb stock
- 3 garlic cloves, minced
- Salt and black pepper to taste

Step-by-Step Directions to Cook It:

1. Preheat the air fryer to 360^{0}F.
2. Add the potatoes to a bowl that fits into the air fryer, add the remaining

ingredients, and transfer into the air fryer. Set time to 45 minutes.

3. Serve and enjoy!

Nutritional value per serving:

Calories: 273kcal, Fat: 4g, Carb: 24g, Proteins: 28g

Spicy lamb Stew with Chickpeas

This tasty and flavourful meal is spicy, warm, and the perfect comfort food for winter. This hearty meal is well seasoned as well as spiced.
Prep time and cooking time: 50 minutes| Serves: 4

Ingredients To Use:

- 1 lb. lamb stew meat
- 2 tbsp. vegetable oil divided
- 2 tbsp. lemon juice
- 1 cup dried chickpeas, soaked overnight
- 1 tbsp. minced garlic
- 1-1/2 tsp. salt
- 1-1/2 tsp. ground cumin
- 1 tsp. ground cinnamon
- 1 tsp. ground coriander
- 1 can (14 oz.) can tomatoes
- 1 tsp. ground turmeric
- 1/2 cup. chopped dried apricot
- 1/4 tsp. black pepper
- 1/4 cup of freshly chopped parsley
- 1 large onion, chopped
- 1-1/2 cups chicken broth
- 1 tbsp. honey
- Hot cooked couscous

Step-by-Step Directions to Cook It:

1. Drain the chickpea. In a pan that fits into the air fryer, add the meat. Brown for 15 minutes, remove and set aside. Add the remaining oil, garlic, onions, and cook until soft.
2. Stir in the remaining ingredients and

transfer to the air fryer. Cover with the lid and set time to 30 minutes.

3. Serve and enjoy!

Nutritional value per serving:

Calories: 452kcal, Fat: 13g, Carb: 5g, Proteins: 21g

Lamb Stew With Almond and Apricots

Lamb stew with almond and apricot is a classic example of sweet and savory flavor. Popularly eaten in north Africa, enjoy with fresh juice.
Prep time and cooking time: 1hour 15 minutes| Serves: 6

Ingredients To Use:

- 2 lb. lamb shoulder, trimmed and cut into cubes
- 1 tsp. cinnamon
- 1 tsp. freshly cracked black pepper
- 1 tsp. ginger
- 1/4 tsp. ground coriander
- 1 tsp. ground ginger
- 1/2 cup of water
- 1/4 tsp. cardamom
- 1/4 tsp. cayenne
- 1 stick of unsalted butter
- 2 cinnamon stick
- 1 cup. chicken stock
- 1/2 cup. chopped parsley
- 2 tbsp. lemon juice
- 2 medium onion, chopped
- 1-1/2 cup. apricot, chopped
- 1/3 cup. honey
- 1-1/2 cup. almond

Step-by-Step Directions to Cook It:

1. In a bowl, add ginger, coriander, cinnamon, cardamom, pepper, cayenne, water, and mix well. Add the meat and toss to coat; leave to marinate overnight

in the refrigerator.
2. Preheat the air fryer to 300°F.
3. Heat oil in a pan over medium heat, add onions, garlic, cinnamon sticks, and cook until fragrant and translucent. Add the meat, including the marinade and stock. Transfer to the air fryer and cook for 50 minutes.
4. Open the lid and stir in the remaining ingredients, cover with the lid and cook for an additional 20 minutes.
5. Serve and enjoy!

Nutritional value per serving:

Calories: 467kcal, Fat: 13g, Carb: 24g, Proteins: 36g

Irish Lamb Stew with Bacon

Irish lamb stew and bacon is one hearty meal you will always like to have for dinner. It is also a great meal to consume the next day as it allows the flavors to infuse the lamb.
Prep time and cooking time: 2 hours 30 minutes| Serves: 6

Ingredients To Use:

- 1 lb. lamb shoulder
- 1/2 cup. water
- 1-1/2 cup. bacon
- 2 cup chicken stock
- 1/2 cup. plain flour
- 2 onions, finely chopped
- 1 tsp. dried thyme
- 1/2 cup. water
- 2 tsp. white sugar
- 2 cups. chopped carrots
- 1 cup. white wine
- 2 bay leaves
- 3 potatoes
- Salt and black pepper to taste

Step-by-Step Directions to Cook It:

1. Preheat the air fryer to 360°F.

2. heat oil in a pan, add bacon and cook until crispy. In a bowl, add flour, salt, pepper, lamb. Toss to coat, add to the oil, and brown for a few minutes. Remove from heat.
3. Add garlic and onion and cook until fragrant; stir in the remaining ingredients. Transfer to the air fryer, cover with the lid and cook for 1 ½ hour.
4. Serve and Enjoy!

Nutritional value per serving:

Calories: 456kcal, Fat: 24g, Carb: 23g, Proteins: 43g

Basque Lamb Stew

This particular dish is a native of Spain, and a spicy and delicious meal that you will love. It is a stew perfect for winter.
Prep time and cooking time: 2 hours | Serves: 4

Ingredients To Use:

- 1 lb. lamb shoulder, cut into smaller pieces
- 1 tbsp. dried rosemary
- 1 onion, chopped
- 1/2 tsp. red chili flakes
- 6 cloves garlic, minced
- 1/2 cup. white wine
- 3 roasted red bell pepper, cut into thin strips
- 2 tbsp. freshly chopped coriander
- 2 tbsp. olive oil
- 1 cup. vegetable stock
- 1 cup. red wine
- 1 bay leaf
- Salt and black pepper

Step-by-Step Directions to Cook It:

1. In a bowl, combine rosemary, white wine, and garlic, add the lamb and mix well. Leave to marinate overnight. Drain the

meat and pat dry with paper towels.

2. Preheat the air fryer to 360^{0}F, in a pan that fits into the air fryer, heat oil, and brown the meat for 1o minutes. Remove from the pan and add onions and garlic. Cook until soft and fragrant.
3. Stir in the remaining ingredients and transfer to the air fryer. Close the lid and set time to 1 hour.
4. Serve and enjoy!

Nutritional value per serving:

Calories: 523kcal, Fat: 23g, Carb: 16g, Proteins: 31g

Spicy Lamb Stew

The spicy lamb stew is a combination of flavors that you won't be able to resist.
Prep time and cooking time: 95 minutes| Serves:6

Ingredients To Use:

- 2 lb. boneless lamb shoulder
- Salt and black pepper to taste
- 1/4 cup all-purpose flour
- Juice of 1/2 lemon
- 1 tbsp. olive oil
- 1 medium onion, chopped
- 1/2 tsp. ground cumin
- 1 cup chicken stock
- 1/2 tsp. ground ginger
- 2 cloves garlic, minced
- 1/4 tsp. ground cinnamon
- 1 medium carrot, peeled and choppcd
- 1 (14.5-ounce) can. Diced tomatoes

Step-by-Step Directions to Cook It:

1. Trim the lamb and season with salt and pepper; toss with the flour. Preheat the air fryer to 360^{0}F.
2. heat oil in a pan, add the lamb and cook until brown on all sides. Toss to coat, add to the oil, and brown for a few

minutes. Remove from heat.

3. Add garlic and onion and cook until fragrant; stir in the remaining ingredients. Transfer to the air fryer, cover with the lid and cook for 1-1/2 hour.
4. Serve and Enjoy!

Nutritional value per serving:

Calories: 527kcal, Fat: 30g, Carb: 26g, Proteins: 37g

Mutton Couscous

Mutton couscous is just like pork couscous, except it tastes better and has more combinations of flavors.
Prep time and cooking time: 45 minutes| Serves: 6

Ingredients To Use:

- 2 lb. lamb loin
- 3/4 cup. chicken stock
- 2 tbsp. olive oil
- 2 cups cooked couscous
- 1/2 tbsp. sweet paprika
- 1/2 tbsp. garlic powder
- 1 tsp. dried basil
- 1/4 tsp. dried marjoram
- 2 and 1/4 tsp. dried sage
- 1 tsp. oregano
- Salt and black pepper to taste

Step-by-Step Directions to Cook It:

1. Preheat the air fryer to 370^{0}F.
2. In a bowl, add all the ingredients except the couscous, add the lamb, and leave to marinate for 1hour. Pour in a pan that fits into the air fryer.
3. Transfer to the air fryer, cook for 35 minutes.
4. Serve with couscous, enjoy!

Nutritional value per serving:

Calories: 326kcal, Fat: 12g, Carb: 9g, Proteins: 27g

Lamb with Beer Sauce

Lamb with beer sauce is a combination of flavor that you won't be forgetting anytime soon.

Prep time and cooking time: 60 minutes| Serves: 4

Ingredients To Use:

- 4 lb. lamb, cut into smaller piece
- 1 portobello mushroom, dried
- 1 onion, chopped
- 1 cup. chicken stock
- 1/4 cup tomato paste
- 6 thyme sprigs, chopped
- 1 cup dark beer
- Salt and pepper to taste

Step-by-Step Directions to Cook It:

1. Preheat the air fryer to 350^{0}F.
2. Heat oil in a pan over medium heat, add garlic, green onions, and ginger, stir and cook for 1 minute.
3. Add the rib and the remaining ingredients, transfer to the air fryer and cook for 35 minutes.
4. Serve and enjoy.

Nutritional value per serving:

Calories: 321kcal, Fat: 12g, Carb: 20g, Proteins: 14g

Lamb with Onion Sauce

Lamb with onion sauce is creamy, juicy, and tasty. The perfect meal for a weeknight dinner.

Prep time and cooking time: 2 hours 10 minutes| Serves: 6

Ingredients To Use:

- 4 lb. lamb brisket
- 8 earl greys teabags
- 4 cups of water
- 1 lb. yellow onion, chopped

- 1 lb. carrot, chopped
- Salt and black pepper to taste
- 1/2 lb. celery, chopped

For sauce:

- 1 oz. garlic, minced
- 16 oz. canned tomatoes, chopped
- 4 oz. vegetable oil
- 1 cup white vinegar
- 1 lb. sweet onion, chopped
- 1 cup. white vinegar
- 1/2 lb. celery, chopped
- 8 earl grey tea bags

Step-by-Step Directions to Cook It:

1. Preheat the air fryer to 300^{0}F.
2. In a pan that fits into the air fryer, add water, carrot, onion, celery, salt, and pepper. Bring to a boil over medium heat. Add the lamb and transfer to the air fryer and cook for 1 hour 30 minutes.
3. Meanwhile, for the sauce, heat oil in a pan over medium heat, add onion, celery, and sauce ingredients. Cook for 10 minutes.
4. Serve the lamb with the sauce.

Nutritional value per serving:

Calories: 400kcal, Fat: 12g, Carb: 28g, Proteins: 31g

Lamb Kabobs

Lamb kabob is just like its beef counterpart; however, they differ in taste because the lamb comes with its juicy flavor.

Prep time and cooking time: 20 minutes| Serves: 4

Ingredients To Use:

- 2 lb. lamb steak (cut into medium sizes)
- 2 tbsp. chili powder
- 1 red onion (chopped)
- 1/4 cup olive oil
- 2 red peppers (chopped)

- 1/2 tbsp. ground cumin
- 2 tbsp. hot sauce
- Juice from 1 lime
- 1 zucchini (sliced)
- 1/4 cup of salsa
- Salt and pepper to taste

Step-by-Step Directions to Cook It:

1. Preheat the air fryer to Preheat the air fryer to 370^{0}F.
2. In a bowl, mix oil, salsa, hot sauce, cumin, lime juice, black pepper, and salt. Whisk thoroughly.
3. Arrange the meat, bell pepper, onions, and Zucchini on a skewer, brush with salsa mix. Arrange in your air fryer and cook for 10 minutes.
4. Better enjoyed with salad at the side.

Nutritional value per serving:

Calories: 170kcal, Fat: 5g, Carb: 13g, Proteins: 16g

Lamb Rack with wine sauce

The lamb is delicious and easy to prepare; the flavor, herbs, and spice create a wonderful dish.
Prep time and cooking time: 55 minutes|
Serves: 6

Ingredients To Use:

- 2 lb. lamb rack
- 3 carrot (chopped)
- 3 oz. red wine
- 1/2 tsp. smoked paprika
- 5 potatoes chopped
- 1/2 tsp. salt
- 1 yellow onion (chopped)
- 4 garlic clove (pressed)
- 17 oz. chicken stock
- 1/2 tsp. chicken salt

Step-by-Step Directions to Cook It:

1. Preheat the air fryer to 360^{0}F.

2. In a bowl, add salt, paprika, and chicken salt, stir. Rub the lamb with the mixture and transfer to a pan that will fit into the air dryer.
3. Add the remaining ingredients and cook for 45 minutes.
4. Enjoy and serve.

Nutritional value per serving:

Calories: 314kcal, Fat: 21g, Carb: 18g, Proteins: 36g

Mutton fries

Mutton fries are crispy as well as crusty; enjoy with ketchup or as a side dish.
Prep time and cooking time: 20 minutes|
Serves: 4

Ingredients To Use:

- 1 lb. boneless mutton (cut into fingers)
- 2 tsp. red chili flakes
- 2 tsp. oregano
- 2 cups dry breadcrumbs

For the Marinade:

- 4 tbsp. lemon juice
- 6 tbsp. cornflour
- 1-1/2 tbsp. ginger-garlic paste
- 1 tsp. red chili powder
- 4 eggs
- 2 tsp. salt
- 1 tsp. pepper powder

Step-by-Step Directions to Cook It:

1. In a bowl, add all the marinade ingredients and mix. Add the mutton fingers and leave to marinate overnight.
2. Preheat the air fryer to 160^{0}F.
3. In a bowl, mix oregano with breadcrumbs and red chili flakes. Dip the fingers in the breadcrumb mixture and transfer to the air fryer. Close the lid and cook for 15 minutes.
4. Serve and enjoy!

Nutritional value per serving:

Calories: 432kcal, Fat: 13g, Carb: 15g, Proteins: 31g

Tasty Mutton Chops

This is a good option if lamb and beef are not available. It is tender, moist, and juicy, a good choice for weeknight dinner.
Prep time and cooking time: 35 minutes | Serves: 4

Ingredients To Use:

- 8 loin mutton chops
- 2 tbsp. olive oil
- 1 tsp. oregano
- 1 tsp. coriander
- 1 tsp. cumin
- 4 tbsp. grainy mustard
- 1 tsp. thyme
- Salt and pepper

Step-by-Step Directions to Cook It:

1. Preheat the air fryer to 350^0F.
2. In a bowl, mix all the ingredients. Add the mutton chops and toss to coat.
3. Transfer to the air fryer and cook for 10 minutes.
4. Serve and enjoy!

Nutritional value per serving:

Calories: 231kcal, Fat: 7g, Carb: 6g, Proteins: 23g

Burgundy Lamb Shanks

This nice and tasty dish has it all, from aroma to taste. Enjoy with a glass of wine!
Prep time and cooking time: 1 hour 10 minutes | Serves: 6

Ingredients To Use:

- 2 lb. lamb roast, cut into smaller cubes
- 4 carrots (chopped)
- 1 cup of water

- 1 cup. beef stock
- 3 tbsp. almond flour
- 2 yellow onions (chopped)
- 1 tbsp. chopped thyme
- 2 celery ribs (chopped)
- 1/2 lb. mushroom (sliced)
- 15 oz. canned tomatoes(chopped)
- 1/2 tsp. mustard powder
- Salt and black pepper to taste

Step-by-Step Directions to Cook It:

1. Preheat the air fryer to 300^0F.
2. Place a medium pot over high heat; add the meat and brown on all sides for 3-5 minutes. Add the tomato, carrot, onions, celery, mushroom, salt, pepper, mustard, stock, and thyme, stir.
3. In a bowl, add water and flour, stir. Add to the pot and transfer into the air fryer, cook for 1 hour.
4. Serve and enjoy.

Nutritional value per serving:

Calories: 275kcal, Fat: 13g, Carb: 17g, Proteins: 28g

Mutton stew

This recipe will create one big hearty meal that will lift your spirit. Also, it is very easy to prepare.
Prep time and cooking time: 95 minutes| Serves: 4

Ingredients To Use:

- 2 lb. mutton, cut into cubes
- 1 tsp. cinnamon
- 1/4 tsp. cayenne
- 1 tsp. freshly cracked black pepper
- 1 tsp. ginger
- 1/4 tsp. ground coriander
- 1 tsp. ground ginger
- 1/2 cup of water
- 1/4 tsp. cardamom

- 1 stick of unsalted butter
- 2 cinnamon stick
- 1 cup. chicken stock
- 1/2 cup. chopped parsley
- 2 tbsp. lemon juice
- 2 medium onion, chopped

1. In a bowl, add ginger, coriander, cinnamon, cardamom, pepper, cayenne, water, and mix well. Add the meat and toss to coat; leave to marinate overnight in the refrigerator.
2. Preheat the air fryer to 300°F.
3. Heat oil in a pan over medium heat, add onions, garlic, cinnamon sticks, and cook until fragrant and translucent. Add the meat, including the marinade and stock. Transfer to the air fryer and cook for 50 minutes.
4. Open the lid and stir in the remaining ingredients, cover with the lid and cook for an additional 20 minutes.
5. Serve and enjoy!

Nutritional value per serving:

Calories: 451kcal, Fat: 10g, Carb: 18g, Proteins: 38g

Balsamic Lamb

The balsamic lamb is a sweet and savory dish that will take your tongue on a super ride. Enjoy the ride with juice or a glass of wine.
Prep time and cooking time: 1hour 10 minutes | Serves: 3

Ingredients To Use:

- 1/2 lb. lamb
- 4 garlic cloves (pressed)
- 1 cup beef stock
- 1 tbsp. Worcestershire sauce
- 1 tbsp. soy sauce
- 1/2 cup balsamic vinegar
- 1 tbsp. honey

Step-by-Step Directions to Cook It:

1. Preheat the air fryer to 360°F.
2. In a pan, mix beef roast with vinegar, Worcestershire sauce, honey, garlic, stock, and soy sauce. Transfer into the air fryer and cook for 1 hour.
3. Serve and enjoy!

Nutritional value per serving:

Calories: 301kcal, Fat: 9g, Carb: 22g, Proteins: 19

Lamb and Spinach Mix

The lamb and spinach dish is a mildly spiced dish but tastes great. It is rich and highly nutritious.
Prep time and cooking time: 55 minutes | Serves: 4

Ingredients To Use:

- 2 lb. lamb (cut into cubes)
- 1 tsp. turmeric
- 1 red onion chopped
- 2 garlic cloves (minced)
- 2 tbsp. grated ginger
- 1/2 tsp. chili powder
- 2-1/2 tbsp. curry
- 14 oz. can tomatoes
- 1 lb. spinach
- 2 tsp. ground coriander
- Salt and black pepper to taste

Step-by-Step Directions to Cook It:

1. Preheat the air fryer to 360°F.
2. In a pan that fits into the air fryer, add all the ingredients and toss to coat. Transfer into the air fryer and cover with the lid, set time to 35 minutes.
3. Serve and Enjoy!

Nutritional value per serving:

Calories: 160kcal, Fat: 6g, Carb: 17g, Proteins: 20g

Spicy Paprika Lamb

For those looking for a spicy dish on a cold winter night, this is the perfect dish for you. Spicy like its name but tasty!

Prep time and cooking time: 40 minutes | Serves: 4

Ingredients To Use:

- 2 lamb steak
- 1 tbsp. brandy
- 1-1/2 tbsp. olive oil
- 1 tbsp. brandy
- 3 cloves garlic, sliced
- 1/2 ancho chili pepper (soaked in hot water)
- 2 tsp. smoked paprika
- 1 tsp. ground allspice

Step-by-Step Directions to Cook It:

1. Preheat the air fryer to 385^0 F.
2. Season the lamb with paprika, salt, and allspice, transfer to a baking pan that fits your air fryer. Sprinkle the garlic and minced ancho chili on top. Drizzle with brandy and olive oil.
3. Transfer to the air fryer, close the lid. Set time to 14 minutes, turning halfway through.
4. Serve warm.

Nutritional value per serving:

Calories: 430kcal, Fat: 21g, Carb: 4g, Proteins: 48g

Air Fryer Mutton Rack

Air fryer mutton racks is a good lunch or dinner meal with crusty and juicy meat. Better enjoyed with a sauce.

Prep time and cooking time: 30 minutes | Serves: 4

Ingredients To Use:

- 2 rack of mutton

- 1 tbsp. minced rosemary
- 2 garlic cloves, pressed
- 1/2 cup Dijon mustard
- Salt and pepper to taste

Step-by-Step Directions to Cook It:

1. Preheat the air fryer to 360^0F.
2. Rinse the mutton rack and pat dry, season with salt and pepper, set aside. In a bowl, add garlic, rosemary, and mustard, mix well. Rub the lamb with the mixture and transfer to the air fryer basket. set time to 10 minutes.
3. Serve and enjoy!

Nutritional value per serving:

Calories: 342kcal, Fat: 12g, Carb: 7g, Proteins: 27g

Mexican Lamb Mix

Mexicans are known for their spicy and tasty dish; all these qualities are present in this one-pot meal.

Prep time and cooking time: 1hour 30 minutes | Serves:4

Ingredients To Use:

- 2 lb. lamb roast, diced
- 1/2 cup of water
- 2 tbsp. olive oil
- 2 green bell peppers, chopped
- 4 jalapenos, chopped
- 2 yellow onions, chopped
- 2 tbsp. cilantro, chopped
- 1 tsp oregano, dried
- Salt and black pepper to taste
- 1 habanero pepper, chopped
- 14 ounces canned tomatoes, chopped
- 6 garlic cloves, grated
- 1 and 1/2 tsp cumin, ground

Step-by-Step Directions to Cook It:

1. Preheat the air fryer to 300°F.
2. Mix the lamb, oil, bell peppers, jalapenos,

onions, tomatoes, habanero, garlic, cumin, oregano, cilantro, salt, pepper, and water in a cooking pan. Ensure the pan fits your air fryer.
3. Transfer the pan to the air fryer and cook for 1 hour 10 minutes.
4. Serve and enjoy.

Calories: 63kcal, Carbs: 37g, Fat: 60g, Protein: 58g

Stuffed Mutton

This stuffed mutton has it all; although not a common dish, it still manages to capture the tongue with its delicious taste.
Prep time and cooking time: 30 minutes|
Serves: 4

Ingredients To Use:
- 2 limes, zested and grated
- Juice from 2 limes
- 4 pork loin steaks
- 1 orange, zested and grated
- Juice from 1 orange
- 1 cup of mint, chopped
- 4 tsp. garlic, grated
- 1 cup of cilantro, chopped
- 1 tsp. oregano, dried
- 2 tsp. cumin, ground
- 3/4 cup of olive oil
- 4 ham slices
- 2 tbsp. mustard
- 2 pickles, chopped
- 6 Swiss cheese slices
- Salt and black pepper to taste

Step-by-Step Directions to Cook It:
1. preheat the air fryer to 340°F.
2. Add the lime and orange zest, lime and orange juice, oil, garlic, oregano, cilantro, black pepper, salt, cumin, and mint to a food processor. Pulse until a smooth

texture is obtained.
3. In a bowl, season lamb steaks with salt and black pepper, then add the marinade and toss.
4. Put the lamb steak on a chopping board or flat surface, divide equal portions of ham, mustard, pickles, and cheese on them, then roll and spear with toothpicks.
5. Transfer stuffed steaks to the air fryer and cook for 20 minutes.
6. Serve and enjoy with salad!

Calories: 270kcal, Carbs: 13g, Fat: 7g, Protein: 20g

Mushroom Stuffed Lamb Roll

This delicious fragrant dish can be featured for a Sunday get-together lunch. It is full of flavors and tastes you will love.
Prep time and cooking time: 40 minutes |
Serves: 8

Ingredients To Use:
- 2 lb. leg of lamb
- juice from 2 lemons
- zest from 2 lemons
- 3 large onions, chopped
- 2 cups of mixed vegetables
- 1 tsp. thyme leaves
- 1 cup. Portobello mushroom, chopped
- 1 tbsp. Dijon mustard
- 2 tbsp. olive oil
- 3 garlic cloves, pressed
- Salt and freshly cracked black pepper

Step-by-Step Directions to Cook It:
1. Preheat the air fryer to 350⁰F.
2. Place a saucepan over medium heat, add onions and mushroom. Cook for 5 minutes or until golden; add garlic, lemon juice, and thyme. Remove from heat and leave to cool. Pour the mixture

into a food processor and pulse until you achieve a breadcrumb texture. Add lemon zest and season with salt and black pepper.

3. Season the lamb with oil, mustard, salt, and pepper. Place the lamb on a flat working surface, spoon the stuffing on the lamb, roll and secure with a string.
4. Transfer to the air fryer and cook for 45 minutes, open the lid and add the vegetables. Cook for an additional 25 minutes.
5. Allow to rest for 10 minutes, serve.

Nutritional value per serving:

Calories: 645kcal, Fat: 14g, Carb: 12g, Proteins: 48g

Stuffed Lamb Shoulder

Stuffed lamb shoulder is a delicious meal that can be prepared for Halloween or Easter celebrations.
Prep time and cooking time: 2 hours | Serves: 6

Ingredients To Use:

- 2 lb. boneless leg of lamb
- 2 tbsp. freshly chopped parsley
- 3 tbsp. olive oil
- 3 garlic cloves, minced
- 1/2 cup red wine
- 2 tbsp. butter
- 2 bacon strips, cut into smaller piece
- 1/4 cup of beef stock
- 1 tsp. cornstarch
- Salt and black pepper to taste

Step-by-Step Directions to Cook It:

1. Preheat the air fryer to 350⁰F.
2. Trim the lamb, season with salt, pepper, bacon, parsley, garlic, and olive oil. Roll and tie with a string. Transfer to the air fryer and set time to 1 hour.
3. Meanwhile, heat butter in a pan, add

onions, stock, red wine, cornstarch. Cook until the sauce thickens.
4. Serve and enjoy!

Nutritional value per serving:

Calories: 678kcal, Fat: 56g, Carb: 9g, Proteins: 48g

Braised Lamb Shanks

The braised lamb shanks is the perfect definition of a hearty meal. The ingredients are healthy and nutritious.
Prep time and cooking time: 1 hour 15 minutes | Serves:4

Ingredients To Use:

- 1 lb. lamb shank
- 2 large carrots, chopped
- 1 garlic clove, minced
- 1 tsp. freshly chopped rosemary
- 2 tbsp. extra virgin olive oil
- 1 yellow onion, chopped
- 3 potatoes, cut into chunks
- 1 bay leaf
- 1-1/4 cup beef stock
- 1 tsp. dried oregano
- 2 celery stalks, chopped
- Salt and black pepper to taste

Step-by-Step Directions to Cook It:

1. Preheat the air fryer to 350⁰F, season the lamb shank with salt and pepper.
2. In a pan that fits into the air fryer, heat oil and brown the lamb shanks. Remove the lamb from oil and set aside. Add onions, celery, and carrots to the oil. Sauté for 5 minutes. Add the remaining ingredients and transfer to the air fryer. Set time to 1 hour.
3. Serve and enjoy!

Nutritional value per serving:

Calories: 341kcal, Fat: 9g, Carb: 16g, Proteins: 14g

Lamb Stew with Spring Vegetables

The dish is a meal rich in nutrients. It can be easily enjoyed for dinner or lunch or serve as comfort food for chilly nights.

Prep time and cooking time: 40 minutes | Serves: 4

Ingredients To Use:

- 2 lb. lamb, cut into smaller pieces
- 1 bay leaves
- 1 cup chicken stock
- 1 cup dry white wine
- 2 sprigs of rosemary
- Two sprigs of parsley
- 1 shallot, thinly sliced
- 1 lb. asparagus
- 2 cups. frozen peas
- 1 lb. asparagus, trimmed
- 1 onion, chopped
- 2 tbsp. all-purpose flour
- 2 tbsp. olive oil
- 2 tbsp. lemon juice
- Salt and pepper to taste

Step-by-Step Directions to Cook It:

1. Season the lamb piece with salt, lemon juice, pepper, and rosemary. Leave to marinate for 30 minutes.
2. Preheat the air fryer to 360°F.
3. Heat oil in a pan that fits in your air fryer add the meat, and brown for 10 minutes. Remove from heat, add shallots, and cook for 2 minutes. Add the remaining ingredients with the lamb. Transfer into your air fryer and set time 2o minutes.
4. Serve and enjoy!

Nutritional value per serving:

Calories: 486kcal, Fat: 5g, Carb: 3g, Proteins: 31g

Lamb Biryani

Biryani is always a combination of flavor, color, and aroma. Using lamb to prepare this dish creates a taste that is on a whole new level.

Prep time and cooking time: 60 minutes | Serves: 6

Ingredients To Use:

- 2 lb. boneless leg of lamb, cut into small piece
- 1 tbsp. Madras spice paste
- 1 tbsp. ginger, grated
- 1 tbsp. sunflower oil
- 8 curry leaves
- 1 onion, chopped
- 1 tbsp. nigella seeds
- 1 tbsp. cumin seeds
- 2 cups. chicken stock
- 4 garlic cloves, grated
- 1 cup. basmati rice rinsed well
- 1 cup plain yogurt for serving
- Sliced green chilies for serving
- 1 cup. chopped spinach

Step-by-Step Directions to Cook It:

1. In a bowl, season the lamb with ginger, garlic, salt, and pepper. Marinate overnight in the refrigerator.
2. Preheat the air fryer to 300°F.
3. Heat oil in a pan over medium heat, add the lamb, and brown for 5 minutes. Add onions, nigella, cumin and cook for another 5 minutes. Stir in the rest of the ingredients. Transfer to your air fryer and cook for 20 minutes.
4. Serve with the yogurt and chili.

Nutritional value per serving:

Calories: 432kcal, Fat: 12g, Carb: 16g, Proteins: 36g

Creamy Lamb Stroganoff

This recipe tastes just like the original beef stroganoff, which in this case, is substituted with lamb.

Prep time and cooking time: 55 minutes| Serves: 4

Ingredients To Use:

- 1 lb. lamb leg steak
- 1 cup sour cream
- 4 cups beef broth
- 4 tbsp. butter
- 2 tbsp. Worcestershire sauce
- 16 oz. egg noodles, cooked
- 8 oz. mushroom

Step-by-Step Directions to Cook It:

1. Preheat the air fryer to 400^{0}F.
2. Melt butter in a pan over medium heat, and transfer to a bowl. Add sour cream, beef broth, sauce, onion, mushroom, and mix. Pour the mixture over the lamb and set aside for 10 minutes.
3. Transfer the lamb to the air fryer basket, close the lid, and set time to 10 minutes.
4. Open and serve with the cooked egg noodles, enjoy!

Nutritional value per serving:

Calories: 530kcal, Fat: 10g, Carb: 6g, Proteins: 28g

Herb Crusted Lamb Schnitzel

Lamb schnitzel is crispy and crusty on the outside but tasty and juicy on the inside. This nutritious meal is perfect for a dinner date, enjoy with a glass of wine.

Prep time and cooking time: 20 minutes| Serves: 4

Ingredients To Use:

- 4 lamb schnitzel cut into strips
- 2 tbsp. melted butter
- 1 whole lemon
- 2 oz. breadcrumbs
- 1 whole egg, whisked
- 1/2 cup grated parmesan
- 2 tbsp. chopped fresh oregano
- Salt and pepper to taste

Step-by-Step Directions to Cook It:

1. Preheat the air fryer to 356^0 F.
2. In a bowl, add breadcrumbs, vegetable oil, cheese, oregano, and mix. Dip the schnitzel into the egg, then into the breadcrumb mixture to coat. Transfer to the air fryer cooking basket and set time for 12 minutes.
3. Drizzle with lemon juice and serve.

Nutritional value per serving:

Calories: 248kcal, Fat: 16g, Carb: 21g, Proteins: 36g

Air Fryer Lamb Chops

Air fryer Lamb chops is a simple but elegant meal. Ideal for serving during summer picnic or gathering. So tasty!

Prep time and cooking time: 30 minutes| Serves: 8

Ingredients To Use:

- 16 lamb loin, cut into smaller piece
- 2 tbsp. lemon juice
- 4 sprigs rosemary
- 4 cloves garlic, minced
- 1 tbsp. lemon zest
- 1 tbsp. olive oil
- Salt and pepper to taste

Step-by-Step Directions to Cook It:

1. In a Ziploc bag, add all the ingredients with the lamb and leave to marinate in the refrigerator for 1 hour.
2. Preheat the air fryer to 360^{0}F, remove the marinade and transfer to the air fryer basket. Cover the lid and set time to 20

minutes, flipping halfway.

3. Serve and enjoy with any sauce of choice.

Nutritional value per serving:

Calories: 342kcal, Fat: 5g, Carb: 2g, Proteins: 37g

Irish Lamb Stew

This interesting meal is prepared by cooking lamb in a rich broth. This recipe creates a perfect comfort meal.
Prep time and cooking time: 2hour 30 minutes| Serves: 6

Ingredients To Use:

- 1.5 lb. lamb shoulder (cut into chunks)
- 2 large onions (cut into chunks)
- 2 tbsp. olive oil
- 1 tsp. salt
- 1 tsp. pepper
- 1 lb. potatoes, cut into large chunks
- 4 cups chicken broth
- 1/4 cup flour
- 1/2 bottle of beer
- 4 large carrots, peeled and cut into chunks

Step-by-Step Directions to Cook It:

1. In a pan that fits into the air fryer, heat oil on medium heat. Add the lamb and brown for 3 minutes, remove from pan, and set aside. Add onions and carrot into the pan and cook for 5 minutes. Add the flour and cook for another 2 minutes.
2. Meanwhile, Preheat the air fryer to 160⁰F. Add the remaining ingredients to the pan, transfer to the air fryer, and close the lid. Cook for 90 minutes.
3. Serve and Enjoy!

Nutritional value per serving:

Calories: 311kcal, Fat: 2g, Carb: 21g, Proteins: 29g

Greek Lamb Burger with Tzatziki Sauce

This delicious recipe is made of lamb seasoned with herb and spice and topped with the savory tzatziki sauce.
Prep time and cooking time: 30 minutes| Serves: 4

Ingredients To Use:

- 1.5 lb. ground lamb
- 1 cup tzatziki sauce
- 1 tsp. oregano
- 1/2 head lettuce
- 1/3 cup. crumbled feta cheese
- 4 buns
- 1 medium tomato
- Salt and pepper to taste

Step-by-Step Directions to Cook It:

1. Preheat the air fryer to 375⁰F.
2. In a bowl, add lamb, cheese, pepper, and oregano, combine thoroughly. Form into 6 patties sprinkle with salt and pepper. Spray with cooking oil and transfer to the air fryer basket. Close the lid and set time to 10 minutes turning halfway through.
3. Arrange the burger on the buns with lettuce, tomatoes, top with tzatziki sauce.
4. Enjoy!

Nutritional value per serving:

Calories: 340kcal, Fat: 10g, Carb: 23g, Proteins: 28g

Chapter 6: Mouth-watering Pork Recipes

Pork Fritters

Pork fritter is a delicious and tasty meal that can be prepared on special occasions. Enjoy with friends and family!

Prep time and cooking time: 30 minutes | Serves: 4

- 1 lb. sliced pork
- 3 tsp. ginger finely chopped
- 1-2 tbsp. fresh coriander leaves
- 2 or 3 green chilies finely chopped
- 1-1/2 tbsp. lemon juice
- Salt and pepper to taste

Step-by-Step Directions to Cook It:

1. Mix the ingredients in a clean bowl. Wet the galettes slightly with water.
2. Preheat the Air Fryer at 160°F for 5 minutes. Place the galettes in the fry basket and let them cook for another 25 minutes at the same temperature. Keep rolling them over to get a uniform cook.
3. Serve either with mint chutney or ketchup.

Nutritional value per serving:

Calories: 213kcal, Fat: 30g, Carb: 15g, Proteins: 65g

BBQ Pork Strips

This BBQ pork strip has a lot going for it; it is quick and easy to prepare, plus the sauce is amazing. The best recipe for a summer get-together!

Prep time and cooking time: 5 hours | Serves: 4

Ingredients To Use:

- 16 packets pork loin chops
- 1 tsp. balsamic vinegar
- 2 tbsp. soy sauce
- 2 tbsp. honey
- 1 clove garlic, finely chopped
- 1/4 tsp. ground ginger or 1/2 tsp. freshly grated ginger
- Freshly ground pepper

Step-by-Step Directions to Cook It:

1. Tenderize the chops and season with pepper.
2. Prepare the marinade by combining the honey, balsamic vinegar, and soy sauce in a bowl. Add the ginger and garlic into the mixture and stir thoroughly to mix. Set to one side. Combine pork chops and the marinade mixture and let it marinate for 2 hours or overnight.
3. Preheat the air fryer at 350°F for 5 minutes. Finally, pour in a pan that fits into the air fryer. Cook for 15 minutes, flip halfway through.
4. Serve and enjoy!

Nutritional value per serving:

Calories: 345kcal, Fat: 11g, Carb: 6g, Proteins: 21g

Honey Glazed Pork Chops

This honey glazed pork chops is an incredible recipe. The meat is so tender, moist, and flavourful.

Prep time and cooking time: 20 minutes | Serves: 4

- 300g minced pork
- 50g onion (peeled and diced)
- 1tsp. mustard
- 1tsp. honey
- 1tsp. garlic puree
- 1tbsp Cheddar cheese (grated)
- Handful fresh basil (chopped into small pieces)
- Salt and pepper to taste

Step-by-Step Directions to Cook It:

1. Preheat the air fryer to 350^{0}F.
2. In a bowl, mix the pork with all the ingredients, form a ball. Form into balls.
3. Transfer to a pan that fits into the air fryer close the lid, and set time to 14 minutes.
4. Serve and enjoy!

Nutritional value per serving:

Calories: 356kcal, Fat: 9g, Carb: 5g, Proteins: 27g

Pork in the Blanket

The pork in a blanket is small and quaint, unlike those wrapped in pastry. The recipe is traditionally served as lunch in UK and Ireland.
Prep time and cooking time: 20 minutes | Serves: 3

Ingredients To Use:

- 9 Rashers unsmoked back bacon
- 3 large Brazilian sausages
- Salt and pepper

Step-by-Step Directions to Cook It:

1. Preheat the air fryer to 320^{0}F.
2. Chop your sausages into three equal sizes so that they become mini sausages. Wrap the sausage with the bacon and transfer it into the air fryer basket. Set time to 15 minutes.

3. Serve sprinkled with salt and pepper, enjoy!

Nutritional value per serving:

Calories: 311kcal, Fat: 7g, Carb: 2g, Proteins: 31g

Japanese Style Pork Chops

Japanese styled pork chop is quite easy to prepare. Another boon for this recipe is that the ingredients are cheap and easily purchased.
Prep time and cooking time: 35 minutes | Serves: 1

Ingredients To Use:

- 1 tbsp. of oil
- 2 packets of pork loin
- 1 egg
- 1/4 cup of bread crumbs
- 1/4 cup of flour
- 1 tsp. black pepper
- 1 tsp. salt

Step-by-Step Directions to Cook It:

1. Preheat the air fryer to 390F. Rub the pork with salt and pepper and leave for 30 minutes to marinate.
2. Beat the egg in a bowl; place bread crumbs in a bowl and flour in another bowl. Now coat the pork with egg, then the flour, and then the breadcrumbs.
3. Place pork in the air fryer cook for 15 minutes.
4. Serve and Enjoy.

Nutritional value per serving:

Calories: 432kcal, Fat: 21g, Carb: 29g, Proteins: 41g

Bacon-Wrapped with Chicken

Bacon-wrapped with chicken tastes as good as it looks. A fancy meal for a casual family dinner.

Prep time and cooking time: 20 minutes | Serves: 4

- 6 Rashers unsmoked back bacon
- 1 small chicken breast
- 1tbsp garlic soft cheese

Step-by-Step Directions to Cook It:

1. Preheat the air fryer to 320^0F.
2. Chop up your chicken breast into six bite-sized pieces. Layout your bacon rashers and spread them with a small layer of soft cheese. Place your chicken on top of the cheese and roll them up. Secure them with a cocktail stick.
3. Transfer to the air fryer basket and cook for 15 minutes, turning halfway through.

Nutritional value per serving:

Calories: 341kcal, Fat: 11g, Carb: 3g, Proteins: 36g

Air Fried Pork Burger

Air fried burger is simple, easy to prepare, and tastes fantastic, especially when eaten with salad.

Prep time and cooking time: 55 minutes | Serves: 4

Ingredients To Use:

- 300g mixed mince (pork and beef)
- Small onion, diced
- 1 tsp. garlic puree
- 1 tsp. tomato puree
- 1 tsp. mustard
- 1 tsp. basil
- 1 tsp. mixed herbs
- Salt and pepper
- 1/4 cup Cheddar cheese
- 4 bread buns
- Salad (for burger topping)

Step-by-Step Directions to Cook It:

1. Preheat the air fryer to 3600F.
2. In a mixing bowl, add the meat and all the ingredients except salad, cheese, and buns, mix well. Form into four medium-sized burgers and place in the Air Fryer cooking tray.
3. Cook for 25 minutes in the air fryer, flip and reduce the temperature to 3200F. Cook for an additional 20 minutes.
4. Arrange on the buns, top with cheese and salad, serve!

Nutritional value per serving:

Calories: 412kcal, Fat: 12g, Carb: 24g, Proteins: 29g

Chinese Style Pork Kebab and Rice

This Chinese recipe is a meal that can be prepared at any time of the day. The marinade gives the meat a sweet and tangy taste.

Prep time and cooking time: 30 minutes | Serves: 4

Ingredients To Use:

- 1/2 lb. minced pork
- 1 small onion (peeled and diced)
- 1 tsp. garlic puree
- 1 tsp. tomato puree
- 1/2 tbsp. Chinese five spice
- 1 slice whole meal bread (made into breadcrumbs)
- 1 tbsp. soy sauce
- 100g egg fried rice (cooked)
- Salt & pepper

Step-by-Step Directions to Cook It:

1. Preheat the air fryer to 320^0F.
2. In a bowl, add the minced pork with the remaining ingredients. Form into a ball and transfer to the air fryer cooking

basket. Set time to 30 minutes.

3. Serve with the rice and enjoy!

Calories: 341kcal, Fat: 21g, Carb: 26g, Proteins: 29g

Thai Style Bites

These bite-size pieces of pork taste heavenly, especially when drizzled with ketchup or red chili sauce.

Prep time and cooking time: 20 minutes | Serves: 4

Ingredients To Use:

- 400g pork mince
- 1 tsp. Chinese spice
- 1 large onion
- 1 tsp. of freshly chopped coriander
- 1 tsp. garlic puree
- 1 tbsp. Worcester sauce
- 2tsp. Thai curry paste
- 1 tbsp. soy sauce
- 1/2 lime zest and juice)
- 1 tsp. of mixed spice
- Salt and pepper, as desired

Step-by-Step Directions to Cook It:

1. Preheat the air fryer to 320^0F.
2. Pour all the ingredients into a bowl and stir until well-combined. Shape the resultant mixture into balls and transfer them to the air fryer.
3. Set the timer for 15 minutes and leave to cook.
4. Serve and enjoy!

Nutritional value per serving:

Calories: 294kcal, Fat: 3g, Carb: 5g, Proteins: 18g

Air Fried Pork Roast

Preparing this recipe with the air fryer is simply the best; the meat is juicy and tender and the taste is out of this world.

Prep time and cooking time: 5 | Serves: 4

Ingredients To Use:

- 2 lb. pork belly; washed and pat dry

For Dry Rub:

- 2 tsp. garlic and onion seasoning
- 1 tsp. white pepper
- 1-1/2 tsp. five-spice powder
- 1 tsp. salt
- 1-1/2 tsp. rosemary
- 2 tbsps. lemon juice
- 1/2 tsp. salt

Step-by-Step Directions to Cook It:

1. Place the washed pork on a steamer rack over a plate. Blanch the pork belly with boiled water for 12 minutes. Pat dry and air-dry for 3 hours.
2. Meanwhile, combine all ingredients of the dry rub except the lemon. Using a fork, poke holes in the pork belly, flip and make about 3 to 4 cuts. Massage both sides of the pork belly with your dry rub, drizzle with the lemon juice.
3. Preheat air fryer at 160°F for 5 minutes. Cook pork belly for 30 minutes. Increase temperature to 180°F and cook for an additional 25 minutes.
4. Cut into portions and serve.

Nutritional value per serving:

Calories: 321kcal, Fat: 10g, Carb: 3g, Proteins: 26g

Air Fried Garlic Bacon and Potatoes

This recipe is unforgettable. It comes with loads of flavors and aromas.

Prep time and cooking time: 30 minutes | Serves: 4

- 4 medium-sized potatoes, peeled and cut into 2
- 4 strips of streaky bacon
- 2 sprigs of rosemary
- 6 cloves of garlic, smashed, unpeeled
- 3 tsp. of vegetable oil

Step-by-Step Directions to Cook It:

1. Preheat Air fryer to 390°F.
2. Put the smashed garlic, bacon, potatoes, rosemary, and then the oil in a bowl. Stir thoroughly. Place into the air fryer basket and roast until golden for about 25 minutes.
3. Serve and enjoy!

Nutritional value per serving:

Calories: 432kcal, Fat: 11g, Carb: 5g, Proteins: 26g

Bacon-Wrapped with Shrimp

Bacon-wrapped with shrimps is simply irresistible, especially when drizzled with a sauce of choice. It can serve as a good appetizer for any occasion.
Prep time and cooking time: 30 minutes | Serves: 4

Ingredients To Use:

- 1 lb. shrimp (about 20 pieces) peeled and deveined
- 20 bacon strips
- 2 tbsp. melted butter
- 2 tbsp. chili powder
- 2 tbsp. maple syrup

Step-by-Step Directions to Cook It:

1. In a bowl, mix butter with syrup and powder. Brush the shrimp with the mixture. Wrap a slice of bacon around the shrimp completely. Refrigerate the wrapped shrimp for 20 minutes.

2. Preheat the Air fryer to 390°F. Transfer to the air fryer cooking basket and cook for 7 minutes.
3. Serve and enjoy!

Nutritional value per serving:

Calories: 453kcal, Fat: 23g, Carb: 7g, Proteins: 43g

Cheese Bacon Croquettes

Cheese bacon croquettes is super delicious and is a meal you won't want to resist. Enjoy as a main or side dish.
Prep time and cooking time: 50 minutes | Serves: 6

Ingredients To Use:

- 1 lb. bacon, sliced thinly
- 1 lb. sharp cheddar cheese block (cut into 1cm cubes)
- 1 egg, whisked
- 1 cup all-purpose flour
- 4 tbsps. olive oil
- 1 cup seasoned breadcrumbs

Step-by-Step Directions to Cook It:

1. Wrap 2 bacon pieces around each cheddar piece completely. Trim off any excess fat and then freeze the cheddar bacon bites for 5 minutes to make firm, but not to freeze.
2. Preheat Air fryer to 390°F. Combine the breadcrumbs and oil and stir until it becomes loose and crumbly.
3. Put the cheddar block into the flour, place the eggs, and then finally the breadcrumbs, pressing the coating to the croquettes to make sure it sticks. (To prevent cheese from running out, double the coating by dipping twice into the egg and then the breadcrumbs). Place the croquettes in the air fryer basket and cook until golden brown or

for about 8 minutes.
4. Serve and enjoy!

Nutritional value per serving:

Calories: 512kcal, Fat: 21g, Carb: 19g, Proteins: 39g

Air Fried Pork Chops

The Air fryer changes the sad, dry unfavorable taste of oven-roasted pork chops to a savory, moist, and tender fairy tale.
Prep time and cooking time: 25 minutes|
Serves: 4

Ingredients To Use:

- 1/2 tsp. black pepper
- 4 boneless pork chops
- 1/2 cup. Parmesan
- 2 tbsp. of olive oil
- 1 tsp. kosher salt
- 1 tsp. garlic powder
- 1 tsp. paprika
- 1 tsp. onion powder

Step-by-Step Directions to Cook It:

1. Preheat the air fryer to 375^{0}F.
2. Dry the pork chops by dabbing them with paper towels, then rub oil on both sides.
3. In a separate bowl, season the parmesan with the spices. Dribble the parmesan mixture on both sides of the pork chops.
4. Transfer to the air fryer basket and cook for 10 minutes, turning at the halfway point for even cooking.
5. Serve and enjoy!

Nutritional value per serving:

Calories: 390kcal, Fat: 21g, Carb: 28g, Proteins: 36g

Keto Pork Chops with Butter and Sage

Keto fans will love this instant low-carb pork chops meal.
Prep time and cooking time: 30 minutes |
Serves: 4

Ingredients To Use:

- 4 medium boneless pork chops
- 6 tbsp. butter divided
- Salt and pepper
- 3 tbsp. chopped fresh sage
- 1 shallot, chopped
- 1 tbsp. olive oil

Step-by-Step Directions to Cook It:

1. Preheat the air fryer to 370^{0}F.
2. Season the pork with salt, pepper, and rub with oil. Transfer into the air fryer and cook for 25 minutes.
3. Meanwhile, heat butter in a pan over medium heat. Add shallot and sage, season with salt and pepper. Cook for 2 minutes.
4. Serve chops with the sage sauce.

Nutritional value per serving:

Calories: 485kcal, Fat: 36.5g, Carb: 0.7, Proteins: 42.8g

Air Fried Crispy Pork Belly

Air fried pork belly is crispy and delicious. Serve with sauce and enjoy.
Prep time and cooking time: 1hour | Serves: 6

Ingredients To Use:

- 1-1/2 lb. pork belly
- 1 tsp. chicken powder
- 1/2 tbsp. five-spice powder
- 2 tsp. sugar
- 2/3 tsp. salt
- 1 tbsp. Chinese rose wine

- 5 tbsp. white vinegar
- 4 cups. kosher salt

1. Blanch the pork belly in boiling water for 8 minutes and wipe dry. Use a fork to poke holes in the pork belly, pat dry with a paper towel. Mix all the remaining ingredients and marinate the bottom part of the pork belly. Keep the marinade off the skin.
2. Pour the white vinegar into a dish. Lay the pork belly skin side down on the dish and refrigerate overnight. Rinse off the white vinegar with water, poke the pork belly with a fork, and pat dry with a paper towel. Spread coarse salt all over the pork.
3. Preheat the air fryer to 3700F, transfer the pork belly to the air fryer basket and cook for 35 minutes. Remove the coarse salt and increase the temperature to 3800F. Cook for an additional 20 minutes.
4. Slice into portions, serve and enjoy!

Nutritional value per serving:

Calories: 634kcal, Fat: 31g Carb: 7g, Proteins: 81g

Provencal Pork

This Provencal pork chops recipe involves a combination of classic flavors. The pork is juicy, succulent, and just melts in the mouth.
Prep time and cooking time: 25 minutes|
Serves: 2

Ingredients To Use:

- 7 oz. pork tenderloin
- 1 green bell pepper, cut into strips
- 2 tbsp. Provencal herbs
- 1 yellow bell pepper, cut into strips
- 1/2 tbsp. mustard
- 1 red onion, sliced

- 1 tbsp. olive oil
- Salt and black pepper to taste

Step-by-Step Directions to Cook It:

1. Preheat the air fryer to 370^0F.
2. In a pan that fits into the air fryer, add all the ingredients, and mix well. Season the pork with salt, pepper, mustard, and rub with oil. Add to the pan and toss to coat.
3. Transfer into the air fryer and cook for 17 minutes.
4. Serve and Enjoy!

Nutritional value per serving:

Calories: 300kcal, Fat: 8g, Carb: 21g, Proteins: 23g

Creamy Pork

This creamy pork recipe is one way of getting your dinner available on the table in 30 minutes. The steps are simple, and ingredients readily available.
Prep time and cooking time: 32 minutes|
Serves: 6

Ingredients To Use:

- 2 lb. pork meat, cut into cubes
- 2 tbsp. chopped dill
- 2 yellow onions, chopped
- 2 tbsp. white flour
- 3 cup chicken stock
- 2 tbsp. white flour
- 3 cloves garlic, minced
- 2 tbsp. sweet paprika
- 1 and 1/2 cups sour cream
- Salt and black pepper to taste

Step-by-Step Directions to Cook It:

1. Preheat the air fryer to 370^0F.
2. In a pan that fits into the air fryer, mix pork with salt, pepper, and oil. Toss to coat, transfer to the air fryer and cook for 7 minutes.
3. Open the lid and add the remaining

ingredients. Increase the temperature to 370^{0}F and cook for 15 minutes.
4. Serve and enjoy.

Nutritional value per serving:

Calories: 300kcal, Fat: 4g, Carb: 26g, Proteins: 34g

Simple Braised Pork

This pork chop meal is delicious and tasty. To better enjoy it, serve with steamed rice or salad by the side.
Prep time and cooking time: 1 hour 20 minutes| Serves: 4

Ingredients To Use:

- 2 lb. pork loin roast, boneless and cubed
- 1/2 lb. red grapes
- 4 tbsp. melted butter
- 2 cups. chicken stock
- 2 garlic cloves, minced
- 1/2 yellow onion
- 1 thyme spring
- 1/2 cup dry white wine
- 2 tbsp. white flour
- 1 tsp. chopped thyme
- 1 bay leaf
- Salt and black pepper to taste

Step-by-Step Directions to Cook It:

1. Preheat the air fryer to 370^{0}F, season the cubes with salt, pepper, and 2 tbsp. Melted butter. Introduce to your air fryer and cook for 8 minutes.
2. Place a saucepan on heat, add the remaining melted butter, and heat. Add garlic, onions, and cook for 2 minutes. Add the remaining ingredients except for grapes and cook for 3 minutes.
3. Introduce the pork and the grape, stir, and transfer to a pan that fits into your air fryer. Increase the temperature to 370^{0}F and set time to 30 minutes.

4. Serve and enjoy.

Nutritional value per serving:

Calories: 320kcal, Fat: 4g, Carb: 29g, Proteins: 38g

Simple Air fried Pork Shoulder

Simple air-fried pork shoulder is the ideal and perfect meal for a family gathering. Enjoy with salad as a side dish.
Prep time and cooking time: 1 hour 50 minutes| Serves:6

Ingredients To Use:

- 4 lb. pork shoulder
- 3 tbsp. minced garlic
- 3 tbsp. olive oil
- Salt and black pepper to taste

Step-by-Step Directions to Cook It:

1. Preheat the air fryer to 390^{0}F.
2. In a bowl, mix all the ingredients with the pork, toss to coat. Transfer to the air fryer basket and cook for 10 minutes.
3. Reduce the temperature to 300^{0}F and set time to 1 hour 10 minutes.
4. Serve and enjoy!

Nutritional value per serving:

Calories: 221kcal, Fat: 4g, Carb: 7g, Proteins: 10g

Roasted Pork Belly and Apple Sauce

You never can resist the sweet and savory taste of pork belly with apple sauce. Try it for dinner and get hooked!
Prep time and cooking time: 50 minutes| Serves: 6

Ingredients To Use:

- 2 lb. pork belly, scored
- 2 tbsp. sugar
- 17 oz. apples, cored and cut into wedges

- 1 tbsp. lemon juice
- 1/2 cup of water
- Salt and black pepper to taste
- Olive oil for drizzling

1. Preheat the air fryer to 400°F.
2. In a food processor, add all the ingredients except the pork, pulse well. Transfer to a bowl, add the pork, and toss well. Remove from the sauce and transfer to the air fryer basket. Cook for 40 minutes.
3. Meanwhile, pour the sauce into a pan and cook for 15 minutes over medium heat.
4. Slice the pork belly and serve with the sauce, Enjoy!

Nutritional value per serving:

Calories: 456kcal, Fat: 34g, Carb: 10g, Proteins: 25g

Pork Chops and Mushroom Mix

Pork chops with the mushroom mix is a bowl of mouth-watering flavor. The meal tastes wonderful.
Prep time and cooking time: 50 minutes| Serves: 3

Ingredients To Use:

- 3 pork chops, boneless
- 1 tsp. garlic
- 1 tsp. nutmeg
- 1/2 cup. olive oil
- 1 tbsp. balsamic vinegar
- 1 cup. mayonnaise
- 8 oz. mushroom, sliced
- 1 yellow onion, sliced
- Salt and black pepper to taste

Step-by-Step Directions to Cook It:

1. Preheat the air fryer to 330°F.
2. Heat oil in a pan that fits into your air fryer; add onions and mushroom. Stir and cook for 4 minutes. Add the pork chops, garlic powder, and nutmeg, brown on all sides.
3. Transfer to your air fryer and cook for 30 minutes. Open the lid; stir in vinegar and mayonnaise.
4. Serve and Enjoy!

Nutritional value per serving:

Calories: 600kcal, Fat: 10g, Carb: 8g, Proteins: 30g

Pork Chops and Green Beans

Pork chops and green beans combine both flavors and nutrients in one plate.
Prep time and cooking time: 25 minutes| Serves: 4

Ingredients To Use:

- 4 pork chops
- 3 garlic cloves, minced
- 1 tbsp. chopped sage
- 16 oz. green beans
- 2 tbsp. chopped parsley
- 2 tbsp. olive oil
- Salt and black pepper to taste

Step-by-Step Directions to Cook It:

1. Preheat the air fryer to 360°F. In a pan that fits into the air fryer, add all the ingredients and mix. Add the pork and mix well.
2. Transfer to the air fryer and set time to 15 minutes.
3. Serve and enjoy!

Nutritional value per serving:

Calories: 261kcal, Fat: 7g, Carb: 17g, Proteins: 20g

Pork Stew

Who doesn't love a steamed bowl of stew,

with flavors and aromas that can't be easily forgotten.

Prep time and cooking time: 47 minutes| Serves: 4

- 2 lb. pork meat, cubed
- 2 zucchinis, cubed
- 1/2 tsp. smoked paprika
- 1 eggplant, cubed
- 1 tbsp. cilantro, chopped
- 1/2 cup beef stock
- Salt and black pepper to taste

Step-by-Step Directions to Cook It:

1. Preheat the air fryer to 370^{0}F.
2. In a pan that fits into the air fryer, add all the ingredients with the beef. Mix well and transfer into the air fryer, set time to 30 minutes.
3. Serve and enjoy!

Nutritional value per serving:

Calories: 245kcal, Fat: 12g, Carb: 5g, Proteins: 14g

Pork Taquitos

Air frying is a healthy way of cooking this recipe. The pork tortilla can easily be available within 15 minutes, perfect for a stress-free lunch.

Prep time and cooking time: 15 minutes| Serves: 10

Ingredients To Use:

- 3 cups cooked shredded pork
- 2-1/2 cup. Mozzarella cheese
- Juice of 1 lime
- 1o small tortillas

Step-by-Step Directions to Cook It:

1. Preheat the air fryer to 380^{0}F.
2. Sprinkle lime juice over the pork and mix well, set aside. Microwave the pork

tortilla and place a damp paper over them for 10 seconds. Add pork and cheese to each tortilla and roll tightly. Arrange onto a greased foil-lined pan (ensure that the pan fits into the air fryer). Spray the tortillas with cooking spray.
3. Transfer into the air fryer and cook for 10 minutes, flipping halfway through.
4. Serve and enjoy!

Nutritional value per serving:

Calories: 312kcal, Fat: 12g, Carb: 23g, Proteins: 27g

Pork with Couscous

This is another creative way of preparing pork. The meal comes together in 45 minutes, serve and enjoy with your family.

Prep time and cooking time: 45 minutes| Serves: 6

Ingredients To Use:

- 2-1/2 lb. pork loin, boneless and trimmed
- 2 tbsp. olive oil
- 2 cups couscous, cooked
- 3/4 cup. chicken stock
- 1 tsp. dried oregano
- 1/2 tbsp. sweet paprika
- 1/4 tsp. dried marjoram
- 2 and 1/4 tsp. dried sage
- 1/4 tsp. dried rosemary
- 1/2 tbsp. garlic powder
- 1 tsp. dried basil
- Salt and black pepper to taste

Step-by-Step Directions to Cook It:

1. In a pan that fits into the air fryer, add all the ingredients, and mix well. Add the pork and toss to coat, leave to marinate for 1 hour.
2. Preheat the air fryer to 370^{0}F.
3. Transfer to your air fryer and cook for 35

minutes.
4. Serve and enjoy!

Calories: 310kcal, Fat: 4g, Carb: 37g, Proteins: 34g

Fennel Flavoured Pork Roast

The fennel boosts the flavor of the pork roast. You may prepare this dish for a special occasion.
Prep time and cooking time: 1hour 10 minutes| Serves: 10

Ingredients To Use:

- 5-1/2 lb. pork loin roast
- 1/4 cup olive oil
- 2 tbsp. chopped rosemary
- 1 tsp. ground fennel
- 1 tbsp. fennel seeds
- 3 garlic cloves, minced
- 2 tsp. crushed red pepper
- Salt and black pepper to taste

Step-by-Step Directions to Cook It:

1. Preheat the air fryer to 350^{0}F.
2. In a food processor, add all the ingredients except the pork. Pulse until you get a paste-like texture. Season the pork with salt and pepper and rub with the paste.
3. Transfer to your air fryer and cook for 30 minutes; reduce the temperature to 300^{0}F. Cook for another 15 minutes.
4. Slice the pork and divide among the plates, enjoy!

Nutritional value per serving:

Calories: 300kcal, Fat: 14g, Carb: 26g, Proteins: 22g

Stuffed Pork Steak

There is nothing as tasty as juicy and tender pork. The stuffing creates unique and delicious pork infused with flavors.
Prep time and cooking time: 30 minutes| Serves: 4

Ingredients To Use:

- 4 pork loin steak
- 2 tbsp. mustard
- Zest from 2 limes, grated
- Juice from 1 orange
- 2 pickles, chopped
- 6 Swiss cheese, sliced
- Juice from 2 limes
- Zest from 1 orange, grated
- 1 cup. chopped cilantro
- 1 tsp.. dried oregano
- 1 cup. chopped mint
- 4 ham slices
- 2 tbsp. mustard
- 3/4 cup. olive oil
- 2 tsp. ground cumin
- Salt and black pepper to taste

Step-by-Step Directions to Cook It:

1. In a food processor, add lime zest, orange zest, lime juice, orange juice, garlic, oregano, cumin, mint, cilantro, and pulse well.
2. Preheat the air fryer to 340^{0}F, season the steak with salt and pepper. Transfer to a bowl and pour your marinade. Toss to coat and transfer to a working surface.
3. Divide the pickle, cheese, ham, mustard on the pork, roll, and secure with toothpicks. Transfer to the air fryer and cook for 20 minutes.
4. Serve and enjoy with a plate of salad.

Nutritional value per serving:

Calories: 270kcal, Fat: 7g, Carb: 13g, Proteins: 20g

Pork Chops and Roasted Pepper

This piece of a heavenly meal is best enjoyed with cheesy polenta and a glass of good wine.
Prep time and cooking time: 26 minutes|
Serves:4

Ingredients To Use:

- 4 pork chops
- 3 tbsp. olive oil
- 2 tbsp. smoked paprika
- 2 roasted bell peppers, chopped
- 3 tbsp. lemon juice
- 2 tbsp. thyme, chopped
- 3 garlic cloves, minced
- Salt and black pepper to taste

Step-by-Step Directions to Cook It:

1. Preheat the air fryer to 400⁰F.
2. In a bowl that fits into the air fryer, add all the ingredients with the pork chops. Mix thoroughly and transfer into the air fryer. Cook for 16 minutes.
3. Serve and enjoy!

Nutritional value per serving:

Calories: 321kcal, Fat: 6g, Carb: 14g, Proteins: 17g

Pork and Sage Sauce

Feel free to indulge yourself in this irresistible creamy delight. The meat is juicy and tenderwhen combined with the creamy sauce, simply awesome!
Prep time and cooking time: 25 minutes|
Serves: 2

Ingredients To Use:

- 2 pork chops
- 2 tbsp. butter
- 1 tbsp. chopped Sage
- 2 garlic cloves, minced
- 1 tbsp. olive oil
- 1 tsp. lemon juice

- 1/2 cup. milk
- 1 shallot, sliced
- Salt and black pepper to taste

Step-by-Step Directions to Cook It:

1. Preheat the air fryer to 370⁰F.
2. Season the pork chops with salt, pepper, and rub with olive oil. Transfer to the air fryer and cook for 10 minutes, flipping halfway.
3. Meanwhile, heat butter in a pan over medium heat, add garlic, shallot and cook for 2 minutes. Add sage, milk, lemon juice, and cook for 2 minutes. Remove from heat.
4. Serve pork chops with sage sauce, enjoy!

Nutritional value per serving:

Calories: 265kcal, Fat: 6g, Carb: 19g, Proteins: 12g

Bacon-Wrapped Pork Tenderloin

The bacon-wrapped pork tenderloin is soft, juicy, and tender. The addition of the bacon boosts the pork's flavor.
Prep time and cooking time: 25 minutes|
Serves: 4

Ingredients To Use:

- 1 lb. pork tenderloin
- 4 bacon strips
- 1/2 tsp. black pepper
- 2 tbsp. Dijon mustard
- 1 tsp. oregano
- 1/2 tsp. garlic powder

Step-by-Step Directions to Cook It:

1. Preheat the air fryer to 360⁰F.
2. In a bowl, mix mustard with pepper, oregano, and garlic. Coat the tenderloins in the mustard mixture and wrap with the bacon.
3. Transfer to the air fryer basket and cook

for 15 minutes, flipping after 7 minutes

4. Serve with sauce of choice and enjoy!

Nutritional value per serving:

Calories: 319kcal, Fat: 21g, Carb: 3g, Proteins: 28g

Marinated Pork Chops and onions

The recipe simply creates a juicy, and tender meat that you won't be able to resist. Enjoy with salad.
Prep time and cooking time: 50 minutes|
Serves: 6

Ingredients To Use:

- 2 pork chops
- 2 tsp. mustard
- 1/2 cup. olive oil
- 2 yellow onions, sliced
- 1 tsp. sweet paprika
- 2 garlic cloves, minced
- 1/2 tsp. thyme, dried
- 1/2 tsp. dried oregano
- Salt and black pepper to taste
- Pinch of cayenne pepper

Step-by-Step Directions to Cook It:

1. In a bowl, add all the ingredients and mix well; add the meat and toss to coat. Leave to marinate in the refrigerator for 1 day.
2. Preheat the air fryer to 360⁰F, pour the meat and onion in a pan that fits into the air fryer, set time to 25 minutes.
3. Serve and enjoy!

Nutritional value per serving:

Calories: 384kcal, Fat: 4g, Carb: 17g, Proteins: 25g

Indian Pork

Spicy and flavorful are the best two words to

describe this dish. Enjoy with steamed rice at the side.
Prep time and cooking time: 45 minutes|
Serves: 4

Ingredients To Use:

- 14 oz. pork chops, cut into cubes
- 1 tsp. ginger powder
- 3 tbsp. soy sauce
- 7 oz. coconut milk
- 2 tsp. chili paste
- 1 shallot, chopped
- 1 tsp. ground coriander
- 3 oz. ground peanuts
- 2 tbsp. olive oil
- 2 garlic cloves, minced
- Salt and black pepper to taste

Step-by-Step Directions to Cook It:

1. In a bowl, mix ginger with 1 tsp. chili paste, add half of the following ingredients: soy sauce, oil, garlic. Whisk thoroughly and add the meat, toss to coat. Set aside for 10 minutes.
2. Preheat the air fryer to 400⁰F.
3. Transfer the meat into the air fryer basket and cook for 12 minutes, turning halfway.
4. Meanwhile, place a pan over medium heat, add oil and heat until shimmering. Add the rest of the ingredients and cook for 5 minutes.
5. Serve the pork with the coconut mix.

Nutritional value per serving:

Calories: 323kcal, Fat: 11g, Carb: 32g, Proteins: 18g

Pork Burger Cutlets

Pork burger is a tasty and delightful meal.
Prep time and cooking time: 25 minutes |
Serves: 6

- 1/4 tsp. of dried mango powder
- 1/2 lb. of pork
- 1 tsp. of lemon juice
- 1/2 cup of breadcrumbs
- 1 tbsp. Of fresh coriander leaves.
- Salt
- 1/4 tsp. of chopped ginger
- 1/4 tsp. of red chili powder
- 1/4 tsp. of cumin powder
- 1 chopped green chili
- 1/2 cup of cooked peas

Step-by-Step Directions to Cook It:

1. Mix green chilies, masala, coriander leaves, onions, ginger in a bowl. Add peas, lemon juice, breadcrumbs, and ginger.
2. Make round cutlets from the mixture. Roll the cutlets out.
3. Transfer cutlets to the air fryer and cook for 12 minutes at 150^{0}F.
4. Serve immediately with ketchup.

Nutritional value per serving:

Calories: 350kcal, Fat: 13g, Carb: 5g, Proteins: 27g

Barbecue Pork Sandwich

Barbecue pork is made by air frying pork at a particular temperature. Follow the instructions verbatim for a truly tasty meal.
Prep time and cooking time: 20 minutes|
Serves: 3

Ingredients To Use:

- 1/2 tsp. of olive oil
- 1/2 cup of water
- 2 white bread slices
- 1/2 flake of crushed garlic
- Pepper and salt
- 1 tbsp. of softened butter
- 1/4 tbsp. of red chili sauce

- 1/4 cup of chopped onion
- 1/2 lb. of cubed pork
- 1/4 tsp. of mustard powder
- 1 capsicum
- 1/2 tbsp. of sugar
- 1/4 tbsp. of Worcestershire sauce
- 1 tbsp. of tomato ketchup

Step-by-Step Directions to Cook It:

1. Remove the edges of the bread slices. Cut it horizontally.
2. In a pan, cook olive oil, Worcestershire sauce, crushed garlic, and sugar. Add tomato ketchup, onion, mustard powder, red chili sauce, salt, and pepper. Stir well until it thickens.
3. Remove the skin of the capsicum and roast well. Slice the capsicum. Mix the capsicum with the ingredients. Add the cubed pork to it. Put the mixture inside the slices of bread.
4. Transfer the sandwich to the air fryer basket. Cook for 15 minutes at 250^{0}F. Flip while cooking for uniformity.

Nutritional value per serving:

Calories: 311kcal, Fat: 10g, Carb: 42g, Proteins: 18g

Pork Kebab

Pork kebab is another name given to crispy pork. The air fryer makes the pork crispier and tastier.
Prep time and cooking time: 35 minutes|
Serves: 4

Ingredients To Use:

- 3 tbsp. of cream
- 1 lb. of boneless pork cubed
- 2-1/2 tbsp. of white sesame seeds
- 3 tsp. of lemon juice
- 3 onions chopped
- 2 tsp. of garam masala

- 5 chopped green chilies
- 4 tbsp. of fresh mint chopped
- 4 tbsp. of chopped coriander
- 2 tbsp. of coriander powder
- 1-1/2 tbsp. of ginger paste
- 3 eggs
- 1-1/2 tsp. of garlic paste
- 1-1/2 tsp. of salt
- 3 tbsp. of chopped capsicum

1. In a bowl, mix the ingredients. Stir until it is a smooth paste. Put the pork cube in the mixture and coat. Break eggs and whisk, sprinkle salt on it.
2. Put pork cube inside the egg, transfer to a sesame seed, and coat. Place it in the fridge for about 1 hour.
3. Put the pork kebab on the air fryer basket and cook at 290^{0}F for 25 minutes.
4. Serve immediately.

Nutritional value per serving:

Calories: 159kcal, Fat: 6g, Carb: 3g, Proteins: 29g

Pork Wonton

Pork wonton is a great meal if the right recipe is applied. Below is a unique recipe that would surely deliver a tasty meal.
Prep time and cooking time: 30 minutes|
Serves: 4

Ingredients To Use:

- 2 tbsp. of oil
- 1-1/2 cup of all-purpose flour
- 2 tsp. of ginger-garlic paste
- 1/2 tsp. of salt
- 2 tsp. of soya sauce
- 5 tbsp. of water
- 2 tsp. of vinegar
- 2 cups of minced pork

Step-by-Step Directions to Cook It:

1. Mix flour, salt, and water to form a dough.
2. Cook pork, oil, ginger-garlic paste, soya sauce, and vinegar in a pan. Cook till it thickens.
3. Put the mixture on the dough, roll and seal on the edges.
4. Transfer the wonton to the air fryer basket. Cook for 20 minutes at 200^{0}F.

Nutritional value per serving:

Calories: 200kcal, Fat: 3g, Carb: 4g, Proteins: 3g

Chili Cheese Pork

Cheese pork is a great and healthy meal.
Prep time and cooking time: 25 minutes|
Serves: 5

Ingredients To Use:

- 2 tsp. of red chili flakes
- 1 lb. of pork
- 1-1/2 tsp. of ginger garlic paste
- 2-1/2 tsp. of ginger-garlic paste
- 1/2 tbsp. of red chili sauce
- 1 tsp. of red chili sauce
- 2 tbsp. of tomato ketchup
- 1/4 tsp. of salt
- 2 tsp. of soya sauce
- 1/4 tsp. of red chili powder
- Black pepper
- 1-2 tbsp. of honey
- Orange food coloring, edible
- 2 tbsp. of olive oil
- 1/4 tsp. of ajinomoto

Step-by-Step Directions to Cook It:

1. In a pan, cook olive oil, ginger-garlic paste, red chili sauce, tomato ketchup, soya sauce, honey, ajinomoto and red chili flakes over medium heat. Remove from heat and add pork. Allow to rest overnight.

2. In a bowl, mix red chili flakes, breadcrumbs and oregano. Mix well and add to the marinated fingers.
3. Transfer the chili pork to the air fryer basket, cook for 15 minutes at 160^{0}F.
4. Serve immediately.

Calories: 330kcal, Fat: 19g, Carb: 4.5g, Proteins: 37g

Boneless Pork Stick

The air fryer has a crispy effect on the pork sticks and makes the meal tastier than when cooked with a griller.
Prep time and cooking time: 25 minutes| Serves: 5

Ingredients To Use:

- 4 eggs
- 1 lb. of boneless pork
- 4 tbsp. of lemon juice
- 2 cup of dry breadcrumbs
- 2 tsp. of salt
- 2 tsp. of oregano
- 1 tsp. of pepper powder
- 2 tsp. of red chili flakes
- 1 tsp. of red chili powder
- 1-1/2 tbsp. of ginger-garlic paste
- 6 tbsp. of cornflour

Step-by-Step Directions to Cook It:

1. In a bowl, mix ginger-garlic paste, lemon juice, salt, pepper powder, red chili powder, cornflour, and eggs. Leave overnight.
2. In another bowl, mix red chili flakes, breadcrumbs, pork fingers, and oregano. Put the pork on sticks.
3. Transfer the pork sticks to the air fryer basket. Cook for 15 minutes at 160^{0}F.

Nutritional value per serving:

Calories: 240kcal, Fat: 15g, Carb: 0g, Proteins: 28g

Pork Tandoori

The lemon juice added to the pork gives it a sweet and lasting feel.
Prep time and cooking time: 1 hour 10 minutes| Serves: 4

Ingredients To Use:

- 1/2 cup of mint leaves
- 2 cups of sliced pork belly
- 4 tsp. of fennel
- 1 large capsicum
- 2 tbsp. of ginger-garlic paste
- 1 onion
- 5 tbsp. of gram flour
- 7 flakes of garlic
- 1 small onion
- Salt
- 2 cup of fresh green coriander
- 3 tbsp. of lemon juice

Step-by-Step Directions to Cook It:

1. In a bowl, mix coriander, mint leaves, fennel, ginger-garlic paste, onion, garlic, salt, and lemon juice. Cut the pork into pieces and stock the pork pieces with the mixture.
2. Mix salt and gram flour with remaining paste. Pour the pieces of pork and mix.
3. Put the pork mixture on the air fryer basket. Cook for 1 hour at 180^{0}F.

Nutritional value per serving:

Calories: 150kcal, Fat: 8g, Carb: 6g, Proteins: 17g

Bacon Sandwich

Bacon has an exceptional taste and below is a special way of making a bacon sandwich.
Prep time and cooking time: 20 minutes| Serves: 4

- 2 tomatoes
- 1/3 cup of barbecue sauce
- 1 bell pepper, yellow
- 2 tbsp. of honey
- 3 pita pockets
- 8 bacon slices
- 1-1/4 cup of butter lettuce leaves
- 1 bell pepper, red

Step-by-Step Directions to Cook It:

1. Mix barbecue sauce and honey in a bowl. Mix well.
2. Rub the mixture on the bacon and bell peppers. Transfer the bacon and bell peppers to the air fryer.
3. Cook for 6 minutes at 350°F. Mix bacon mixture and stuffed pita in a bowl. Add lettuce and tomatoes.
4. Serve immediately with barbecue sauce.

Nutritional value per serving:

Calories: 187kcal, Fat: 7g, Carb: 1g, Proteins: 15g

Chinese Pork Mix

Chinese pork mix is a combination of different Chinese spices and herbs. It is also an incredibly delicious meal.
Prep time and cooking time: 25 minutes|
Serves: 4

Ingredients To Use:

- Chinese five-spice
- 2 eggs
- Black pepper and salt
- 2 pounds of cubed pork,
- 3 tbsp. of canola oil
- 1 cup of cornstarch
- Sweet tomato sauce
- 1 tsp. of sesame oil

Step-by-Step Directions to Cook It:

1. Mix pepper, five-spice, corn starch, and

salt. Mix well.

2. Mix sesame oil and eggs in a bowl and whisk.
3. Dip the cubed pork in the cornstarch mixture, transfer to the egg mixture. Transfer it to the greased air fryer with canola oil.
4. Cook for 12 minutes at 340°F.
5. Serve immediately with tomato sauce.

Nutritional value per serving:

Calories: 320kcal, Fat: 12g, Carb: 1g, Proteins: 21g

Pork and Potato Mix

Pork and potatoes make a hale and hearty meal. You would be too filled up to crave for snacks, which is extremely helpful when trying to lose weight.
Prep time and cooking time: 35 minutes|
Serves: 2

Ingredients To Use:

- 2 pounds of pork loin
- 1/2 tsp. of red pepper flakes
- Black pepper and salt
- 1 tsp. of parsley
- 2 red potatoes
- Balsamic vinegar
- 1/2 tsp. of garlic powder

Step-by-Step Directions to Cook It:

1. In a bowl, mix salt, pepper flakes, potatoes, parsley, pork, salt, garlic powder, vinegar, and pepper flakes. Mix well.
2. Transfer the mixture to the air fryer. Cook for 25 minutes at 390°F.
3. Serve pork and potatoes.

Nutritional value per serving:

Calories: 400kcal, Fat: 16g, Carb: 2g, Proteins: 27g

Bacon Pudding

The minced garlic used in this meal adds a cool taste to pork.

Prep time and cooking time: 40 minutes|
Serves: 6

- 2 tsp. of minced garlic
- Cooking spray
- 4 boiled and chopped bacon strips
- 3 eggs
- 1/2 cup of red bell pepper
- 1 tbsp. of soft butter
- 1/2 cups of milk
- 1 tsp. of thyme
- 2 cups of corn
- 3 cups of cubed bread
- 1 chopped yellow onion
- Black pepper and salt
- 1/4 cup of celery
- 1/2 cup of heavy cream
- 4 tbsp. of grated parmesan

Step-by-Step Directions to Cook It:

1. Spray the air fryer with cooking spray.
2. Mix corn, heavy cream, salt, bell pepper, and milk in a bowl. Add butter, eggs, bacon, celery, garlic, bread cubes, thyme, and onion.
3. Pour the mixture into the greased pan. Spray with cheese.
4. Cook at 320^0F for 30 minutes.
5. Serve immediately.

Nutritional value per serving:

Calories: 277kcal, Fat: 11g, Carb: 2g, Proteins: 22g

Garlic and Bacon Pizzas

Cooking bacon with garlic gives a soothing taste and flavor.

Prep time and cooking time: 20 minutes|

Serves: 4

Ingredients To Use:

- 1-1/4 cups of cheddar cheese,
- 4 frozen dinner rolls
- 1 cup of tomato sauce
- Cooking spray
- 4 minced garlic cloves
- 8 slices of bacon
- 1/2 tsp. of oregano dried
- 1/2 tsp. of garlic powder

Step-by-Step Directions to Cook It:

1. Put the dinner roll on a flat surface, cut 4 flat ovals from it.
2. Spray cooking spray on the ovals. Place them in the air fryer. Cook for 2 minutes at 370^0F.
3. Add garlic, tomato sauce, garlic, cheese, oregano, and bacon to the oval. Cook for another 8 minutes at the same temperature.
4. Serve immediately.

Nutritional value per serving:

Calories: 218kcal, Fat: 6g, Carb: 2g, Proteins: 13g

Japanese Fried Pork Chop

The Japanese have a special way of making pork chop and this recipe has been modified to accommodate the particularities of Japanese cooking with air frying.

Prep time and cooking time: 35 minutes|
Serves: 2

Ingredients To Use:

- 1 tbsp. of oil
- 1 tsp. of black pepper
- 2 packets of pounded pork loin
- 1 tsp. of salt
- 1 egg
- Bread crumbs Flour

1. Sprinkle pepper and salt on the pork. Allow to rest for about 30 minutes.
2. Whisk egg in a bowl.
3. Put flour and bread crumbs in separate bowls.
4. Put the pork in the egg mixture and transfer to the flour and then bread crumbs.
5. Put coated pork in the air fryer and cook at 390°F for 15 minutes.

Nutritional value per serving:

Calories: 430kcal, Fat: 24g, Carb: 20g, Proteins: 35g

Cheesy Bacon Potato Stuffed

This meal is particularly made during the Thanksgiving and special occasions.
Prep time and cooking time: 55 minutes|
Serves: 4

Ingredients To Use:

- 4 medium sized potatoes
- 4 ounces of grated cheese
- 1 chopped small onion
- 2 tbsp. of olive oil
- 2 bacon rashers

Step-by-Step Directions to Cook It:

1. Rub oil on the potatoes. Place it in the air fryer, cook at 356°F for about 10 minutes. Cook till potato is baked.
2. Place bacon and onion in a skillet and fry over medium heat. Add cheese and stir.
3. Mix the potatoes and fried bacon in the air fryer, add cheese and cook for 6 minutes at 356°F.

Nutritional value per serving:

Calories: 198kcal, Fat: 4g, Carb: 36g, Proteins: 7g

Italian Pork

The prosciutto added to the pork adds a delightful taste to this meal.
Prep time and cooking time: 50 minutes|
Serves: 5

Ingredients To Use:

- 2 tbsp. of fresh sage, chopped
- 2 tbsp. of sun-dried tomatoes, chopped
- 2 tbsp. of olive oil
- 1/2 tsp. of black pepper, ground
- 1/4 cup of chopped onion
- 1/4 cup of chopped prosciutto
- 1/2 cup of heavy cream
- 2 tbsp. of fresh parsley, chopped
- 1-1/2 pound of pork tenderloin
- 1/4 tsp. of salt
- 1/2 cup of chicken broth

Step-by-Step Directions to Cook It:

1. Mix tomatoes, pepper, onion, parsley, sage, and prosciutto in a bowl. Add salt and pork tenderloin. Mix the pork and mixture well.
2. Top with cheese. Grease the air fryer with olive oil, place the pork tenderloin on it. Cook for 20 minutes at 350°F.
3. Serve immediately.

Nutritional value per serving:

Calories: 357kcal, Fat: 26g, Carb: 5g, Proteins: 30g

Honey Pork Tenderloin

Honey is naturally sweet and adds a unique flavor to meals. In this recipe, the honey transforms the air fried pork's taste and gives it an unforgettable flavor.
Prep time and cooking time: 1 hour 20 minutes| Serves: 6

- 1 tbsp. of brown sugar
- 1/3 cup of honey
- 2 tbsp. of balsamic vinegar
- 1 tbsp. of mustard
- 2 pounds of pork tenderloin
- 2 tbsp. of sesame oil.
- 2 tbsp. of soy sauce

1. In a bowl, brown sugar, honey, balsamic vinegar, mustard, sesame oil, and soy sauce.
2. Place the pork tenderloin on the air fryer and cook for about 5 minutes. Add the honey mix and cook for 55 minutes.
3. Serve immediately.

Calories: 211kcal, Fat: 8g, Carb: 20g, Proteins: 19g

Capers and Pork Chop

The combination of capers and pork chops results in a dashing meal.
Prep time and cooking time: 40 minutes| Serves: 4

- 4 of 8 ounces of pork chop
- 3 tbsp. of capers
- 1 sliced lemon
- 3 tbsp. of melted butter
- 4 chopped green onions
- 4 cloves of garlic
- Black pepper and salt

1. Rub butter on the pork chop. Spray with pepper and salt. Transfer it to the baking dish in the air fryer.
2. Add slices of lemon, capers, onion, and garlic. Toss well to coat. Place the mixture in the air fryer.
3. Cook for 30 minutes at 370^0F.
4. Serve immediately.

Calories: 200kcal, Fat: 9g, Carb: 1g, Proteins: 25g

Pork Chop and asparagus

Asparagus helps neutralize the pork's fatty content and contributes some beneficial nutrients to the body.
Prep time and cooking time: 40 minutes| Serves: 4

- 8 ounces of pork chop
- Black pepper and salt
- 1 tsp. of ground cumin
- 8 spears of asparagus
- 1 tbsp. of chopped rosemary

1. Sprinkle pork chop with pepper and salt. Add cumin and rosemary. Transfer the mixture to the air fryer basket.
2. Place the asparagus spears on it. Cook for 30 minutes at 360^0F.
3. Serve immediately.

Calories: 378kcal, Fat: 16g, Carb: 40g, Proteins: 24g

Chapter 7: Meatless Cuisines

Masala Galette

A masala is a combination of grounded spices. It is a great vegetable, and it is very nutritious. It also contains high protein.
Prep time and cooking time: 40 minutes|
Serves: 4

Ingredients To Use:

- 1-1/2 tbsp. of coriander leaves, fresh
- Black pepper and salt
- 3 tsp. of chopped ginger
- 2 medium mashed potatoes, boiled
- 1-1/2 tbsp. of lemon juice
- 3 chopped chili
- 1-1/2 cup of crushed peanuts
- 2 tbsp. of masala

Step-by-Step Directions to Cook It:

1. In a bowl, mix lemon juice, coriander leaves, salt, and pepper. Add mashed potatoes, chili, and masala. Mix well till it forms round but flat galettes.
2. Sprinkle water on the galettes. Coat with crushed peanuts.
3. Heat the air fryer for about 5 minutes at 160⁰F. Transfer the galettes to the air fryer, leave to cook for 25 minutes at 160⁰F.
4. Serve immediately with ketchup.

Nutritional value per serving:

Calories: 290kcal, Fat: 13g, Carb: 17g, Proteins: 25g

Sago Galette

Sago is also called saksak. It is loaded with starch obtained from the spongy part of the palm stem. It is also a good source of antioxidant.
Prep time and cooking time: 40 minutes|
Serves: 5

Ingredients To Use:

- 1-1/2 tbsp. of lemon juice
- 2 cups of soaked sago
- 2 tbsp. of coriander leaves, fresh
- Black pepper and salt
- 3 chopped green chilies
- 3 tsp. of chopped ginger
- 1-1/2 cup of crushed peanuts

Step-by-Step Directions to Cook It:

1. In a bowl, mix sago, lemon juice, coriander leaves, pepper, salt ginger, and chilies. Mix well till it forms 5 flat and round galettes.
2. Sprinkle with water, coat with crushed peanuts.
3. Heat the air fryer for about 5 minutes at 160⁰F. Put the galettes on the basket that fits the air fryer. Leave to cook at the same temperature for 25 minutes.
4. Serve immediately with mint chutney.

Nutritional value per serving:

Calories: 330kcal, Fat: 1g, Carb: 80g, Proteins: 1g

Stuffed Capsicum

Capsicum is similar to bell pepper and can also be used to make stuffed peppers.
Prep time and cooking time: 35 minutes|
Serves: 4

Ingredients To Use:

- 1/2 tsp. of pepper powder
- 4 capsicums, long

- 1/2 tsp. of salt
- 1 tsp. of fenugreek
- 1 chopped green chili
- 1 tsp. of ground cumin
- 3 big boiled potatoes, mashed
- 1 tsp. of mango powder, dried
- 1 medium of chopped onion
- 1-1/2 tbsp. of coriander leaves, chopped
- Black pepper and salt
- 1 tsp. of chili flakes, red
- 1/2 tsp. of basil
- 3 tbsp. of grated cheese
- 1/2 tsp. of parsley
- 1/2 tsp. of oregano

1. In a bowl, mix mashed potatoes, mango powder, chopped green chili, and onion. Add ground cumin, fenugreek, and coriander leaves.
2. In another bowl, take the stem, cap, and seeds of the capsicum off. Spray with pepper and salt. Leave for some minutes.
3. Fill the capsicum with the potato mixture. Spray cheese on them, top with red chili flakes, oregano, basil, and parsley.
4. Heat the air fryer for about 5 minutes at 150⁰F. Place stuffed capsicum on the air fryer basket. Leave to cook for about 20 minutes at the same temperature.
5. Serve immediately.

Calories: kcal, Fat: g, Carb: g, Proteins: g

Baked Macaroni Pasta

Pasta is a really starchy meal, but the carrots and oregano balance this recipe's starch content.
Prep time and cooking time: 20 minutes|
Serves: 2

- 1 cup of pasta
- Black pepper and salt
- 1-1/2 tsp. of oregano
- 5 tbsp. of olive oil
- 7 cups of boiling water
- Black pepper and salt
- 1 tsp. of dried basil
- 1/2 cup of chopped carrot
- 1/2 tsp. of dried parsley
- 2 cups of milk
- 2 tbsp. of all-purpose flour

1. Cook the pasta, sieve when done. Add salt, pepper, 1-1/2 tbsp. of olive oil, 1/2 tsp. of oregano, chopped carrot, 1/2 tsp. of basil.
2. In a pan, put 2 tbsp. of olive oil, all-purpose flour, milk, 1 tsp. of oregano, 1/2 tsp. of basil, 1/2 tsp. of parsley, pepper, and salt. Cook and stir till it is thick.
3. Put the sauce and pasta in a bowl, sprinkle cheese on it.
4. Place the bowl in the air fryer basket. Cook for about 10 minutes at 160⁰F.
5. Serve immediately.

Calories: 220kcal, Fat: 43g, Carb: 2g, Proteins: 9g

Veg Momos

Veg momo is a good and healthy vegetarian snack. It is an irresistible meal and is also low in calories.
Prep time and cooking time: 30 minutes|
Serves: 4

- 5 tbsp. of water
- 1-1/2 cup of all-purpose flour
- 2 cups of grated carrots

- 2 tsp. of soya sauce
- 2 cups of grated cabbage
- 1/2 tsp. of salt
- 2 tsp. of ginger-garlic paste
- 2 tbsp. of oil
- 2 tsp. of vinegar

1. In a bowl, mix flour, water, and salt till it forms a dough.
2. In a pan, put oil, carrots, cabbage, ginger-garlic paste, soya sauce, and vinegar. Cook till the sauce is done.
3. Place the dough on a working surface, put the sauce inside it and wrap.
4. Place the dough inside the air fryer basket. Cook for 20 minutes at 200^0F.
5. Serve immediately with ketchup.

Nutritional value per serving:

Calories: 40kcal, Fat: 2g, Carb: 5g, Proteins: 1g

Cornflakes French Toast

Cornflakes is one of the most popular breakfast world-wide because they are sweet and crunchy.
Prep time and cooking time: 30 minutes|
Serves: 2

Ingredients To Use:

- 1 tsp. of sugar
- 2 Slices of bread
- Crushed cornflakes
- 1 egg white

Step-by-Step Directions to Cook It:

1. In a bowl, put sugar and egg white. Whisk well. Dip bread inside the egg mix. Coat the bread with crushed cornflakes.
2. Transfer the bread to the air fryer basket. Cook for 20 minutes at 180^0F.
3. Serve immediately with any berries.

Nutritional value per serving:

Calories: 155kcal, Fat: 4g, Carb: 25g, Proteins: 7g

Cottage Cheese Pops

This recipe tastes just like popcorn but has an additional creamy taste.
Prep time and cooking time: 30 minutes|
Serves: 3

Ingredients To Use:

- 1 tsp. of dried basil
- 1-1/2 tsp. of garlic paste
- 1 tsp. of chili flakes, red
- Black pepper and salt
- 1 cup of cottage cheese
- 1/2 cup of hung curd
- 1 tsp. of dried oregano
- 1 tsp. of lemon juice

Step-by-Step Directions to Cook It:

1. Cut the cheese into 3 rectangular and thick pieces.
2. In a bowl, mix garlic paste, pepper, oregano, and basil. Add hung curd, lemon juice, red chili flakes, and salt.
3. Put the cheese in the mixture and coat. Put aside for some minutes.
4. Set the cheese on the air fryer basket. Cook for about 20 minutes at 180^0F.
5. Serve immediately with ketchup.

Nutritional value per serving:

Calories: 45kcal, Fat: 2g, Carb: 12g, Proteins: 3g

Mint Galette

Mint Galette is an ideal meal for vegetarians. It is a healthy meal and is usually made for special occasions.
Prep time and cooking time: 40 minutes|
Serves: 4

- 1-1/2 cup of crushed peanuts
- 2 cup of mint leaves
- 2 tbsp. of coriander leaves
- Black pepper and salt
- 2 medium cooked and mashed potatoes
- 3 chopped green chilies
- 1-1/2 tbsp. of lemon juice
- 3 tsp. of ground ginger

Step-by-Step Directions to Cook It:

1. In a bowl, mix slices of mint leaves, coriander leaves, potatoes, green chilies, lemon juice, and ground ginger.
2. Mix till it forms 4 flat and round galettes.
3. Sprinkle the galettes with water. Put the galettes in crushed peanut and coat well.
4. Transfer the galettes to the air fryer basket. Cook at 160^{0}F for about 25 minutes.
5. Serve immediately with ketchup.

Nutritional value per serving:

Calories: 251kcal, Fat: 18g, Carb: 0.6g, Proteins: 22g

Palak Galette

Here is another vegetarian meal that has incredible flavor and taste.
Prep time and cooking time: 35 minutes|
Serves: 6

Ingredients To Use:

- 3 tsp. of chopped ginger
- 2 cups of palak leaves
- 2 tbsp. of coriander leaves, fresh
- 1-1/2 tbsp. of lemon juice
- 1-1/2 cup of crushed peanuts
- Black pepper and salt
- 2 tbsp. of garam masala
- 3 chopped green chilies

Step-by-Step Directions to Cook It:

1. In a bowl, mix garam masala, palak leaves, ginger, coriander leaves, green chilies, lemon juice, pepper, and salt. Mix into 6 flat and round galettes.
2. Sprinkle with water. Put the galettes in crushed peanuts.
3. Transfer the galettes into the air fryer basket. Cook at 160^{0}F for 25 minutes.
4. Serve immediately with chutney.

Nutritional value per serving:

Calories: 460kcal, Fat: 40g, Carb: 8g, Proteins: 23g

Masala French Fries

All gym instructors tell their members to cut down on their fries, but this masala French fries meal is an exception. With your air fryer, the potatoes are fried without any oil and have minimal fat compared to French fries served at restaurants.
Prep time and cooking time: 25 minutes|
Serves: 2

Ingredients To Use:

- 1 tbsp. of olive oil
- 1/2 tsp. of red chili flakes
- 2 medium sized potatoes
- 1 tbsp. of lemon juice
- Salt
- 1 tsp. of mixed herbs

Step-by-Step Directions to Cook It:

1. Cook the potatoes. Cut potatoes into smaller pieces.
2. In a bowl, mix olive oil, mixed herbs, red chili flakes, salt, and lemon juice. Add the potatoes and coat.
3. Place the coated potatoes in the air fryer basket. Cook for 25 minutes at 200^{0}F. Toss the fries when cooking.
4. Serve immediately.

Nutritional value per serving:

Calories: 140kcal, Fat: 8g, Carb: 19g, Proteins: 3g

Barbeque Corn Sandwich

A corn sandwich is an amazing sandwich that screams classic taste.
Prep time and cooking time: 35 minutes| Serves: 1

Ingredients To Use:

- 1 cup of sweet corn kernels
- 2 slices of bread
- 1 small capsicum
- 1 tbsp. of soft butter
- 1/2 flake of crushed garlic
- 1/4 tbsp. of Worcestershire sauce
- 1/4 tbsp. of red chili sauce
- 1/2 tsp. of olive oil
- 1/2 cup of water
- 1/4 cup of chopped onion

Step-by-Step Directions to Cook It:

1. Put the slice of bread on a working surface and cut horizontally.
2. In a pan, put olive oil, red chili sauce, crushed garlic, Worcestershire sauce, chopped onion, and water. Stir till the mixture is thick.
3. Roast the capsicum, peel the skin and cut into smaller slices. Put the sauce on the capsicum slices. Place the sauce in between the slices of bread.
4. Transfer the sandwich to the air fryer basket. Cook at 250^0F for about 15 minutes.
5. Serve immediately with chutney.

Nutritional value per serving:

Calories: 196kcal, Fat: 13g, Carb: 12g, Proteins: 6g

Burger Cutlet

Not all burgers cause weight gain, and this recipe is an amazing example that helps people shed some weight by majorly contributing healthy protein and carbs.
Prep time and cooking time: 20 minutes| Serves: 4

Ingredients To Use:

- 1 tsp. of lemon juice
- Salt
- 1 big cooked and mashed potatoes
- 1/2 cup of boiled peas
- 1 chopped green chili
- 1/4 tsp. of cumin powder
- 1 tbsp. of ground coriander leaves
- 1/2 cup of breadcrumbs
- 1/4 tsp. of ground dried mango
- 1/4 tsp. of ginger powder
- 1/4 tsp. of red chili powder

Step-by-Step Directions to Cook It:

1. In a bowl, mix all the ingredients. Make 3-4 round cutlets out of the mixture.
2. Transfer the cutlets to the air fryer basket. Cook for 1o minutes at 150^0F. Flip the cutlets for cooking uniformity.
3. Serve immediately.

Nutritional value per serving:

Calories: 205kcal, Fat: 18g, Carb: 0g, Proteins: 16g

Pizza

This recipe combines several original pizza recipes to produce the tastiest pizza. The mozzarella cheese adds an amazing texture to the pizza draw.
Prep time and cooking time: 30 minutes| Serves: 1

Ingredients To Use:

- 1 pizza base

- Cooking spray
- Mozzarella cheese
- 2 chopped tomatoes
- 2 medium of chopped onion
- 2 tsp. of pizza seasoning
- 2 chopped capsicum
- 1 tbsp. of mushroom

Step-by-Step Directions to Cook It:

1. Place the pizza base inside the air fryer for about 5 minutes at 340^0F.
2. Remove the base from the air fryer, spray with oil and sprinkle mozzarella cheese on it.
3. In another bowl, mix chopped onion, capsicum, tomatoes, mushrooms, and pizza seasoning. Pour the mixture on the pizza base. Sprinkle with mozzarella cheese.
4. Transfer the pizza to the air fryer basket. Cook for about 10 minutes at 170^0F. If it is not done to your satisfaction. Cook for 2 more minutes.

Nutritional value per serving:

Calories: 267kcal, Fat: 11g, Carb: 34g, Proteins: 12g

Cheese French Fries

Cheese French fries are not as healthy as the other meals in this cookbook, and their contribution to weight loss is minimal, but the taste is worth a try.
Prep time and cooking time: 35 minutes| Serves: 2

Ingredients To Use:

- 1 tsp. of mixed herbs
- 1 tbsp. of lemon juice
- 2 medium sized peeled potatoes
- Salt
- 1 tbsp. of olive oil
- 1/2 tsp. of red chili flakes

- 1 cup of cheddar cheese

Step-by-Step Directions to Cook It:

1. In a bowl, mix olive oil, mixed herbs, red chili flakes, salt, and lemon juice to make a marinade.
2. Boil the potatoes, drain it, and cut into pieces. Dry with a towel. Put the potatoes inside the marinade.
3. Place the coated potatoes inside the air fryer basket. Cook for 20 minutes at 220^0F.
4. Serve immediately with melted cheddar cheese.

Nutritional value per serving:

Calories: 280kcal, Fat: 22g, Carb: 9g, Proteins: 14g

Baked Chickpea

Chickpeas are tasty and great for weight loss. With your air fryer, you can prepare delicious chickpeas that can serve as snacks or side dishes for your premium meals.
Prep time and cooking time: 1 hour 35 minutes| Serves: 3

Ingredients To Use:

- 1 tsp. of dry mint
- 1 cup of overnight soaked white chickpeas
- 4 tbsp. of thick curd
- 1 tsp. of ginger-garlic paste
- Black pepper and salt
- 2 chopped onions
- 1/2 tsp. of ground cumin
- 4 tbsp. of chopped coriander leaves
- 2 chopped green chilies
- Olive oil
- 4 tbsp. of roasted sesame seeds
- 1/2 tsp. of coriander powder

Step-by-Step Directions to Cook It:

1. Put the chickpeas in a pressure cooker,

add salt and water. Cook for about 25 minutes. Mash the chickpeas when it is done.
2. In a bowl, put coriander powder, ginger-garlic paste, ground cumin, onion, green chili, pepper, coriander leaves, and salt.
3. Mix the 2 mixtures in a bowl. Cut in a star shape. Sprinkle mint leaves and curd. Pour sesame seed on it.
4. Transfer the star-shaped mixture to the air fryer basket. Cook for 1 hour at 200^0F.
5. Serve immediately with ketchup.

Nutritional value per serving:

Calories: 69kcal, Fat: 5g, Carb: 8g, Proteins: 16g

Cheesy Spinach Toasties

After experiencing the incredible taste of this cheesy spinach toast, you will drop all your old toast recipes.
Prep time and cooking time: 25 minutes| Serves: 2

Ingredients To Use:
- 1 tsp. of crushed green chilies
- 1 tbsp. of butter
- 2 flakes of chopped garlic
- 2 tbsp. of grated pizza cheese
- 1/2 bunch of cooked and crushed spinach
- 1 tbsp. of fresh cream
- Pepper and salt
- 1 cup of milk
- 1 chopped small onion
- 2 slices of toast bread
- 1 tbsp. of all-purpose flour

Step-by-Step Directions to Cook It:
1. Put butter in a pan and melt. Add garlic and onions. Roast till it turns brown. Add all-purpose flour, milk, spinach, green chilies, seasoning, and cream. Cook till

the mixture is thick.
2. Put a slice of the toasted bread, put the mixture on it, cover with the second slices.
3. Transfer it to the air fryer basket. Cook for about 10 minutes at 290^0F.
4. Serve immediately.

Nutritional value per serving:

Calories: 66kcal, Fat: 4g, Carb: 7g, Proteins: 5g

Garlic Toast and Cheese

Toast has never tasted better than with this delightful air fryer recipe.
Prep time and cooking time: 20 minutes| Serves: 3

Ingredients To Use:
- 5 crushed garlic
- 6 s of French bread
- 1/2 tsp. of black pepper
- 2 tbsp. of soft butter
- Salt
- 1 tbsp. of olive oil
- 2 tsp. of oregano seasoning
- 3/4 cup of grated cheese
- Flakes of red chilies

Step-by-Step Directions to Cook It:
1. Mix butter, crushed garlic, salt, and black pepper in a bowl. Mix till it forms a paste.
2. Put the garlic paste in between 2 slices of French bread. Top with cheese, chili flakes, and oregano seasoning. Spray with oil.
3. Transfer the slices of bread to the air fryer basket. Cook for about 10 minutes at 160^0F.
4. Serve immediately.

Calories: 200kcal, Fat: 18g, Carb: 15g, Proteins: 10g

Mixed Vegetable Pancake

This is the combination of edible leafy vegetables to make a nutrient-rich air fryer pancake recipe.

Prep time and cooking time: 20 minutes| Serves: 2

Ingredients To Use:

- 2 tsp. of dried parsley
- 1-1/2 cups of almond
- Pepper and salt
- 2 tsp. of dried basil
- 3 tbsp. of butter
- 3 eggs
- 2 cups of shredded vegetables.

Step-by-Step Directions to Cook It:

1. Heat the air fryer at 250°F.
2. In a container, mix vegetables, almond flour, eggs, basil, parsley, butter, pepper, and salt. Meld the mixture in a pancake shape. Rub with butter.
3. Place it in the air fryer basket. Cook till they are brown on both sides.
4. Serve immediately with maple syrup.

Nutritional value per serving:

Calories: 200kcal, Fat: 7g, Carb: 31g, Proteins: 10g

Potato Club Sandwich

With this flavor-packed air fryer recipe, making a sandwich with the right proportion of ingredients is possible.

Prep time and cooking time: 30 minutes| Serves: 3

Ingredients To Use:

- 1 cup of boiled potato
- 6 white bread slices
- 1 medium of small capsicum
- 1 tbsp. of soft butter
- 1/4 cup of chopped onion
- 1/4 tbsp. of Worcestershire sauce
- 1/2 flake of crushed garlic
- 1/4 tbsp. of red chili sauce
- 1/2 tsp. of olive oil

Step-by-Step Directions to Cook It:

1. Cut the edges of the slices of bread.
2. In a bowl, mix olive oil, garlic, onion, chili sauce, and Worcestershire sauce. Remove the capsicum skin and roast. Put the ingredients on the bread slices.
3. Place the sandwich in the air fryer basket. Cook for about 15 minutes at 250°F.
4. Serve immediately with mint chutney.

Nutritional value per serving:

Calories: 510kcal, Fat: 10g, Carb: 84g, Proteins: 26g

Vegetable Pie

Vegetables always add amazing nutritional benefits to meals. In this recipe, the roasted vegetables do the job exceptionally.

Prep time and cooking time: 30 minutes| Serves: 3

Ingredients To Use:

- 4 tsp. of powdered sugar
- 1 cup of plain flour
- 2 cups of cold milk
- 1 tbsp. of unsalted butter
- 2 tbsp. of sugar
- 1/2 cup of roasted nuts
- 2 tsp. of lemon juice
- 2 cups of roasted vegetable
- 1/2 tsp. of cinnamon
- 2 tbsp. of sugar

1. Mix butter, sugar, and flour in a bowl. Add cold milk, mix till it forms a dough. Allow resting for 10 minutes.
2. Cut a circle out of the dough. Put the dough in a pie tin.
3. In a pan, mix roasted nuts, roasted vegetables, sugar, cinnamon, and lemon juice. Cook over low flame. Pour the mixture inside the pie tin.
4. Transfer the pie tin to the air fryer basket. Cook till it is brown.
5. Allow the pan to cool and serve with cream.

Nutritional value per serving:

Calories: 195kcal, Fat: 6g, Carb: 33g, Proteins: 5g

Cottage Cheese Kebab

The lemon juice used in this recipe adds a unique flavor to this cheese kebab recipe.
Prep time and cooking time: 35 minutes|
Serves: 5

Ingredients To Use:

- 1-1/2 tsp. of salt
- 5 chopped green chilies
- 3 tsp. of lemon juice
- 3 eggs
- 2 tbsp. of coriander powder
- 2 cups of cubed cottage cheese
- 1-1/2 tbsp. of ginger paste
- 3 tbsp. of chopped capsicum
- 1-1/2 tsp. of garlic paste
- 2 tbsp. of peanut flour
- 3 tsp. of lemon juice

Step-by-Step Directions to Cook It:

1. Put the cubed cheese in the cornflour and coat. Add onion, green chilies, ginger paste, garlic paste, salt, lemon juice, coriander powder, and capsicum.

2. Break egg inside another bowl, add salt, and whisk.
3. Put the cubed cheese in the egg mixture. Spray with sesame seeds. Put in the fridge for about an hour.
4. Put the cheese kebab in the air fryer basket. Cook at 290^{0}F for 25 minutes. Flip while cooking to give uniformity.

Nutritional value per serving:

Calories: 30kcal, Fat: 0.3g, Carb: 1.5g, Proteins: 4g

Cottage Cheese Fingers

Cheese fingers can be made by frying or baking. The air fryer makes the cooked cheese fingers crispy.
Prep time and cooking time: 25 minutes|
Serves: 4

Ingredients To Use:

- 2 cups of dry breadcrumbs
- 2 tsp. of red chili flakes
- 2 cups of cottage cheese fingers
- 2 tsp. of oregano
- 1 tsp. of pepper powder
- 1-1/2 tbsp. of ginger-garlic paste
- 1 tsp. of pepper powder
- 4 eggs
- 1 tsp. of red chili powder
- 2 tsp. of salt
- 6 tbsp. of cornflour

Step-by-Step Directions to Cook It:

1. In a bowl, mix ginger-garlic paste, lemon juice, salt, pepper powder, red chili powder, cornflour, and eggs.
2. In another bowl, mix red chili flakes, breadcrumbs, and oregano. Mix the 2 mixtures. Add cottage cheese fingers. Cover the mixture and leave for a while.
3. Place the cheese fingers inside the air fryer basket. Cook for about 15 minutes

at 160^{0}F.

Calories: 85kcal, Fat: 3g, Carb: 5g, Proteins: 12g

Onion Galette

Onion is rich in vitamins, and it reduces the risk of having cancer. It also helps to moderate blood pressure. And all these benefits explain why an onion galette is a healthy meal.

Prep time and cooking time: 35 minutes| Serves: 3

Ingredients To Use:

- 2 tbsp. of coriander leaves, fresh
- 2 medium sized onion
- Pepper and salt
- 3 tsp. of chopped ginger
- 3 chopped green chilies
- 1-1/2 cup of crushed peanuts
- 1-1/2 tbsp. of lemon juice
- 2 tbsp. of garam masala

Step-by-Step Directions to Cook It:

1. In a bowl, mix garam masala, onion, chopped ginger, coriander leaves, green chilies, salt, pepper, and lemon juice. Mix well till it forms a flat and round galette.
2. Sprinkle water on the galettes. Place the galettes in the crushed peanuts.
3. Transfer the galettes to the air fryer basket. Cook for about 25 minutes at 160^{0}F.
4. Serve immediately with ketchup.

Nutritional value per serving:

Calories: 310kcal, Fat: 14g, Carb: 43g, Proteins: 13g

Cauliflower Galette

Try out this recipe for a truly delectable meal. Prep time and cooking time: 35 minutes|

Serves: 3

Ingredients To Use:

- 2 tbsp. of coriander leaves, fresh
- Pepper and salt
- 3 tsp .of chopped ginger
- 1-1/2 tbsp. of lemon juice
- 2 cups of cauliflower
- 1-1/2 cup of crushed peanuts
- 2 tbsp. of garam masala
- 3 chopped green chilies

Step-by-Step Directions to Cook It:

1. In a bowl, mix garam masala, cauliflower, ginger, coriander leaves, green chilies, lemon juice, pepper, and salt. Mix till it forms flat and round galettes.
2. Spray the galette with water. Place the galette inside the crushed peanuts.
3. Transfer the galettes into the air fryer basket. Cook at 160^{0}F for 25 minutes. Flip while cooking.
4. Serve immediately with ketchup.

Nutritional value per serving:

Calories: 300kcal, Fat: 20g, Carb: 30g, Proteins: 10g

Cabbage Fritters

Cabbage fritters are a high-calorie meal, but the cabbage reduces the unhealthy calories. Prep time and cooking time: 30 minutes| Serves: 4

Ingredients To Use:

- 2 chopped green chilies
- 2 cups of cabbage
- Pepper and salt
- 3 tsp. of chopped ginger
- 2 tbsp. of garam masala
- 1-1/2 tbsp. of lemon juice
- 1-1/2 cup of crushed peanuts
- 2 tbsp. of coriander leaves, fresh

1. In a bowl, mix garam masala, cabbage, ginger, coriander leaves, green chilies, lemon juice, pepper, and salt. Mix until it forms 4 flat and round fritters.
2. Sprinkle water on the fritters. Place the fritters inside the crushed peanuts and coat.
3. Transfer the fritters inside the air fryer basket. Cook at 160°F for 20-25 minutes. Flip while cooking.
4. Serve immediately with chutney.

Nutritional value per serving:

Calories: 360kcal, Fat: 23g, Carb: 25g, Proteins: g

Cottage Cheese Galettes

Cottage cheese galettes is a creamy meal that provides vitamins to the body.
Prep time and cooking time: 35 minutes|
Serves: 3

Ingredients To Use:

- 1-1/2 cup of crushed peanuts
- Pepper and salt
- 3 tsp. of chopped ginger
- 2 tbsp. of garam masala
- 2 tbsp. of coriander leaves, fresh
- 1-1/2 tbsp. of lemon juice
- 2 cups of grated cottage cheese
- 3 chopped green chilies

Step-by-Step Directions to Cook It:

1. In a bowl, mix all the ingredients except crushed peanuts. Mix till it forms flat and round galettes.
2. Sprinkle water on the galettes. Place the galettes in the crushed peanuts.
3. Transfer the galettes to the air fryer basket. Cook at 160°F for 25 minutes.
4. Serve immediately with ketchup.

Nutritional value per serving:

Calories: 131kcal, Fat: 7g, Carb: 9g, Proteins: 10g

Gourd Galette

With your air fryer, you can prepare a rare delicacy such as gourd galette.
Prep time and cooking time: 30 minutes|
Serves: 4

Ingredients To Use:

- 1-1/2 cup of crushed peanuts
- Pepper and salt
- 3 tsp. of chopped ginger
- 2 tbsp. of garam masala
- 2 tbsp. of coriander leaves, fresh
- 1-1/2 tbsp. of lemon juice
- 2 cups of the sliced gourd
- 3 chopped green chilies

Step-by-Step Directions to Cook It:

1. In a bowl, mix garam masala, slices of gourd, ginger, coriander leaves, green chilies, lemon juice, pepper, and salt. Make 3 flat and round galettes out of it.
2. Spray the galette with water. Place the galette inside the crushed peanuts.
3. Transfer the galettes into the air fryer basket. Cook at 160°F for 25 minutes. Flip while cooking.
4. Serve immediately with ketchup.

Nutritional value per serving:

Calories: 344kcal, Fat: 23g, Carb: 29g, Proteins: 15g

Cottage Cheese Patties

Using an air fryer to create these patties makes the meal soft and palatable.
Prep time and cooking time: 25 minutes|
Serves: 2

- Pepper and salt
- 1/4 tsp. of red chili powder
- 1/4 tsp. of chopped ginger
- 1 tbsp. of coriander leaves, fresh
- 1 tbsp. of lemon juice
- 1/4 tsp. of cumin powder
- 1 cups of grated cottage cheese
- 1 chopped green chilies

Step-by-Step Directions to Cook It:

1. In a bowl, mix cottage cheese, ginger, green chili, lemon juice, coriander leaves, red chili powder, cumin powder. Make patties out of the mixture.
2. Place the patties in the air fryer basket. Cook for 10 minutes at 150^{0}F. Flip while cooking.
3. Serve immediately with chutney.

Nutritional value per serving:

Calories: kcal, Fat: g, Carb: g, Proteins: g

Garlic and Cheese French Fries

Everyone loves French fries but may avoid it due to the high-calorie. Well, you do not need to avoid this recipe because the starch is well balanced to provide a healthy meal.
Prep time and cooking time: 30 minutes|
Serves: 4

Ingredients To Use:

- 1 cup of molten cheese
- 1 tbsp. of olive oil
- 1 tbsp. of lemon juice
- 2 medium sized potatoes
- 1 tsp. of mixed herbs
- 1/2 tsp. of red chili flakes
- 2 tsp. of garlic powder
- salt

Step-by-Step Directions to Cook It:

1. boil and bleach the potatoes. Cut it into

pieces.

2. In a pan, mix olive oil, mixed herbs, red chili flakes, salt, molten cheese, garlic powder, and lemon juice. Cook over medium heat till it thickens.
3. Put the potatoes in the marinade. Place the coated fries in the air fryer basket. Cook for 25 minutes at 200^{0}F.
4. Serve immediately.

Nutritional value per serving:

Calories: 690kcal, Fat: 50g, Carb: 50g, Proteins: 10g

Pineapple Kebab

All the ingredients in this recipe can be purchased at the local grocery store, therefore fulfilling this book's major promises to provide healthy, accessible meals.
Prep time and cooking time: 35 minutes|
Serves: 4

Ingredients To Use:

- 1-1/2 tsp. of salt
- 2 cups of pineapple cubes
- 3 tbsp. of cream
- 3 tsp. of lemon juice
- 3 eggs
- 5 chopped green chilies
- 1-1/2 tsp. of salt
- 3 tbsp. of chopped capsicum
- 3 medium chopped onion
- 2-1/2 tbsp. of white sesame seeds
- 1-1/2 tbsp. of ginger paste
- 2 tsp. of garam masala
- 1-1/2 tsp. of garlic paste

Step-by-Step Directions to Cook It:

1. In a food processor, blend all the ingredients except eggs and pineapple.
2. Put the pineapple in the mixture and coat.

3. Break the eggs in a bowl, sprinkle salt to taste. Put the coated pineapple inside the egg mixture. Put the coated pineapple on a stick.
4. Place it in the air fryer basket. Cook at 160^{0}F for 25 minutes. Flip while cooking.
5. Serve immediately.

Nutritional value per serving:

Calories: 177kcal, Fat: 6g, Carb: 30g, Proteins: 10g

Banana Croquette

Banana is highly recommended for weight loss, and its addition to this croquette recipe makes it a great meal for vegetarians.
Prep time and cooking time: 35 minutes|
Serves: 3

Ingredients To Use:

- 1-1/2 tsp. of salt
- 2 cups of banana slices
- 3 tbsp. of cream
- 3 tsp. of lemon juice
- 3 eggs
- 5 chopped green chilies
- 1-1/2 tsp. of salt
- 3 tbsp. of chopped capsicum
- 3 medium of chopped onion
- 2-1/2 tbsp. of white sesame seeds
- 1-1/2 tbsp. of ginger paste
- 2 tsp. of garam masala
- 1-1/2 tsp. of garlic paste

Step-by-Step Directions to Cook It:

1. In a blender, grind the ingredients except for banana and eggs. Blend till it forms a paste. Put the banana slices inside the paste.
2. Whisk the egg in a bowl, place the coated banana inside the egg mixture. Then back to the paste. Put the coated banana slice on a stick.
3. Transfer it to the air fryer basket. Cook

for about 20-25 minutes at 160^{0}F. Flip over while cooking.
4. Serve immediately.

Nutritional value per serving:

Calories: 90kcal, Fat: 0.5g, Carb: 23g, Proteins: 2g

Apricot Kebab

Apricot is an amazing fruit and adds an incredible flavor to this kebab recipe.
Prep time and cooking time: 25 minutes|
Serves: 2

Ingredients To Use:

- 3 eggs
- 2 cups of fresh apricots
- 3 medium chopped onions
- 3 tsp. of lemon juice
- 5 chopped green chilies
- 2 tsp. of garam masala
- 2-1/2 tbsp. of white sesame seeds
- 1-1/2 tbsp. of ginger paste
- 1-1/2 tsp. of garlic paste
- 1-1/2 tsp. of salt

Step-by-Step Directions to Cook It:

1. Blend onion, green chilies, ginger paste, garlic paste, salt, lemon juice, and garam masala in a blender. Blend till it forms a paste.
2. Whisk eggs in a bowl and put the apricot in it.
3. Put the apricot in the paste and coat. Then inside the sesame seed and coat again
4. Put the apricot on a stick. Transfer it to the air fryer basket. Cook at 160^{0}F for 25 minutes.
5. Serve immediately.

Nutritional value per serving:

Calories: 141kcal, Fat: 2g, Carb: 15g, Proteins: 23g

Cauliflower Kebab

Cauliflower kebab is another super flavorful meal. Lemon juice is used to give the meal an exceptional and great feel.
Prep time and cooking time: 30 minutes | Serves: 5

Ingredients To Use:

- 2 cups of cauliflower florets
- 1-1/2 tsp. of salt
- 3 medium chopped onions
- 2-1/2 tbsp. of white sesame seeds
- 3 tsp. of lemon juice
- 5 green chopped chilies
- 2 tsp. of garam masala
- 3 eggs
- 1-1/2 tbsp. of ginger paste
- 1-1/2 tsp. of garlic paste

Step-by-Step Directions to Cook It:

1. In a blender, grind the ingredients except for cauliflower florets and eggs. Blend till it forms a paste. Put the floret inside the paste.
2. Whisk the egg in a bowl, place the coated floret inside the egg mixture. Then back to the paste. Put the coated floret slice on a stick.
3. Transfer the floret stick to the air fryer basket. Cook for about 20-25 minutes at 160^0F. Flip over while cooking.
4. Serve immediately.

Nutritional value per serving:

Calories: 82kcal, Fat:6 g, Carb: 10g, Proteins: 5g

Broccoli Tikka

Though broccoli may not be the tastiest of all vegetables, it adds an incredible flavor to this meal.
Prep time and cooking time: 35 minutes|

Serves: 3

Ingredients To Use:

- 2 cups of broccoli florets
- 1-1/2 tsp. of garlic paste
- 3 medium chopped onions
- 3 tsp. of lemon juice
- 5 green chopped chilies
- 1-1/2 tsp. of salt
- 2 tsp. of garam masala
- 1-1/2 tbsp. of ginger paste
- 2-1/2 tbsp. of white sesame seeds
- 3 eggs

Step-by-Step Directions to Cook It:

1. In a food processor, grind the ingredients except for cauliflower florets and eggs. Blend till it forms a paste. Put the broccoli inside the paste.
2. Whisk the eggs in a bowl, place the coated broccoli inside the egg mixture. Then back to the sesame seeds and coat well. Put the coated broccoli on a stick.
3. Transfer the broccoli stick to the air fryer basket. Cook for about 20-25 minutes at 160^0F. Flip over while cooking.
4. Serve immediately.

Nutritional value per serving:

Calories: 420kcal, Fat: 31g, Carb: 10g, Proteins: 27g

Cottage Cheese Gnocchis

Cheese gnocchi is a meal with a sweet and amazing taste.
Prep time and cooking time: | Serves:

Ingredients To Use:

- 2 tsp. of vinegar
- 1-1/2 cup of all-purpose flour
- 2 tbsp. of oil
- 1/2 tsp. of salt
- 2 tsp. of ginger-garlic paste
- 5 tbsp. of water

- 2 tsp. of soya sauce
- 2 cups of grated cottage cheese

1. In a bowl, mix flour, water, and salt to form a dough. Knead well.
2. In a pan, cook cottage cheese, oil, ginger-garlic paste, soya sauce, and vinegar. Cook till it thickens.
3. Put the filling mixture on each dough and wrap. Put the gnocchi in the air fryer basket. Cook for 20 minutes at 200^0F.
4. Serve immediately with ketchup.

Nutritional value per serving:

Calories: 7kcal, Fat: 0.04g, Carb: 0.5g, Proteins: 0.1g

Cauliflower Gnocchi

Cauliflower gnocchi is a healthy and delicious meal; soya sauce gives the gnocchi an amazing taste.
Prep time and cooking time: 35 minutes| Serves: 3

Ingredients To Use:

- 1-1/2 cup of all-purpose flour
- 2 cups of grated cauliflower
- 1/2 tsp. of salt
- 2 tbsp. of oil
- 5 tbsp. of water
- 2 tsp. of soya sauce
- 2 tsp. of ginger-garlic paste
- 2 tsp. of vinegar

Step-by-Step Directions to Cook It:

1. In a bowl, mix flour, water, and salt to form a dough. Knead well until it is smooth.
2. In a pan, cook grated cauliflower, oil, ginger-garlic paste, soya sauce, and vinegar. Cook till it thickens.
3. Put the filling mixture on each dough, wrap and seal at the edge. Put the

gnocchi in the air fryer basket. Cook for 20 minutes at 200^0F.
4. Serve immediately with chili sauce.

Nutritional value per serving:

Calories: 142kcal, Fat: 4g, Carb: 23g, Proteins: 3g

Broccoli Momos

Broccoli is an edible plant that has beta-carotene, which converts to vitamin A when consumed. As promised, this cookbook has your health on focus when creating recipes.
Prep time and cooking time: 30 minutes| Serves: 4

Ingredients To Use:

- 1-1/2 cup all-purpose flour
- 2 cups grated broccoli
- 1/2 tsp. salt
- 2 tbsp. oil
- 2 tsp. vinegar
- 2 tsp. ginger-garlic paste
- 5 tbsp. water
- 2 tsp. soya sauce

Step-by-Step Directions to Cook It:

1. Mix flour, water, and salt in a bowl until it forms a dough. Knead well until it is smooth.
2. Cook grated broccoli, oil, ginger-garlic paste, soya sauce, and vinegar over medium heat. Cook till it thickens.
3. Put the filling mixture on each dough, wrap and seal at the edge. Put the momos in the air fryer basket. Cook for 20 minutes at 200^0F.
4. Serve immediately with ketchup.

Nutritional value per serving:

Calories: 35kcal, Fat: 0.5g, Carb: 8g, Proteins: 4g

Aloo Patties

Aloo patties can be made with different kinds of plants, but potatoes will be used in this recipe.

Prep time and cooking time: 20 minutes| Serves: 7

- 1 cup of mashed potato
- 1 tsp. of lemon juice
- 1 chopped green chili
- Salt
- 1 tbsp. of fresh coriander leaves
- 1/4 tsp. of red chili powder
- 1/4 tsp. of ginger finely chopped
- 1/4 tsp. of cumin powder

Step-by-Step Directions to Cook It:

1. In a bowl, mix all the ingredients. Make round patties as much as possible from the mixture.
2. Place the patties on the air fryer basket. Cook for about 10-12 minutes at 150^{0}F.
3. Serve immediately with ketchup.

Nutritional value per serving:

Calories: 136kcal, Fat: 9g, Carb: 13g, Proteins: 4g

Mixed Vegetable Patties

Mixed vegetables contain different ingredients like cabbage, cauliflower, chickpea, carrot, green peas, etc. This recipe results in sandwich patties that are incredibly healthy and tasty.

Prep time and cooking time: 20 minutes| Serves: 6

Ingredients To Use:

- 1 cup of grated mixed vegetables
- 1/4 tsp. of cumin powder
- Salt
- 1 tsp. of lemon juice

- 1/4 tsp. of ginger finely chopped
- 1 tbsp. of fresh coriander leaves
- 1 chopped green chili
- 1/4 tsp. of red chili powder

Step-by-Step Directions to Cook It:

1. Mix all the ingredients in a bowl. Make many round patties from the mixture.
2. Place the patties on the air fryer basket. Cook at 150^{0}F for 12 minutes.
3. Serve immediately.

Nutritional value per serving:

Calories: 310kcal, Fat: 10g, Carb: 54g, Proteins: 11g

Mushroom Galette

Mushroom is excellent for weight loss and eating this recipe would help you achieve those summer body goals.

Prep time and cooking time: 35 minutes| Serves: 4

Ingredients To Use:

- 2 tbsp. of fresh coriander leaves
- 2 tbsp. of garam masala
- 3 tsp. of ground ginger
- 3 chopped green chilies
- Pepper and salt
- 2 cups of sliced mushrooms
- 1-1/2 tbsp. of lemon juice
- 1-1/2 cup of crushed peanuts

Step-by-Step Directions to Cook It:

1. In a bowl, mix garam masala, mushroom slices, chopped ginger, coriander leaves, green chilies, salt, pepper, and lemon juice. Make flat and round galettes from the mixture.
2. Sprinkle water on the galettes. Place the galettes in the crushed peanuts.
3. Transfer the galettes to the air fryer basket. Cook for about 25 minutes at 160^{0}F.

4. Serve immediately with ketchup.

Calories: 22kcal, Fat: 0.5g, Carb: 4g, Proteins: 4g

Zucchini Samosa

Zucchini is an edible fruit vegetable that looks like a cucumber. It has many nutritional benefits, which explains why it is used to make samosas.
Prep time and cooking time: 45 minutes| Serves: 5

Ingredients To Use:

- 2 tbsp. of unsalted butter
- 1 tsp. of powdered ginger
- 1-1/2 cup of all-purpose flour
- 1/2 tsp. red of chili power
- 2 chopped green chilies
- Salt
- 1/2 tsp. of cumin
- Water
- 3 medium mashed zucchinis
- 1/4 cup of boiled peas
- 1 dried red chili
- 1/2 tsp. of dried mango powder.
- 2 tbsp. of coriander, 1 tsp of coarsely crushed coriander

Step-by-Step Directions to Cook It:

1. Mix butter, flour, salt, and water in a bowl. Mix till it forms a smooth dough.
2. In a pan, over medium heat, cook zucchini, boiled peas, ginger, green chilies, cumin, coriander, red chili, mango powder, and salt. Cook till it thickens.
3. Make the dough flat and cut out as many as you want. Put the filling mixture inside it and wrap it. Use water to seal the edges.
4. Transfer the samosa to the air fryer basket. Cook for 25 minutes at 200^{0}F. After that, change the temperature to 250^{0}F and fry for about 10 minutes.
5. Serve immediately with mint chutney.

Nutritional value per serving:

Calories: 191kcal, Fat: 2g, Carb: 42g, Proteins: 8g

Vegetable Skewer

There are different ways of making mixed vegetables, but you will find that this recipe is different. Try it now to find out why this recipe is unique.
Prep time and cooking time: 30 minutes| Serves: 6

Ingredients To Use:

- 1-1/2 tsp. of garlic paste
- 2 cups of mixed vegetables
- 1-1/2 tsp. of salt
- 3 medium chopped onions
- 2-1/2 tbsp. of white sesame seeds
- 3 tbsp. of cream
- 3 eggs
- 5 chopped green chilies
- 1-1/2 tbsp. of ginger paste

Step-by-Step Directions to Cook It:

1. Mix all the ingredients except the eggs and mixed vegetables. Mix well to form a paste.
2. Pour the mixed vegetable in it and coat.
3. Break the eggs in a bowl and put the mixed vegetable in the eggs, and coat. Put the vegetables on sticks.
4. Transfer it to the air fryer basket. Cook for 25 minutes at 160^{0}F. Flip while cooking for uniformity.
5. Serve immediately.

Nutritional value per serving:

Calories: 174kcal, Fat: 4g, Carb: 38g, Proteins: 8g

Stuffed Eggplants

Eggplant is highly nutritious, and the ingredients stuffed into it contributes to great flavor.
Prep time and cooking time: 30 minutes|
Serves: 6

Ingredients To Use:

- 1 tsp. of dried mango powder
- 6 eggplants
- 1 tsp. of fenugreek
- 1/2 tsp. of basil
- 1/2 tsp. of salt
- 1 tsp. of cumin powder
- 1/2 tsp. of pepper powder
- 1/2 tsp. of parsley
- 3 tbsp. of grated cheese
- 1 medium of chopped onion
- 1 chopped green chili
- 1 tsp. of red chili flakes
- 1-1/2 tbsp. of chopped coriander leaves
- Salt and pepper
- 1/2 tsp. of oregano

Step-by-Step Directions to Cook It:

1. Mix onion, green chili, coriander leaves, fenugreek, cumin powder, pepper, and salt in a bowl.
2. Cut the stem and the cap of eggplant away. Pray with pepper and salt. Leave for a while.
3. Put the onion mixture inside the eggplant. Top with cheese, red chili flake, oregano, basil, and parsley.
4. Transfer it to the air fryer basket. Cook for 20 minutes at 140°F.

Nutritional value per serving:

Calories: 312kcal, Fat: 10g, Carb: 34g, Proteins: 29g

Mushroom Pasta

The ingredients used in this recipe all contribute to giving the meal an irresistible taste.
Prep time and cooking time: 20 minutes|
Serves: 4

Ingredients To Use:

- 1-1/2 tsp. dried oregano
- 1 cup pasta
- 2 tbsp. all-purpose flour
- 1-1/2 tbsp. olive oil
- 2 cups sliced mushroom
- Salt
- 2-1/2 tbsp. olive oil
- 2 cups of milk
- 1 tsp. dried basil
- Salt and pepper to taste
- 1/2 tsp. dried parsley

Step-by-Step Directions to Cook It:

1. Cook the pasta, sieve after it is done. Add 1-1/2 tbsp. of olive oil, 1/2 tsp. of oregano, 1/2 tsp. of basil, pepper, and salt.
2. In a pan, cook 2 tbsp. of olive oil, mushroom, all-purpose flour, milk, 1/2 tsp. of oregano, 1/2 tsp. of basil, parsley, pepper, and salt. Mix the pasta and the sauce. Mix till it thickens. Place the mixture in another glass bowl and top with cheese.
3. Put the bowl on the air fryer basket. Cook for 10 minutes at 160°F.
4. Serve immediately.

Nutritional value per serving:

Calories: 280kcal, Fat: 10g, Carb: 34g, Proteins: 16g

French Bean Toast

Bean is one of the most nutritious food

globally. It contains a very high protein , and a combination of baked beans and bread crispy gives you a great meal.

Prep time and cooking time: 30 minutes| Serves: 1

Ingredients To Use:

- 2 slices of bread
- Crushed cornflakes
- 1 egg white
- 2 cups of baked beans
- 1 tsp. of sugar

Step-by-Step Directions to Cook It:

1. Mix egg and sugar in a bowl, put bread in the mixture, and coat. Transfer to the crushed cornflakes and coat.
2. Transfer the coated bread to the air fryer basket. Cook for 20 minutes at 180^0F.
3. Serve immediately with baked beans.

Nutritional value per serving:

Calories: 72kcal, Fat: 4g, Carb: 10g, Proteins: 5g

Mushroom Pops

The lemon juice used in this recipe gives the mushroom pops an attractive feel.

Prep time and cooking time: 30 minutes| Serves: 4

Ingredients To Use:

- 1 cup whole mushrooms
- 1 tsp. dry basil
- 1-1/2 tsp. garlic paste
- 1 tsp. lemon juice
- Salt and pepper
- 1 tsp. red chili flakes
- 1 tsp. dry oregano

Step-by-Step Directions to Cook It:

1. In a bowl, mix all the ingredients.
2. Put the mushroom in the mixture. Leave for some minutes.
3. Put the coated mushroom in the air fryer

basket. Cook for 20 minutes for 180^0C.
4. Serve immediately with ketchup.

Nutritional value per serving:

Calories: 20kcal, Fat: 0.3g, Carb: 0.6g, Proteins: 2.5g

Potato Flat Cakes

Potatoes add a unique flavor to this flat cake recipe.

Prep time and cooking time: 30 minutes| Serves: 4

Ingredients To Use:

- 2 tbsp. of garam masala
- 1-1/2 tbsp. of lemon juice
- 2 cups of sliced potato
- Pepper and salt
- 3 tsp. of ginger finely chopped
- 2 tbsp. of fresh coriander leaves
- 3 chopped green chilies

Step-by-Step Directions to Cook It:

1. In a bowl, mix all the ingredients, add water. Make it form a paste. Put the slices of potatoes in it and coat.
2. Transfer the potato slices to the air fryer basket. Bake for 25 minutes at 160^0F.
3. Serve immediately.

Nutritional value per serving:

Calories: 211kcal, Fat: 4g, Carb: 43g, Proteins: 7g

Fenugreek Galette

Fenugreek has low-calorie and is an awesome addition to a weight loss diet.

Prep time and cooking time: 35 minutes| Serves: 3

Ingredients To Use:

- 2 cups of fenugreek
- 1-1/2 tbsp. of lemon juice
- 2 medium cooked and mashed potatoes

- Salt and pepper
- 3 tsp. of ginger finely chopped
- 2 tbsp. of fresh coriander leaves
- 3 chopped green chilies

1. In a bowl, mix all the ingredients. Mix and form 3-4 flat and round galette.
2. Spray the mixture with water.
3. Transfer the galettes into the basket of the air fryer. Cook for 25 minutes at 160^0F temperature. Then flip halfway for uniformity.
4. Serve immediately with ketchup.

Calories: 15kcal, Fat: 0.5g, Carb: 2g, Proteins: 2g

Snake Gourd Galette

Though snake gourds look tasteless, the vegetable's actual taste is far from it. Try this recipe now to discover the overwhelming flavor of snake gourd galettes.
Prep time and cooking time: 30 minutes|
Serves: 4

- 2 tbsp. of fresh coriander leaves
- 2 tbsp. of garam masala
- 3 tsp. of fine ground ginger
- 1 cup of snake gourd slices
- Pepper and salt
- 3 chopped green chilies
- 1-1/2 cup of crushed peanuts
- 1-1/2 tbsp. of lemon juice

1. In a bowl, mix all the ingredients. Mix and form 4 flat and round galette.
2. Spray water on the mixture.
3. Transfer the galettes into the basket of the air fryer.
4. Cook at 160^0F for about 25 minutes. Flip

while cooking for uniformity.
5. Serve immediately with mint chutney.

Calories: 89kcal, Fat: 5g, Carb: 7g, Proteins: 6g

Potato Wedges

Potato wedge is a baked or fried dish of potatoes; it is a tempting and savory meal.
Prep time and cooking time: 30 minutes|
Serves: 4

- 1/2 tsp. of red chili flakes
- 2 medium sized potatoes
- Salt
- 1 tbsp. of olive oil
- 1 tbsp. of lemon juice
- 1 tsp. of mixed herbs

1. Boil and bleach the potatoes.
2. In the pan, cook olive oil, mixed herb, red chili flakes, salt, and lemon juice. Stir the marinade till it thickens. Add the bleached potatoes to the marinade.
3. Put the coated potatoes in your air fryer basket. Cook at 200^0F for 25 minutes.
4. Serve immediately with ketchup.

Calories: 125kcal, Fat: 3g, Carb: 27g, Proteins: 4g

Bottle Gourd Flat Cakes

With the use of bottle gourds in this recipe, the taste is totally unique, with an outburst of flavors on the tastebuds.
Prep time and cooking time: 30 minutes|
Serves: 4

- 2 tbsp. of garam masala

- 3 chopped green chilies
- 2 cups of bottle gourd slices
- 1-1/2 tbsp. of lemon juice
- 3 tsp. of chopped ginger
- Pepper and salt
- 2 tbsp. of fresh coriander leaves

1. Mix all the ingredients in a bowl, add water until it forms a paste. Put the bottle gourd in it and coat well.
2. Transfer the coated bottle gourd to the air fryer basket. Cook for 25 minutes at 160^0F.
3. Serve immediately with ketchup.

Nutritional value per serving:

Calories: 16kcal, Fat: 0.1g, Carb: 4g, Proteins: 1g

Snake Gourd Cakes

Snake gourd cake is a great and healthy cake. Try this recipe and enjoy the wonderful taste. Prep time and cooking time: 30 minutes| Serves: 4

Ingredients To Use:

- 2 tbsp. of garam masala
- 3 chopped green chilies
- 2 cups of sliced snake gourd
- 1-1/2 tbsp. of lemon juice
- 3 tsp. of chopped ginger
- Pepper and salt
- 2 tbsp. of fresh coriander leaves

Step-by-Step Directions to Cook It:

1. In a bowl, mix all the ingredients, add water till it forms a paste. Put the slices of snack gourd in it and coat.
2. Transfer the slices of snack gourd to the air fryer basket. Bake for 25 minutes at 160^0F.
3. Serve immediately.

Nutritional value per serving:

Calories: 89kcal, Fat: 5g, Carb: 8g, Proteins: 6g

Cabbage Flat Cakes

Cabbage is a low-calorie fruit vegetable, and on its addition to the regular ingredients of a pound cake, it transforms the snack into a delicious and healthy combination. It is best made during a special gathering or occasion. Prep time and cooking time: 35 minutes| Serves: 4

Ingredients To Use:

- 3 tsp. of ginger finely chopped
- 2 tbsp. of garam masala
- 3 chopped green chilies
- 2 cups of halved cabbage leaves
- 1-1/2 tbsp. of lemon juice
- 2 tbsp. of fresh coriander leaves
- Pepper and salt

Step-by-Step Directions to Cook It:

1. Mix all the ingredients in a bowl, add water until it forms a paste. Avoid adding too much water. Put the cabbage in it and coat well.
2. Transfer the coated cabbage to the air fryer basket. Bake for 25 minutes at 160^0F.
3. Serve immediately with ketchup.

Nutritional value per serving:

Calories: 22kcal, Fat: 0.5g, Carb: 6g, Proteins: 2g

Bitter Gourd Cakes

Bitter gourd, also known as bitter melon, has many nutritional benefits. Bitter gourd helps to reduce and maintain sugar level in the blood.
Prep time and cooking time: 35 minutes|

Serves: 4

- 1-/2 tbsp. of lemon juice
- 2 tbsp. of garam masala
- 2 tbsp. of fresh coriander leaves
- 2 cups of sliced bitter gourd
- Pepper and salt
- 3 chopped green chilies
- 3 tsp. of ginger finely chopped

Step-by-Step Directions to Cook It:

1. Mix all the ingredients in a bowl, add water until it forms a paste. Avoid adding too much water. Put the bitter gourd in it and coat well.
2. Transfer the coated bitter gourd to the air fryer basket. Bake for 25 minutes at 160^{0}F.
3. Serve immediately with ketchup.

Nutritional value per serving:

Calories: 21kcal, Fat: 0.1g, Carb: 4g, Proteins: 1g

Pumpkin Galette

Pumpkin is a good source of vitamin A; it also has low calories. Pumpkin galette can be made in different ways. Below is a unique way of making it.
Prep time and cooking time: 30 minutes|
Serves: 4

Ingredients To Use:

- 2 tbsp. of garam masala
- 3 chopped green chilies
- 1 cup of sliced pumpkin
- 1-1/2 tbsp. of lemon juice
- 3 tsp. of chopped ginger
- Pepper and salt
- 2 tbsp. of fresh coriander leaves

Step-by-Step Directions to Cook It:

1. In a bowl, mix the ingredients. Make 4 flat and round galettes from it. Sprinkle water on the galettes.
2. Transfer the galettes to the air fryer and cook for 25 minutes at 160^{0}F.
3. Serve with ketchup.

Nutritional value per serving:

Calories: 350kcal, Fat: 22g, Carb: 29g, Proteins: 15g

Radish Flat Cakes

Radish is mostly served as a salad due to its high fiber content.
Prep time and cooking time: 35 minutes|
Serves: 5

Ingredients To Use:

- 2 tbsp. of garam masala
- 3 chopped green chilies
- 2 cups of sliced radish
- 1-1/2 tbsp. of lemon juice
- 3 tsp. of chopped ginger
- Pepper and salt
- 2 tbsp. of fresh coriander leaves

Step-by-Step Directions to Cook It:

1. Mix all the ingredients in a bowl, add water until it forms a paste. Put the radish in it and coat well.
2. Transfer the coated radish to the air fryer basket. Bake for 25 minutes at 160^{0}F.
3. Serve immediately with ketchup.

Nutritional value per serving:

Calories: 523kcal, Fat: 24g, Carb: 53g, Proteins: 12g

Mushroom Wonton

Mushroom wonton can also be called mushroom pie. It is prepared in almost the same way as a regular pie, but the ingredients are quite different.

Prep time and cooking time: 20 minutes | Serves: 2

Ingredients To Use:

- 1-1/2 cup of all-purpose flour
- 2 tbsp. of oil
- 1/2 tsp. of salt
- 2 tsp. of ginger-garlic paste
- 5 tbsp. of water
- 2 tsp. of soya sauce
- 2 tsp. of vinegar
- 2 cups of cubed mushroom

Step-by-Step Directions to Cook It:

1. In a big bowl, mix the flour, salt, and water. Knead well to form a smooth dough.
2. In a pan, put oil, mushroom, ginger-garlic paste, soya sauce, vinegar, and cook.
3. Place the dough on a working surface. Fill the dough with the mushroom mixture. Use water to seal the edges.
4. Transfer the wonton to your air fryer basket. Set the air fryer to 200^0F and cook for 20 minutes.

Nutritional value per serving:

Calories: 71kcal, Fat: 2g, Carb: 13g, Proteins: 3g

Mushroom Patties

Mushrooms are incredibly beneficial for the immune system and try this recipe as a health-boosting meal.
Prep time and cooking time: 20 minutes| Serves: 8

Ingredients To Use:

- 1 cup of minced mushroom
- 1 tsp. of lemon juice
- Salt
- 1 tbsp. of fresh coriander leaves
- 1/4 tsp. of cumin powder

- 1/4 tsp. of ginger finely chopped
- 1/4 tsp. of chili powder
- 1 chopped green chili

Step-by-Step Directions to Cook It:

1. Mix all the ingredients in a bowl. Make 8 round patties from the mixture.
2. Place the patties on your air fryer basket. Cook for about 12 minutes at 250^0F.
3. Serve immediately.

Nutritional value per serving:

Calories: 151kcal, Fat: 5g, Carb: 15g, Proteins: 15g

Asparagus Galette

Asparagus is also called sparrow grass. Asparagus is fast and easy to cook, and it improves digestive health, and also lowers blood pressure.
Prep time and cooking time: 30 minutes| Serves:

Ingredients To Use:

- 2 cups of minced asparagus
- 1-1/2 tbsp. of lemon juice
- 3 tsp. of chopped ginger
- Pepper and salt
- 2 tbsp. of freshly chopped coriander leaves
- 3 chopped green chilies

Step-by-Step Directions to Cook It:

1. In a bowl, mix all the ingredients. Make flat and round galettes from the mixture. Spray the galettes with water.
2. Transfer it to your air fryer. Set the air fryer to 160^0F, cook for 25 minutes.
3. Serve with tomato ketchup.

Nutritional value per serving:

Calories: 378kcal, Fat: 28g, Carb: 24g, Proteins: 10g

Chapter 8: Side Snacks and Appetizers

Coconut Chicken Bites

Coconut is nutritious with high protein and vitamin B. The taste of chicken, when paired with chicken, is simply amazing.
Preparation time and cooking time: 25 minutes| Serves: 4

Ingredients To Use:

- 2 eggs
- Cooking spray
- 3/4 cup of bread crumbs
- 2 tsp of garlic powder
- 8 tender chickens
- 3/4 cup of shredded coconut

Step-by-Step Directions to Cook It:

1. Mix the pepper, eggs, garlic powder, and salt in a bowl. Stir until well-combined.
2. Mix the panko and coconut in a separate bowl.
3. Coat the tender chicken with the egg mixture, then pour it into the coconut mixture, and toss well.
4. Spray cooking spray on the coated chicken bites.
5. Transfer it to the air fryer basket. Set the air fryer to 350^0F. Cook for 30 minutes.
6. Serve immediately as an appetizer.

Nutritional value per serving:

Calories: 255kcal, Fat: 5g, Carb: 15g, Proteins: 27g

Buffalo Cauliflower Snack

Cauliflower is a healthy veggie that adds flavor to fish and meat meals. This recipe is no different.
Preparation time and cooking time: 25 minutes| Serves: 4

Ingredients To Use:

- 1 cup of bread crumbs, panko
- 1/4 cup of buffalo sauce
- 4 cups of cauliflower florets
- Mayonnaise
- 1/4 cup of melted butter

Step-by-Step Directions to Cook It:

1. Mix the butter and buffalo sauce in a bowl and mix well.
2. Put the cauliflower floret in the mixture. Transfer it to panko bread crumbs.
3. Put the coated buffalo in the air fryer's basket. Set the air fryer to 350^0F. Cook for 16 minutes.
4. Serve immediately with mayonnaise.

Nutritional value per serving:

Calories: 240kcal, Fat: 6g, Carb: 10g, Proteins: 8g

Banana Snack

Banana is an edible fruit that improves digestive health. Eat healthy with this air-fryer recipe.
Prep time and cooking time: 15 minutes| Serves: 8

Ingredients To Use:

- 1 sliced banana
- 16 cups of baking crust
- 3/4 cup of chocolate chips
- 1 tbsp. of vegetable oil
- 1/4 cup of peanut butter

Step-by-Step Directions to Cook It:

1. Heat chocolate chips in a small pot over medium heat until it melts.

2. Mix the coconut oil and peanut butter in a bowl and mix well.
3. Scoop 1 tsp. of the chocolate mixture in a cup, add in one or two banana slice and 1 tsp. of the butter mixture.
4. Repeat the process for the remaining cups. Put it all in a baking dish that fits the air fryer. Set the air fryer to 320⁰F. Cook for 5 minutes.
5. Place in the refrigerator until it is cool.

Nutritional value per serving:

Calories: 72kcal, Fat: 6g, Carb: 12g, Proteins: 3g

Potato Spread

Potato is an edible tuber crop. It is divided into 2 varieties; Irish potato and sweet potato, and they are both good sources of vitamin C and vitamin B6. Start eating healthy with this recipe.
Prep time and cooking time: 20 minutes| Serves: 10

Ingredients To Use:
- 1 tbsp. of olive oil
- 1 cup of sweet potatoes
- 5 cloves of garlic
- 2 tbsp. of water
- 19 ounces of canned garbanzo beans
- 1/4 cup of tahini
- White pepper and salt
- 2 tbsp. of lemon juice
- 1/2 tsp. of ground cumin

Step-by-Step Directions to Cook It:
1. Place the potatoes in the air fryer basket. Set the air fryer to 360⁰F. Cook for 14 minutes. Allow to cool down and peel. Place it in the food processor and blend well.
2. Add the garlic, cumin, oil, and lemon juice. Add the sesame paste, beans, and

water. Pulse well.
3. Add the pepper and salt. Pulse the food processor. Serve immediately.

Nutritional value per serving:

Calories: 201kcal, Fat: 5g, Carb: 22g, Proteins: 13g

Mexican Apple Slice

Apple is an edible fruit that is rich in fiber. It also benefits your heart and is good for weight loss. As a snack, apple is with a bundle of health benefits and delicacy.
Prep time and cooking time: 15 minutes| Serves: 4

Ingredients To Use:
- 1/2 cup of dark chocolate chips
- 3 large apples
- 1/2 cup of caramel sauce
- 2 tsp. of lemon juice
- 1/4 cup of chopped pecans

Step-by-Step Directions to Cook It:
1. Mix lemon juice and apples. Put it in the air fryer pan.
2. Add pecans, caramel sauce, and chocolate chips. Set the air fryer to 320⁰F. Cook for 5 minutes.
3. Serve with small bowls as snacks.

Nutritional value per serving:

Calories: 203kcal, Fat: 5g, Carb: 23g, Proteins: 5g

Shrimps Muffins

Shrimps are nutrient-rich, low-calorie seafood. They are also incredibly delicious and can make you feel good. Try this recipe to discover the pleasure of adding shrimps to your snacks.
Prep time and cooking time: 30 minutes| Serves: 6

- 1-1/2 cups of panko
- 2 tbsp. of mayonnaise
- Cooking spray
- 1 spaghetti squash
- 1 glove of garlic
- Black pepper and salt
- 1 cup of shredded mozzarella
- 1 tsp. of parsley flakes
- 8 ounces of shrimps

Step-by-Step Directions to Cook It:

1. Place spaghetti squash inside the air fryer. Set the air fryer to 350^{0}F. Cook for 15 minutes. Transfer to a bowl and allow to cool down.
2. Add parsley flakes, salt, shrimps, mozzarella, and peppers. Add mayonnaise and panko. Mix well.
3. Spray muffins tray with cooking spray. Put the muffins in a basket that fits the air fryer. Divide the shrimps and squash mixture into different cups.
4. Set the air fryer to 360^{0}F. Cook for 10 minutes.
5. Serve the muffins as snacks.

Nutritional value per serving:

Calories: 62kcal, Fat: 4g, Carb: 8g, Proteins: 8g

Zucchini Cakes

Zucchini Is also called courgette, which has low fat and carbohydrate. This makes it an ideal meal for eating healthy and living right. Prep time and cooking time: 25 minutes| Serves: 12

Ingredients To Use:

- 1 egg
- 2 cloves of garlic
- 1/2 cup of whole wheat flour
- Cooking spray

- 1 chopped onion, yellow
- 1/2 cup of chopped dill
- Black pepper and salt to taste
- 3 grated zucchini

Step-by-Step Directions to Cook It:

1. Mix onion, pepper, flour, and garlic in a bowl. Add egg, zucchini, and dill. Mix well. Scoop a small part out of the mixture. Spray each scoop with cooking spray.
2. Put them in the basket that fits the air fryer. Set the air fryer to 370^{0}F temperature. Cook for 5 minutes on both sides.
3. Serve immediately as snacks.

Nutritional value per serving:

Calories: 62kcal, Fat: 3g, Carb: 8g, Proteins: 4g

Cauliflower Bars

Cauliflower has high fiber content that strengthens the bone and boosts the heart. Eat right with vegetables in your snacks. Prep time and cooking time: 35 minutes| Serves: 12

Ingredients To Use:

- 1 tsp. of Italian seasoning
- 1 large cauliflower head
- 1/2 cup of shredded mozzarella
- Black pepper and salt
- 1/4 cup of egg white

Step-by-Step Directions to Cook It:

1. In a food processor, put cauliflower floret and pulse. Pour it on the baking dish that fits the air fryer. Set the air fryer to 360^{0}F. Cook for 10 minutes.
2. Pour the cauliflower into a bowl. Add cheese, Italian seasoning, salt, egg white, and pepper. Pour the mixture into the air fryer. Set the air fryer at 360^{0}F. Cook for 15 minutes.

3. Cut the cooked snacks into 12 bars.

Calories: 52kcal, Fat: 3g, Carb: 6g, Proteins: 6g

Pesto Crackers

Pesto cracker is a biscuit snack that can be eaten with any kind of drink.
Prep time and cooking time: 30 minutes| Serves: 3

Ingredients To Use:

- 1 clove of minced garlic
- 3 tbsp. of butter
- 1/2 tsp. of baking powder
- 1/4 tsp. of dried basil
- 2 tbsp. of basil pesto
- Black pepper and salt
- 1-1/4 cups of flour

Step-by-Step Directions to Cook It:

1. Mix fl0ur, pepper, basil, and salt in a bowl. Add baking powder, cayenne, and butter. Mix until you get a dough.
2. Place the dough of the baking sheet on the air fryer.
3. Set the air fryer to 325^0F. Allow baking for 18 minutes.
4. Allow cooling before serving.

Nutritional value per serving:

Calories: 201kcal, Fat: 22g, Carb: 5g, Proteins: 10g

Pumpkin Muffins

Pumpkin is an edible vegetable that's rich in vitamin A, which helps to boost body immunity.
Prep time and cooking time: 25 minutes| Serves: 18

Ingredients To Use:

- 1 tsp. of cinnamon powder

- 2 tbsp. of flaxseed meal
- 1/4 cup of butter
- 1/2 cup of sugar
- 1/2 tsp. of baking powder
- 3/4 cup of pumpkin puree
- 1/4 cup of flour
- 1 egg
- 1/2 tsp. of ground nutmeg
- 1/2 tsp. of baking soda

Step-by-Step Directions to Cook It:

1. Mix pumpkin puree, egg, and butter in a bowl.
2. Add baking soda, flaxseed meal, cinnamon, and baking soda. Add sugar, flour, nutmeg, and baking powder. Mix well.
3. Scoop the mixture inside a muffin pan that fits the air fryer. Set the air fryer to 350^0F. Bake for 14 minutes.
4. Allow cooling before serving as a snack.

Nutritional value per serving:

Calories: 52kcal, Fat: 4g, Carb: 5g, Proteins: 5g

Zucchini Chips

Zucchini chips are yummy and rare. You get to experience a privileged delicacy with this recipe.
Prep time and cooking time: 70 minutes| Serves: 6

Ingredients To Use:

- 2 tbsp. of olive oil
- 3 slices of zucchinis
- 2 tbsp. of balsamic vinegar
- Black pepper and salt

Step-by-Step Directions to Cook It:

1. Mix salt, oil, pepper, and vinegar in a bowl. Mix well.
2. Put zucchini slices in the mixture and coat. Set the air fryer to 200^0F. Cook for 1

hour.

3. Serve when it is cool.

Calories: 43kcal, Fat: 5g, Carb: 5g, Proteins: 10g

Beef Jerky Snack

Jerky snack stuffed with beef is an irresistible and yummy recipe.
Prep time and cooking time: 3 hours 30 minutes| Serves: 6

Ingredients To Use:

- 2 tbsp. of black pepper
- 2 cups of soy sauce
- 2 tbsp. of black peppercorns
- 2 pounds of sliced beef round
- 1/2 cup of Worcestershire sauce

Step-by-Step Directions to Cook It:

1. Mix black pepper, soy sauce, Worcestershire sauce, and black peppercorns in a bowl. Mix well.
2. Put beef slices and coat. Place in the refrigerator for about 6 hours for the sauce to enter the beef.
3. Put the coated beef in the air fryer. Set the air fryer at 370^0F temperature. Cook for 1 hour 30 minutes.
4. Serve when cool.

Nutritional value per serving:

Calories: 305kcal, Fat: 15g, Carb: 5g, Proteins: 11g

Honey Party Wings

Honey is very sweet and helps to reduce the duration of digestion in the body. Add honey to your chicken wings to improve the flavor and taste.
Prep time and cooking time: 1 hour 25 minutes| Serves: 8

Ingredients To Use:

- 2 tbsp. of honey
- 2 tbsp. of lime juice
- 16 wings of chicken
- 2 tbsp. of soy sauce
- Black pepper and salt

Step-by-Step Directions to Cook It:

1. Mix honey, chicken wings, pepper, soy sauce, lime juice, and salt in a bowl. Mix well and leave in the refrigerator for about 1 hour.
2. Place the chicken wings in the air fryer. Cook for 12 minutes at 360^0F temperature.
3. Serve immediately as an appetizer.

Nutritional value per serving:

Calories: 212kcal, Fat: 6g, Carb: 18g, Proteins: 5g

Salmon Party Patties

Salmon may be fatty, but it is still a good source of protein and other nutrients. This recipe will help you create a well-seasoned salmon.
Prep time and cooking time: 35 minutes| Serves: 4

Ingredients To Use:

- 1 egg
- 2 tbsp. of chopped parsley
- 3 large boiled and mashed potatoes
- 2 tbsp. of bread crumbs
- Black pepper and salt
- 1 large boneless and skinless salmon fillet
- 2 tbsp. of chopped dill
- Cooking spray

Step-by-Step Directions to Cook It:

1. Put salmon in the air fryer basket. Coot at 360^0F for 10 minutes.

2. Put the salmon on a flat surface. Allow to cool down. Cut it into tiny slice and transfer it to a bowl.
3. Add pepper, bread crumbs, mashed potatoes, and parsley. Add dill, salt, and egg. Stir well.
4. Transfer it to a greased air fryer basket with cooking spray. Cook for 13 minutes at 360°F temperature.
5. Serve immediately as an appetizer.

Calories: 230kcal, Fat: 12g, Carb: 0g, Proteins: 20g

Banana Chips

Banana is rich in vitamin C and vitamin B6 that benefits the body. Air frying does not reduce its nutritional value. Try this recipe now for a nutritious and delicious snack.
Prep time and cooking time: 25 minutes|
Serves: 4

- 1 tsp. of olive oil
- Salt
- 1/2 tsp. of chai masala
- 4 sliced bananas
- 1/2 tsp. of turmeric powder

1. Mix turmeric, banana, oil, salt, and chai masala in a bowl. Mix well and leave for about 10 minutes.
2. Put the banana slices in the heat air fryer. Cook for 15 minutes at 360°F.
3. Serve immediately as snacks,

Calories: 120kcal, Fat: 30g, Carb: 50g, Proteins: 7g

Spring Rolls

Spring rolls can always get people delight because they don't know what to expect in there until they bite it. With Spring rolls, every bite is a surprise.
Prep time and cooking time: 35 minutes|
Serves: 8

- 1 tsp. of soy sauce
- 2 tbsp. of water
- 1 grated carrot
- Black pepper and salt
- 2 chopped onions, yellow
- 1 tsp. of sugar
- 10 spring roll sheets
- 2 cups of shredded cabbage
- 3 cloves of garlic
- 1/2 minced chili pepper
- 2 tbsp. of cornflour
- 1 tbsp. of grated ginger
- 2 tbsp. of olive oil

1. Put oil in a pan, heat over medium heat. Add chili pepper, salt, onions, and cabbage. Add sugar, soy sauce, garlic, and pepper. Mix well and cook for about 3 minutes.
2. Roll out the spring roll and cut it into a square shape. Put cabbage mixture on each of square roll.
3. Get another bowl, mix water and cornflour in it. Mix well and use the mixture to seal the spring roll.
4. Put the spring roll in the air fryer basket. Cook for about 11 minutes at 360°F on both sides.
5. Serve immediately as an appetizer or serve when cool.

Calories: 200kcal, Fat: 7g, Carb: 8g, Proteins: 15g

Radish Chips

Radish chips are snacks with low carbohydrates and low calories.
Prep time and cooking time: 20 minutes|
Serves: 4

Ingredients To Use:

- 1 tbsp of chopped chives
- 15 sliced radish
- Cooking spray
- Black pepper and salt.

Step-by-Step Directions to Cook It:

1. Place the radish in the air fryer back. Spray cooking spray on it. Spray black pepper and salt as well.
2. Cook for 10 minutes on both sides at 350^{0}F.
3. Serve immediately with chives.

Nutritional value per serving:

Calories: 50kcal, Fat: 2g, Carb: 2g, Proteins: 2g

Crab sticks

Crabs are tender and very tasty, and crab sticks are not different.
Prep time and cooking time: 25 minutes|
Serves: 4

Ingredients To Use:

- 2 tsp. of sesame oil
- 10 halved crabsticks
- 2 tsp. of Cajun seasoning

Step-by-Step Directions to Cook It:

1. In a bowl, put sesame oil, crab sticks, and Cajun seasoning. Mix well.
2. Put the mixture in the air fryer basket.
3. Cook for 10-12 minutes at 350^{0}F.
4. Serve immediately and appetizer.

Nutritional value per serving:

Calories: 100kcal, Fat: 0g, Carb: 18g, Proteins: 9g

Fried Dill Pickles

Who doesn't love a good air fried pickle? Try this recipe out when you want to try something new.
Prep time and cooking time: 15 minutes|
Serves: 4

Ingredients To Use:

- 1 egg
- Cooking spray
- 1/2 tsp3 of sweet paprika
- 16 ounces of jarred dill pickles
- 1/4 cup of ranch sauce
- 1/2 tsp3 of garlic powder
- 1/2 cup of flour
- 1/4 cup of milk

Step-by-Step Directions to Cook It:

1. Mix egg and milk in a bowl.
2. Get another bowl, mix garlic powder, flour, paprika, and salt. Stir well.
3. Dip the pickles in flour. Dip it in the egg mixture and dip it back in the flour mixture. Transfer it to the air fryer.
4. Spray it with cooking spray. Cook for 5 minutes at 400^{0}F temperature.
5. Serve immediately with ranch sauce.

Nutritional value per serving:

Calories: 12kcal, Fat: 0.3g, Carb: 2.5g, Proteins: 0.5g

Chickpeas Snack

Chickpeas are excellent snacks. They satisfy your palate easily while adding health benefits to your body.
Prep time and cooking time: 20 minutes|
Serves: 4

Ingredients To Use:

- 1 tbsp. of olive oil
- 15 ounces of canned chickpeas

- 1 tsp. of smoked paprika
- 1/2 tsp. of ground cumin
- Black pepper and salt

1. Mix paprika, oil, salt, chickpea, pepper, and cumin in a bowl.
2. Transfer the mixture to the air fryer basket. Cook for about 10 minutes at 390^{0}F.
3. Serve immediately as a snack.

Calories: 365kcal, Fat: 8g, Carb: 63g, Proteins: 20g

Sausage Ball

Sausage ball is a dough containing a variety of fillings such as meat. It is mostly called sausage roll.
Prep time and cooking time: 25 minutes| Serves: 9

- 1 tsp. of sage
- 4 ounces of ground sausage meat
- 1/2 tsp. of minced garlic
- 3 tbsp. of bread crumbs
- Black pepper and salt
- 1 chopped onion, small

1. Mix pepper, bread crumbs, sausage, and sage in a bowl. Add garlic, salt, and onion. Stir well.
2. Transfer it to the air fryer basket. Cook for about 15 minutes at 360^{0}F.
3. Serve immediately as snacks.

Calories: 125kcal, Fat: 8g, Carb: 5g, Proteins: 15g

Air-Baked Chicken

In this recipe, the chicken is seasoned then baked to finesse.
Prep time and cooking time: 35 minutes| Serves: 10

- 1 cup of yogurt
- 4 chopped scallions
- 12 ounces of cream cheese
- 1/3 cup of raisins
- 2 cups of shredded chicken
- 2 tsp. of curry powder
- 1/2 cup of chutney
- 3 tbsp. of melted butter
- 1/4 cup of chopped cilantro
- Black pepper and salt
- 6 ounces of grated cheese, Monterey jack
- 1/2 cup of sliced almond

1. Mix yogurt and cream cheese in a bowl. Use a mixer to whisk it.
2. Add chicken meat, curry powder, cilantro, scallions, cheese, salt, raisins, and pepper. Stir well.
3. Transfer the mixture to a baking sheet that fits the air fryer. Bake for about 25 minutes at 300^{0}F.
4. Serve immediately as appetizer and top with chutney.

Calories: 300kcal, Fat: 20g, Carb: 2g, Proteins: 26g

Sweet Popcorn

Sweet popcorn is prepared by air-frying corn kernels or corn seed with sugar and butter at a very high temperature.
Prep time and cooking time: 15 minutes|

Serves: 4

- 2 ounces of brown sugar
- 2 tbsp. of corn kernels
- 2-1/2 tbsp. of butter

Step-by-Step Directions to Cook It:

1. In the air fryer pan, put corn kernel, butter, and sugar.
2. Set the air fryer to 400^{0}F temperature. Cook until popcorn starts popping out.
3. Allow to cool or serve immediately as snacks.

Nutritional value per serving:

Calories: 270kcal, Fat: 4.5g, Carb: 75g, Proteins: 15g

Apple Chips

This is another apple chip recipe to help spice up your regular meal. In this recipe, cayenne pepper is added to make the apple chips spicy.
Prep time and cooking time: 20 minutes|
Serves: 2

Ingredients To Use:

- 1 tbsp. of sugar
- Salt,
- 1 sliced apple
- 1/2 tsp. of cayenne powder

Step-by-Step Directions to Cook It:

1. Mix salt, cayenne pepper, apple slices, and sugar in a bowl.
2. Put the mixture in the air fryer basket. Cook at 390^{0}F for 10 minutes on both sides.
3. Share in a bowl and serve immediately as snacks.

Nutritional value per serving:

Calories: 72kcal, Fat: 1g, Carb: 6g, Proteins: 4g

Bread Sticks

The cinnamon powder used in this recipe gives the bread an exceptional taste.
Prep time and cooking time: 20 minutes|
Serves: 2

Ingredients To Use:

- 1 tbsp. of honey
- 4 slices of bread
- 2 eggs
- Nutmeg powder
- 1/4 cup of milk
- 1 tsp. of cinnamon powder

Step-by-Step Directions to Cook It:

1. Mix brown sugar, honey, milk, nutmeg, egg, and cinnamon in a bowl. Mix well.
2. Add the breadsticks to the mixture and mix well.
3. Transfer the soaked breadsticks to the air fryer and cover it.
4. Cook for 10 minutes at 360^{0}F.
5. Serve immediately as a snack in a bowl.

Nutritional value per serving:

Calories: 143kcal, Fat: 3g, Carb: 12g, Proteins: 8g

Crispy Shrimps

Shrimps are extremely delicious when fried until crunchy and make an awesome appetizer.
Prep time and cooking time: 15 minutes|
Serves: 4

Ingredients To Use:

- 1 cup of panko bread crumbs
- Black pepper and salt
- 12 large peeled shrimps
- 1 cup of flour
- 1 cup of coconut
- 2 egg whites

1. Mix coconut and panko in a bowl.
2. Get another bowl, mix pepper, flour, and salt.
3. In the third bowl, put egg whites and whisk.
4. Put the shrimps inside egg mixture, flour mixture, and coconut mixture.
5. Put it in the air fryer basket. Cook for 10 minutes at 350^{0}F. Serve immediately as an appetizer.

Nutritional value per serving:

Calories: 142kcal, Fat: 10g, Carb: 2g, Proteins: 10g

Cajun Shrimp

Cajun shrimp is mostly cooked during the Thanksgiving or special occasions. The old bay seasoning gives the Cajun shrimp a great taste.
Prep time and cooking time: 15 minutes| Serves: 2

Ingredients To Use:

- 1 tbsp. of olive oil
- Black pepper and salt
- 1/4 tsp. of smoked paprika
- 20 peeled tiger shrimps
- 1/2 tsp. of old bay seasoning

Step-by-Step Directions to Cook It:

1. Mix salt, paprika, shrimps, pepper, oil, and old bay seasoning in a bowl.
2. Put the shrimps in the air fryer basket. Cook for about 5 minutes at 390^{0}F.
3. Serve immediately as an appetizer.

Nutritional value per serving:

Calories: 160kcal, Fat: 10g, Carb: 12g, Proteins: 18g

Crispy Fish Sticks

Whitefish is a delicacy for fancy days. This crispy fish snack is always ready to serve you.
Prep time and cooking time: 25 minutes| Serves: 2

Ingredients To Use:

- 1 egg
- 4 ounces of bread crumbs
- Black pepper and salt
- 4 tbsp. of olive oil
- 4 skinless and boneless whitefish fillets

Step-by-Step Directions to Cook It:

1. Mix oil and bread crumbs in a bowl.
2. Get another bowl, put pepper, egg, and salt. Mix well.
3. Put fish inside the egg and transfer to the bread crumb mixture.
4. Put the fish in the air fryer basket. Cook for 10-12 minutes at 360^{0}F.
5. Put the fish sticks on the platter and serve immediately as an appetizer.

Nutritional value per serving:

Calories: 165kcal, Fat: 8g, Carb: 1g, Proteins: 15g

Fish Nuggets

Fish nuggets are like chicken nuggets, but with fewer calories
Prep time and cooking time: 25 minutes| Serves: 4

Ingredients To Use:

- 1 tbsp. of smoked paprika
- 5 tbsp. of flour
- 28 ounces of skinless fish fillets
- Cooking spray
- 5 tbsp. of water
- 1 tsp. of dried dill
- 3 ounces of panko bread crumbs
- 1 egg

- 4 tbsp. of homemade mayonnaise
- Black pepper and salt
- 1/2 lemon juice
- 1 tbsp. of garlic powder

1. Mix water and flour in a bowl. Add pepper, egg, and salt. Whisk.
2. In another bowl, mix paprika, panko, and garlic powder.
3. Put pieces of fish inside the egg mixture and the flour mixture. Transfer it to the air fryer basket. Cook for 10-12 minutes at 400^0F.
4. Mix lemon juice, mayonnaise, and dill in another bowl.
5. Serve fish nugget with lemon juice mixture.

Nutritional value per serving:

Calories: 300kcal, Fat: 11g, Carb: 21g, Proteins: 17g

Chestnut and Shrimp Rolls

Chestnut is an edible nut with low protein and fat content. It also contains vitamin C, which makes it a good addition for a healthy snack.
Prep time and cooking time: 25 minutes| Serves: 4

Ingredients To Use:

- 1 clove of minced garlic
- 1 egg yolk
- 8 ounces of chopped water chestnuts
- 3 chopped scallions
- 2 tbsp. of olive oil
- 2 cups of chopped cabbage
- 1/2 pounds of chopped shiitake mushrooms
- Black pepper and salt
- 1/2 pound of chopped cooked shrimp
- 1 tsp. of grated ginger

- 1 tbsp. of water
- 6 wrappers of spring roll

Step-by-Step Directions to Cook It:

1. Put oil in a pan and heat over medium heat. Add mushrooms, ginger, cabbage, and salt. Add shrimps, garlic, pepper, and scallions. Cook for about 2 minutes
2. Mix water and egg in a bowl. Stir.
3. Place the roll wrappers on a flat surface. Put veggie mix and shrimps on it. Seal it with egg wash. Transfer it to the air fryer basket. Cook for 16 minutes at 360^0F.
4. Serve immediately as an appetizer.

Nutritional value per serving:

Calories: 142kcal, Fat: 5g, Carb: 15g, Proteins: 5g

Seafood Appetizer

This recipe is an explosion of seafood. Crabmeat and shrimp paired together produce an exotic taste.
Prep time and cooking time: 35 minutes| Serves: 4

Ingredients To Use:

- 1 cup of flaked crabmeat
- 1 tbsp. of butter
- 1 cup of chopped green bell pepper
- 2 tbsp. of bread crumbs
- 1/2 cup of chopped yellow onion
- 1 cup of chopped celery
- 1 tsp. of sweet paprika
- 1 tsp. of Worcestershire sauce
- 1 cup of homemade mayonnaise
- Black pepper and salt
- 1 cup of peeled baby shrimp

Step-by-Step Directions to Cook It:

1. Mix bell pepper, mayonnaise, shrimps, pepper, onion, salt, crab meat, and celery in a bowl.
2. Put Worcestershire sauce and stir.

Transfer the mixture to a baking sheet that fits the air fryer.

3. Add butter and spray bread crumbs. Cook for 20-25 minutes at 320°F.
4. Serve immediately as an appetizer, top with paprika.

Nutritional value per serving:

Calories: 201kcal, Fat: 5g, Carb: 10g, Proteins: 5g

Salmon Meatballs

Salmon is rich in fatty acid and protein, and when prepared as meatballs, it's incredible.
Prep time and cooking time: 25 minutes| Serves: 4

Ingredients To Use:

- 1 egg white
- 1/2 tsp. of paprika
- 3 tbsp. of minced cilantro
- Cooking spray
- 1 pound of chopped and skinless salmon
- 1/2 tsp. of ground oregano
- 1 chopped small onion, yellow
- 2 cloves of garlic
- Black pepper and salt
- 1/4 cup of panko

Step-by-Step Directions to Cook It:

1. Get a food processor, mix salt, cilantro, paprika, salmon, salt, and garlic cloves. Add egg white, oregano, panko, and onion. And blend well. Shape into meatball form.
2. Transfer the meatball to the air fryer basket. Sprinkle with cooking spray. Cook for about 10-12 minutes at 320°F.
3. Serve the meatballs as an appetizer.

Nutritional value per serving:

Calories: 290kcal, Fat: 15g, Carb: 25g, Proteins: 27g

Chicken Wings

Chicken wings are healthy and taste great. What could be better?
Prep time and cooking time: 1 hour 10 minutes| Serves: 2

Ingredients To Use:

- 1/4 cup of honey
- 16 pieces of chicken wings
- 3/4 cup of potato starch
- 4 tbsp. of minced garlic
- 1/4 cup of butter
- Black pepper and salt

Step-by-Step Directions to Cook It:

1. Mix pepper, chicken wings, potato starch, and salt in a bowl. Put the mixture in the air fryer basket.
2. Cook at 360°F for about 25 minutes, increase the temperature to 400°F for 5 minutes.
3. Get another pan, put butter, and heat over medium heat. Put garlic and mix. Cook for about 5 minutes. Add honey, salt, and pepper. Cook for 20 minutes over medium heat.
4. Place chicken wings in bowls and serve with honey sauce as an appetizer.

Nutritional value per serving:

Calories: 90kcal, Fat: 7g, Carb: 0g, Proteins: 14g

Chicken Breast Rolls

Chicken breast roll is mostly eaten as an appetizer. It is taste perfect and is healthy.
Prep time and cooking time: 35 minutes| Serves: 4

Ingredients To Use:

- 1 cup of chopped dried tomatoes
- 2 cups of baby spinach
- Olive oil

- Black pepper and salt
- 4 skinless and boneless chicken breasts
- 4 slices of mozzarella
- 1-1/2 tbsp. of Italian seasoning

1. Use a meat tenderizer to flatten chicken breasts. Put spinach, pepper, mozzarella, Italian seasoning, and salt. Roll it and seal.
2. Transfer it to the air fryer basket. Spray oil on the chicken breast roll. Cook for 18 minutes on both side at 375^0F.
3. Serve the chicken breast roll immediately as an appetizer.

Nutritional value per serving:

Calories: 170kcal, Fat: 4g, Carb: 0g, Proteins: 35g

Chicken Breast Sticks Crispy

This crispy chicken recipe will leave you drooling for more. outturn on your air fryer and start cooking.
Prep time and cooking time: 30 minutes|
Serves: 4

Ingredients To Use:

- 1 cup of panko bread crumbs
- 1 grated lemon zest
- 1 pound of boneless and skinless chicken breast
- 3/4 cup of white flour
- Black pepper and salt
- 1 tsp. of sweet paprika
- 1 egg
- 1/2 tbsp. of olive oil

Step-by-Step Directions to Cook It:

1. Mix salt, lemon zest, paprika, pepper, and flour in a bowl.
2. Put the egg in a separate bowl and whisk.
3. Put panko bread crumbs in another bowl. Coat the chicken in flour mixture, egg,

and panko. Transfer them to the air fryer basket. Spray oil on them. Cook for 9 minutes on both sides at 400^0F.
4. Place them on a platter, serve immediately as an appetizer.

Nutritional value per serving:

Calories: 168kcal, Fat: 4g, Carb: 0g, Proteins: 33g

Beef Rolls

Beef roll is an amazing appetizer with high protein.
Prep time and cooking time: 25 minutes|
Serves: 4

Ingredients To Use:

- 1 cup of baby spinach
- 3 tbsp. of pesto
- 2 pounds of flattened beef steak
- 6 slices of provolone cheese
- Black pepper and salt
- 3 ounces of chopped, roasted red bell pepper.

Step-by-Step Directions to Cook It:

1. Place the flattened beef steak on a flat surface, put pesto over it. Put bell peppers, cheese, pepper, spinach, and salt.
2. Roll the beefsteak, use a toothpick to hold it, sprinkle pepper and salt again.
3. Transfer it to the air fryer basket. Cook for 14 minutes at 400^0F.
4. Allow cooling before serving as an appetizer.

Nutritional value per serving:

Calories: 296kcal, Fat: 17g, Carb: 5g, Proteins: 36g

Empanadas

This empanadas recipe combines beef and other flavor-rich ingredients to make a filling.

Prep time and cooking time: 35 minutes|
Serves: 4

- 1 chopped onion, yellow
- 1 chopped green bell pepper
- 1 empanada shells, package
- 4cup of tomato salsa
- 1 tbsp. of olive oil
- 1/2 tsp. of ground cumin
- Black pepper and salt
- 1 pound of ground beef meat
- 2 cloves of garlic
- 1 egg yolk and 1 tbsp. of water

Step-by-Step Directions to Cook It:

1. Put oil in a pan and heat over medium heat. Add beef, make it brown on every side.
2. Add bell pepper, onion, pepper, tomato salsa, garlic, and salt. Cook for about 14 minutes.
3. Put the meat into empanadas shells. Rub egg wash all over it and seal.
4. Put it in the steam basket in the air fryer. Cook for 10 minutes at 350⁰F.
5. Serve immediately in a bowl as an appetizer.

Nutritional value per serving:

Calories: 300kcal, Fat: 20g, Carb: 33g, Proteins: 15g

Lamb Meatballs

Lamb is rich in protein, and as meatballs, it can serve as a fantastic appetizer.
Prep time and cooking time: 20 minutes|
Serves: 10

Ingredients To Use:

- 1 slice of toasted, crumbled bread
- 4 ounces of minced lamb meat
- 1/2 tbsp. of grated lemon peels
- Black pepper and salt

- 1 tbsp. of chopped oregano
- 4 ounces of minced lamb meat

Step-by-Step Directions to Cook It:

1. Mix salt, feta, lemon peels, bread crumbs, pepper, and oregano in a bowl. Scoop into 10 meatball shape.
2. Transfer it to the air fryer basket. Cook for 8-10 minutes at 400⁰F.
3. Serve immediately as an appetizer.

Nutritional value per serving:

Calories: 250kcal, Fat: 15g, Carb: 22g, Proteins: 35g

Beef Party Rolls

When white wine is used to make beef party rolls, it results in an exceptional taste.
Prep time and cooking time: 35 minutes|
Serves: 4

Ingredients To Use:

- 1 tbsp. of melted butter
- 7 ounces of white wine
- Black pepper and salt
- 4 slices of ham
- 4 cutlets of beef
- 14 ounces of beef stock
- 8 sage leaves

Step-by-Step Directions to Cook It:

1. Put beef stock in a pan and heat over medium heat. Put wine and cook. For some minutes.
2. Sprinkle pepper and salt over cutlets. Pour sage on it and roll it in ham slices.
3. Rub butter on rolls. Transfer it to the air fryer basket. Cook for about 15 minutes at 400⁰F.
4. Serve immediately with gravy.

Nutritional value per serving:

Calories: 296kcal, Fat: 16g, Carb: 2g, Proteins: 36g

Pork Rolls

Pork rolls smell good and taste great. The cumin and chili powder introduces a sharp spicy taste to the rolls
Prep time and cooking time: 50 minutes|
Serves: 4

Ingredients To Use:

- 1 chopped red onion
- 1 tsp. of cinnamon powder
- 2 tbsp. of olive oil
- 15 ounces of pork fillet
- 1 clove of garlic
- 1-1/2 tsp. of ground cumin
- 1/2 tsp. of chili powder
- 2 tbsp. of olive oil
- 3 tbsp. of chopped parsley

Step-by-Step Directions to Cook It:

1. Mix salt, onion, garlic, chili powder, cinnamon powder, and parsley. Add cumin, oil, and pepper. Mix well.
2. Place the pork fillet on a flat surface. Use a meat tenderizer to flatten it.
3. Put the onions on the pork and roll it tight.
4. Transfer the rolled pork to the air fryer basket. Cook at 360^0F for 30-35 minutes.
5. Serve immediately as an appetizer.

Nutritional value per serving:

Calories: 290kcal, Fat: 15g, Carb: 0g, Proteins: 30g

Beef Patties

You don't need to queue at a burger shop before you get a great burger. You can air-fry an even healthier, tastier burger by making patties with this recipe.
Prep time and cooking time: 20 minutes|
Serves: 4

Ingredients To Use:

- 1 chopped leek
- 14 ounces of minced beef
- 1/2 tsp. of ground nutmeg
- 2 tbsp. of ham
- Black pepper and salt
- 3 tbsp. of bread crumbs

Step-by-Step Directions to Cook It:

1. Mix pepper, nutmeg, leek, salt, beef, bread crumbs, and ham in a bowl. Scoop into small patties.
2. Transfer it to the basket that fits the air fryer. Cook for about 8 minutes at 400^0F.
3. Serve immediately as an appetizer.

Nutritional value per serving:

Calories: 255kcal, Fat: 11g, Carb: 0.8g, Proteins: 16g

Pepper Rolls

Do you love your peppers without a kick? Then, this is the perfect recipe for you.
Prep time and cooking time: 20 minutes|
Serves: 8

Ingredients To Use:

- 1 chopped green onion
- 1 halved orange bell pepper
- 4 ounces of crumbled feta cheese
- 2 tbsp. of chopped of oregano
- 1 halved bell pepper, yellow
- Black pepper and salt

Step-by-Step Directions to Cook It:

1. Mix oregano, pepper, onion, salt, and cheese in a bowl. Mix well
2. Put the halves bell pepper in the air fryer basket. Cook for 10 minutes at 400^0F.
3. Put the cheese mixture in halved bell pepper and roll. Use a toothpick to hold it.
4. Serve immediately as an appetizer.

Nutritional value per serving:

Calories: 100kcal, Fat: 5g, Carb: 10g, Proteins: 12g

Easy Stuffed Pepper

This is another recipe that combines peppers with some rice and cheese.
Prep time and cooking time: 20 minutes|
Serves: 8

Ingredients To Use:

- 1 tbsp. of olive oil
- 1 cup of cooked white rice
- 3.5 ounces of goat cheese in 8 pieces
- 8 bell peppers, small
- Black pepper and salt

Step-by-Step Directions to Cook It:

1. Mix salt, cheese, rice, pepper, and oil in a bowl. Mix well.
2. Put goat cheese in the pepper and stuff well. Put it in the air fryer basket.
3. Cook for 8 minutes at 400^{0}F. Serve immediately as an appetizer.

Nutritional value per serving:

Calories: 300kcal, Fat: 11g, Carb: 33g, Proteins: 27g

Herbed Tomato Appetizer

Tomato has never tasted better than with this well-seasoned tomato appetizer recipe.
Prep time and cooking time: 30 minutes|
Serves: 2

Ingredients To Use:

- 1 tsp. of dried basil
- Cooking spray
- 1 tsp. of rosemary
- Black pepper and salt
- 2 halved tomatoes
- 1 tsp. of parsley
- 1 tsp. of oregano

Step-by-Step Directions to Cook It:

1. Drizzle the halved tomato with cooking spray. Add basil, rosemary, salt, oregano, parsley, and pepper.
2. Transfer to the air fryer basket. Cook for 20 minutes at 320^{0}F.
3. Serve immediately as an appetizer.

Nutritional value per serving:

Calories: 90kcal, Fat: 5g, Carb: 6g, Proteins: 5g

Olive Pepperoni Snack

Are you ready for a combination of unusual but delicious ingredients? Then this is the right recipe for you. Here, you get to combine olives, tomato pesto, pepperoni, cheese and many more.
Prep time and cooking time: 15 minutes|
Serves: 6

Ingredients To Use:

- 1 tbsp. of chopped basil
- 2 tbsp. of tomato pesto, sun-dried
- 8 minced black olives
- 4 ounces of cream cheese
- Black pepper and salt
- 14 slices of chopped pepperoni

Step-by-Step Directions to Cook It:

1. Mix pepper, pesto, cream cheese, basil, salt, black olives, and pepperoni in a bowl. Mix well. Scoop in a small ball shape and transfer them to the air fryer basket.
2. Cook for 5 minutes at 350^{0}F. Serve immediately as snacks.

Nutritional value per serving:

Calories: 90kcal, Fat: 3g, Carb: 8g, Proteins: 6g

Jalapeno Balls

Jalapeno balls are awesome. It's spicy, meaty, and delicious.
Prep time and cooking time: 15 minutes|
Serves: 3

Ingredients To Use:

- 1 chopped jalapeno pepper
- 3 slices of cooked and crumbled bacon
- 1/4 tsp. of garlic powder
- Black pepper and salt
- 3 ounces of cream cheese
- 1/2 tsp. of dried parsley
- 1/4 tsp. of onion powder

Step-by-Step Directions to Cook It:

1. Mix jalapeno pepper, garlic powder, salt, parsley in a bowl. Add pepper, onion powder, and bacon. Mix well.
2. Scoop into a small ball shape. Transfer to the air fryer basket. Cook for 5 minutes at 350^{0}F.
3. Serve immediately as an appetizer.

Nutritional value per serving:

Calories: 130kcal, Fat: 6g, Carb: 10g, Proteins: 12g

Wrapped Shrimp

Wrapped shrimp is an incredible appetizer; it's very nutritious and tasty.
Prep time and cooking time: 20 minutes|
Serves: 16

Ingredients To Use:

- 11 slices of prosciutto
- 2 tbsp. of olive oil
- 1/3 cup of red wine
- 1 tbsp. of chopped mint
- 10 ounces of peeled and deveined shrimp, cooked
- 1/3 cup of ground blackberries

Step-by-Step Directions to Cook It:

1. Put shrimps inside slices of prosciutto. Spray oil on them. Put it in the air fryer. Cook for about 8 minutes at 390^{0}F.
2. Get a pan and heat over medium heat, put ground blackberries, add wine, and mint. Cook for about 3 minutes and remove the heat.
3. Set shrimp in the dish. Serve with blackberry sauce.

Nutritional value per serving:

Calories: 225kcal, Fat: 15g, Carb: 2g, Proteins: 20g

Broccoli Patties

For vegetarians who don't love burgers, here is an amazing veggie patties recipe to help you satisfy those cravings.
Prep time and cooking time: 20 minutes|
Serves: 12

Ingredients To Use:

- 1 tsp. of garlic powder
- 4 cups of broccoli florets
- 2 egg
- 1/2 tsp. of baking soda
- 1 tsp. of paprika
- 2 cups of grated cheddar cheese
- 1-1/2 cup of almond flour
- 1/2 tsp. of apple cider vinegar
- 1/4 cup of olive oil
- Black pepper and salt

Step-by-Step Directions to Cook It:

1. In a food processor, put broccoli floret, pepper, and salt. Blend well. Put the mixture in a bowl.
2. Add baking soda, almond flour, pepper, eggs. Add paprika, oil, salt, cheese, vinegar. Stir well. Scoop into 12 patties shapes.
3. Put them in the air fryer basket. Cook for

about 10 minutes at 350⁰F.
4.   Serve the patties as an appetizer.

Calories: 200kcal, Fat:14 g, Carb: 22g,
Proteins: 13g

Meat-Stuffed Peppers

If you want more than rice in your peppers,
here is an incredible recipe for meat lovers.
Prep time and cooking time: 30 minutes|
Serves: 6

Ingredients To Use:
- 1 pound of ground beef meat
- 1 pound of halved mini bell pepper
- 1/4 tsp. of red pepper flakes
- Black pepper and salt
- 1 tbsp. of chili powder
- 1/2 tsp. of dried oregano
- 1 tsp. of ground cumin
- 1 tsp. of sweet paprika
- 1-1/2 cup of shredded cheese
- Sour cream
- 1 tsp. of garlic powder

Step-by-Step Directions to Cook It:
1.   Mix paprika, cumin, chili powder, salt,
      and garlic powder in a bowl. Add pepper
      flakes.
2.   Heat a pan over medium heat. Put beef
      and stir. Cook for about 10 minutes until
      it is brown. Put the chili powder mixture.
      Remove the heat. Put the mixture inside
      halved pepper.
3.   Spray cheese on it. Put them in the air
      fryer basket. Cook for 6 minutes at 350⁰F.
4.   Serve immediately with sour cream.

Nutritional value per serving:

Calories: 300kcal, Fat: 10g, Carb: 20g,
Proteins: 25g

Zucchini Cheese Snack

Zucchini is also called courgette, which is a
very healthy fruit. It is high in antioxidants
and makes a nutritious appetizer.
Prep time and cooking time: 20 minutes|
Serves: 4

Ingredients To Use:
- 1 sliced zucchini
- 1 cup of shredded mozzarella
- Cooking spray
- 1/4 cup of tomato sauce
- Cumin
- Black pepper and salt.

Step-by-Step Directions to Cook It:
1.   Place zucchini in the air fryer basket.
      Drizzle with cooking spray. Put tomato
      sauce all over it. Sprinkle cumin, salt,
      pepper, and mozzarella.
2.   Cook for about 8 minutes at 320⁰F.
3.   Serve immediately as a snack.

Nutritional value per serving:

Calories: 120kcal, Fat: 1g, Carb: 6g, Proteins:
5g

Spinach Balls

Spinach as balls? Woah! You're in for a
delicious snack that is seasoned with the
perfect spices.
Prep time and cooking time: 20 minutes|
Serves: 30

Ingredients To Use:
- 1 cup of flour
- 1 tsp. of garlic powder
- 1/3 cup of grated parmesan
- 4 tbsp. of melted butter
- 3 tbsp. of whipping cream
- 1/4 tsp. of ground nutmeg
- 16 ounces of spinach
- 1 tbsp. of onion powder

- 2 eggs
- Black pepper and salt
- 1 cup of flour

1. Put eggs, feta cheese, nutmeg, and onion in a blender. Add spinach, whipping cream, pepper, flour, parmesan, butter, garlic, and salt. Blend well. Leave the mixture in the refrigerator for about 10 minutes.
2. Scoop the spinach into a ball shape in 30 pieces. Put it in the air fryer basket.
3. Cook for about 7 minutes at 300^0F.
4. Serve immediately as an appetizer.

Nutritional value per serving:

Calories: 50kcal, Fat: 6g, Carb: 3g, Proteins: 5g

Mushroom Appetizer

Mushrooms always taste great as meals or appetizers, and this is no different.
Prep time and cooking time: 20 minutes| Serves: 4

Ingredients To Use:

- 1 tsp. of curry powder
- 1 chopped onion, small and yellow
- 1/4 cup of mayonnaise
- 1/2 cup of shredded Mexican cheese
- 1 cup of cooked and deveined shrimps
- 24 ounces of white mushroom caps
- 1/4 cup of sour cream
- 1 tsp. of garlic powder
- 4 ounces of soft cream cheese
- Black pepper and salt.

Step-by-Step Directions to Cook It:

1. Mix cream cheese, mayonnaise, shrimps, and garlic powder in a bowl. Add sour cream, pepper, onion, Mexican cheese, curry powder, and salt. Sir well.
2. Put mushroom inside the mixture.

Transfer it to the air fryer basket. Cook for about 10 minutes at 300^0F.
3. Serve immediately as an appetizer.

Nutritional value per serving:

Calories: 400kcal, Fat: 30g, Carb: 20g, Proteins: 15g

Party Cheesy Wings

Party cheesy wing is a delightful meal. The chicken wings are mixed with cheese to create a great and perfect appetizer.
Prep time and cooking time: 25 minutes| Serves: 6

Ingredients To Use:

- 1 tsp. of garlic powder
- 6 pounds of halved chicken wings
- 1/2 cup of grated parmesan cheese
- Black pepper and salt
- 1 egg
- 1/2 tsp. of Italian seasoning
- Crushed red pepper flakes
- 2 tbsp. of butter

Step-by-Step Directions to Cook It:

1. Place the chicken wings on the air fryer basket. Cook for about 9 minutes at 390^0F.
2. Blend egg, garlic powder, butter, pepper flakes, salt, cheese, pepper, and Italian seasoning. Blend well.
3. Pour the cheese mixture on the chicken wings. Cook for about 3 minutes at 390^0F.
4. Serve immediately as an appetizer.

Nutritional value per serving:

Calories: 200kcal, Fat: 10g, Carb: 1g, Proteins: 20g

Cheese Sticks

Perfect comfort food for days when you

crave for sweet, delicious snacks.
Prep time and cooking time: 1 hour 20 minutes| Serves: 15

- 1 cup of grated parmesan
- 2 eggs
- 1 minced clove of garlic
- Black pepper and salt
- 1 tbsp. of Italian seasoning
- 8 strings of mozzarella cheese
- Cooking spray

Step-by-Step Directions to Cook It:

1. Mix pepper, garlic, salt, parmesan, and Italian seasoning in a bowl.
2. In another bowl, put the egg and whisk.
3. Put mozzarella in the egg mixture. Transfer to the cheese mixture. Put it inside egg again and then parmesan mixture. Put them in the refrigerator for about 1 hour.
4. Drizzle the cheese sticks with cooking spray. Transfer it to the air fryer. Cook for about 8 minutes at 390^{0}F.
5. Serve immediately as an appetizer.

Nutritional value per serving:

Calories: 400kcal, Fat: 35g, Carb: 2g, Proteins: 26g

Bacon Snack

Bacon in a meal is great but it is even greater as a snack.
Prep time and cooking time: 40 minutes| Serves: 16

Ingredients To Use:

- 1 tbsp. of avocado
- 1/2 tsp. of cinnamon powder
- 1 tsp. of maple extract
- 16 slices of bacon
- 3 ounces of avocado oil

Step-by-Step Directions to Cook It:

1. Put slices of bacon on the air fryer basket. Spray cinnamon powder on it. Cook for about 30 minutes at 300^{0}F.
2. Put oil inside a pot and heat over medium heat. Put chocolate and mix until the chocolate melts. Put maple extract. Remove the heat and allow it to cool down.
3. Put the bacon inside the chocolate mixture. Put it on a platter and allow it to cool down.
4. Serve when it is cold as a snack.

Nutritional value per serving:

Calories: 540kcal, Fat: 45g, Carb: 2g, Proteins: 40g

Chicken Rolls

You can enjoy these chicken rolls with a beer and some TV shows.
Prep time and cooking time: 2 hours 20 minutes| Serves: 12

Ingredients To Use:

- 2 chopped green onions
- Cooking spray
- 4 ounces of crumbled blue cheese
- 12 wrappers of egg roll
- 2 cups of cooked and chopped chicken
- 1/2 cup of tomato sauce
- Black pepper and salt
- 2 chopped celery stalks

Step-by-Step Directions to Cook It:

1. Mix pepper, tomato sauce, blue cheese, and celery in a bowl. Add chicken meat, green onion, and salt.
2. Put the egg wrappers on a flat surface. Put the chicken mixture on it. Roll the wrapper and seal the edges.
3. Put the chicken rolls on the air fryer basket. Cook for about 10 minutes at

350^0F.

4. Serve immediately as an appetizer.

Nutritional value per serving:

Calories: 260kcal, Fat: 6g, Carb: 40g, Proteins: 15g

Celery and Kale Crackers

This recipe creates an incredibly delicious snack.
Prep time and cooking time: 30 minutes|
Serves: 6

Ingredients To Use:

- 1 bunch of chopped basil
- 2 cups of ground flax seed
- 4 bunches of chopped kale
- 4 cloves of minced garlic
- 2 cups of overnight soaked flaxseed, drained
- 1/2 bunch of chopped celery
- 1/3 cup of olive oil

Step-by-Step Directions to Cook It:

1. Mix kale, garlic, celery, ground flaxseed, and celery in a food processor. Blend well.
2. Put soaked flaxseed and oil, then blend again. Pour the mixture on a pan that fits the air fryer.
3. Cook for about 20 minutes at 380^0F.
4. Serve immediately as an appetizer.

Nutritional value per serving:

Calories: 145kcal, Fat: 5g, Carb: 7g, Proteins: 5g

Egg White chips

Egg white chips may seem weird at first, but you won't feel this way when you taste it's delicious crunchiness.
Prep time and cooking time: 15 minutes|
Serves: 2

Ingredients To Use:

- 4 egg whites
- 1/2 tbsp. of water
- Black pepper and salt
- 2 tbsp of shredded parmesan

Step-by-Step Directions to Cook It:

1. Mix pepper, egg whites, water, and salt in a bowl. Mix well.
2. Scoop the mixture into a muffin pan in the air fryer. Spray cheese on it. Cook for 8 minutes at 350^0F.
3. Serve immediately as a snack.

Nutritional value per serving:

Calories: 50kcal, Fat: 0.3g, Carb: 0.8g, Proteins: 12g

Tuna Cake

A cake infused with seafood flavor. It tastes just right.
Prep time and cooking time: 20 minutes|
Serves: 12

Ingredients To Use:

- 1 tsp. of garlic powder
- 15 ounces of canned tuna
- 1/2 tsp. of dried dill
- Black pepper and salt
- 1/2 cup of chopped red onion
- Cooking spray
- 3 eggs
- 1 tsp. of dried parsley

Step-by-Step Directions to Cook It:

1. Mix pepper, parsley, eggs, and onion in a bowl. Add dill, salt, garlic, and tuna. Make a medium cake shape out of it.
2. Put the tuna in the basket that fits the air fryer. Drizzle with cooking spray. Cook for 10 minutes at 350^0F.
3. Serve immediately as an appetizer.

Nutritional value per serving:

Calories: 132kcal, Fat: 5g, Carb: 6g, Proteins: 17g

Shrimp and Calamari Snack

Get a slice of the sea with this seafood combination recipe.

Prep time and cooking time: 30 minutes| Serves: 2

Ingredients To Use:

- 1 tsp. of tomato paste
- 8 ounces of calamari
- 1 tsp. of lemon juice
- 2 tbsp. of chopped avocado
- 7 ounces of deveined shrimps
- 1tbsp of olive oil
- ½ tsp. of turmeric powder
- Worcestershire sauce
- 1 tbsp. of mayonnaise
- Black pepper and salt
- 3 tbsp. of white flour
- 1 egg

Step-by-Step Directions to Cook It:

1. Put oil and egg in a bowl and whisk. Add shrimps and calamari rings.
2. Get another bowl, put pepper, flour, turmeric, and salt. Stir well.
3. Put shrimps and calamari in the flour mixture. Transfer it to the air fryer basket. Cook for about 9 minutes at 350⁰F.
4. Get another bowl, put mayonnaise, tomato paste, and avocado. Use a fork to mash well. Add lemon juice, pepper, Worcestershire sauce, and pepper. Stir well.
5. Serve shrimps and calamari with sauce.

Nutritional value per serving:

Calories: 131kcal, Fat: 6g, Carb: 6g, Proteins: 17g

Chapter 9: Dessert Recipes

Tasty Banana Cake

Banana cake has an irresistible taste and smell. Try it out with your air fryer when you are in the mood for a delicious dessert.
Prep time and cooking time: 40 minutes|
Serves: 4

Ingredients To Use:

- 1 tsp. of baking powder
- 1 egg
- 1 cup of flour
- 1 tbsp. of soft butter
- 1 peeled banana
- 1/2 tsp. of cinnamon powder
- 1/3 cup of brown sugar
- Cooking spray
- 2 tbsp. of honey

Step-by-Step Directions to Cook It:

1. Grease a cake pan with cooking spray.
2. Add honey, flour, and sugar to a bowl. Add banana, cinnamon, whisk, and baking powder. Mix thoroughly.
3. Pour the mixture inside the greased cake pan.
4. Set the air fryer to 350^{0}F. Cook for 30 minutes.
5. Serve the banana cake hot or let it cool down before serving.

Nutritional value per serving:

Calories: 230kcal, Fat: 5g, Carb: 1.2g, Proteins: 4.3g

Cheesecake

Vanilla is the main ingredient in this cheesecake recipe. It results in a lasting flavor and reforms the taste of the dessert.

Prep time and cooking time: 25 minutes|
Serves: 13

Ingredients To Use:

- 1 cup of crumbled crackers
- 2 eggs
- 1 pound of cream cheese
- 2 tbsp. of butter
- 4 tbsp. of sugar
- 1/2 tsp. of vanilla extract

Step-by-Step Directions to Cook It:

1. Mix the butter and crackers in a bowl.
2. Line the mixture on the cake pan. Set the air fryer to a temperature of 350^{0}F. Cook for 4 minutes.
3. In another bowl, mix the vanilla and sugar. Add the eggs and cream cheese, mix thoroughly.
4. Spread the mixture on the crackers crust. Lower the air fryer temperature to 310^{0}F, cook for 15 minutes.
5. Serve immediately or allow to cool before serving.

Nutritional value per serving:

Calories: 250kcal, Fat: 13g, Carb: 21g, Proteins: 4g

Bread Pudding

Bread pudding is an amazing recipe with a pleasant taste.
Prep time and cooking time: 70 minutes|
Serves: 5

Ingredients To Use:

- 1/2 cup of raisins
- 4 egg yolks
- 1/2 cup of chocolate chips

- 6 crumbled glazed doughnuts
- 1 cup of cherries
- 1/4 cup of sugar
- 1-1/2 cups of whipping cream

Step-by-Step Directions to Cook It:

1. Mix the whipping cream, cherries, and egg yolks in a bowl.
2. Get another bowl, add the chocolate chips, doughnuts, and sugar. Stir.
3. Combine the two mixtures in a separate bowl and add it to a greased pan that can fit your air fryer. Set the temperature to 310^0 and cook for 1 hour.
4. Leave to cool before serving.

Nutritional value per serving:

Calories: 300kcal, Fat: 9g, Carb: 24g, Proteins: 11g

Amaretto and Bread Dough

Amaretto has a sweet flavor and is best taken with your favorite fruit juice or chilled beer.
Prep time and cooking time: 25 minutes| Serves: 12

Ingredients To Use:

- 1 cup of sugar
- 1 cup of heavy cream
- 2 tbsp. of amaretto liqueur
- 1 pound of bread dough
- 12 ounces of chocolate chips
- 1/2 cup of butter

Step-by-Step Directions to Cook It:

1. Roll the bread dough and slice it into 19-20 pieces. Cut each piece into half.
2. Rub the dough with butter and spray with sugar, then put it in the air fryer basket. Set the air fryer to 350^0F and cook for 5 minutes each on both sides.
3. Put heavy cream in a pan and heat, mix

chocolate chips and stir until they melt. Add liqueur and stir.
4. Serve immediately with sauce.

Nutritional value per serving:

Calories: 201kcal, Fat: 2g, Carb: 7g, Proteins: 7g

Cream Cheese Dip in Cinnamon Rolls

This dessert is a classic one and is usually prepared for a special family occasion.
Preparation time and cooking time: 2 hours 15 minutes | Serves: 7

Ingredients To Use:

- 2 cups of sugar
- 1-1/2 tbsp. of cinnamon
- 2-1/4 cup of butter
- 1 pound of bread dough
- 1/2 tsp. of vanilla
- 4 ounces of cream cheese

Step-by-Step Directions to Cook It:

1. Roll the bread dough on a flat floured surface. Cut in a rectangle shape, rub 1/4 cup of butter on the dough.
2. Get a bowl, mix the sugar and cinnamon. Stir and sprinkle it over the dough. Roll the dough. Seal the dough, cut into 7 pieces.
3. Leave the dough rolls for 2 hours to ferment. Put the roll on the air fryer's basket. Set the air fryer temperature to 350^0F, cook on both sides for 4 minutes.
4. In another bowl, mix the sugar, cream cheese, vanilla, and butter. Stir well.
5. Serve the cream cheese mixture dip in a cinnamon roll.

Nutritional value per serving:

Calories: 201kcal, Fat: 2g, Carb: 5.5g, Proteins: 6.2g

Pumpkin Pie

Pumpkin is rich in antioxidants and still retains its nutrients when baked with an air fryer. Try this dessert and keep eating healthy with your air fryer.
Preparation time and cooking time: 25 minutes| Serves: 9

Ingredients To Use:

- 1 tbsp. of butter
- 3.5 ounces of pumpkin flesh
- 2 tbsp. of sugar
- 5 tbsp. of water
- 1 egg
- 1 tsp. of mixed spice
- 2 tbsp. of flour
- 1 tsp. of nutmeg

Step-by-Step Directions to Cook It:

1. To a pot, add 3 ounces of water, egg, spice, nutmeg. Add pumpkin, 1 tbsp. of sugar, and boil for about 20 minutes.
2. Remove the mixture from heat and blend.
3. Mix 2 tbsp. of water, flour, 1 tbsp. of sugar, and butter in a bowl. Press the dough until it is smooth.
4. Grease the air fryer's pan with butter, place the dough in the pan. Fill the dough with pumpkin filling. Put it on the air fryer's basket. Set the air fryer temperature to 360^0F, cook for 15 minutes.
5. Serve immediately or leave to cool.

Nutritional value per serving:

Calories: 201kcal, Fat: 6g, Carb: 6g, Proteins: 7g

Wrapped Pears

Pear is a sweet fruit that can be enjoyed with oats or bread. Mixing pears with vanilla custard is an incredible combination.
Prep time and cooking time: 25 minutes|
Serves: 5

Ingredients To Use:

- 1 egg
- 2 tbsp. of sugar
- 4 puff of pastry sheets
- 2 pears
- 1/2 tsp. of cinnamon powder
- 14 ounces of vanilla custard

Step-by-Step Directions to Cook It:

1. Set the pastry slices on the flat surface. Put the vanilla custard in the center. Put on pears and wrap.
2. Rub the pear with egg, sprinkle it with cinnamon and sugar. Put it in the air fryer's basket. Set the air fryer to a temperature of 320^0F, cook for 15 minutes.
3. Serve immediately.

Nutritional value per serving:

Calories: 199kcal, Fat: 2g, Carb: 15g, Proteins: 3g

Strawberry Doughnut

A delicious dessert that is designed to put you in a good mood.
Prrep time and cooking time: 25 minutes|
Serves: 4

Ingredients To Use:

- 1 egg
- 1 tbsp. of brown sugar
- 4-1/2 tbsps. of butter
- 3.5 ounces of icing sugar
- 1 tbsp. of white sugar
- 1 tbsp. of whipped cream
- 1 tbsp. of brown sugar
- 1/2 tsp. of pink coloring
- 4 ounces of whole milk
- 1/4 cup of strawberries

- 1 tsp. of baking powder

1. Mix 1 tbsp. of white sugar, butter, flour, and 1 tbsp. of brown sugar in a bowl and stir.
2. In another bowl, put 1-1/2 tbsp. of butter, milk, and egg. Mix thoroughly.
3. Combine the two mixtures. Mix well. Cut into a doughnut shape. Transfer to the air fryer's basket. Set the air fryer to a temperature of 360^{0}F, cook for 15 minutes.
4. In a bowl, mix the icing sugar, whipped cream, 1 tbsp. of butter. Add the strawberry puree and food coloring. Stir thoroughly.
5. Place the doughnut on a plate and top with strawberry icing.

Nutritional value per serving:

Calories: 250kcal, Fat: 13g, Carb: 33g, Proteins: 5g

Air Fried Banana

Banana is an edible fruit that contains many nutrients like vitamins, magnesium, copper, and potassium. It also contains a high carbohydrate content.
Prep time and cooking time: 25 minutes|
Serves: 4

Ingredients To Use:

- 1 cup of panko
- 2 eggs
- 1/2 cup of cornflour
- 3 Tbsp. of butter
- 8 bananas
- 3 Tbsp. of cinnamon sugar

Step-by-Step Directions to Cook It:

1. Put the butter in a pan. Heat it over medium heat. Put in the panko and stir. Leave to cook for about 4 minutes. Move

it into another bowl.
2. Add the egg to the panko mixture, roll it in flour. Place it on the air fryer's basket. Sprinkle with cinnamon sugar. Set the air fryer to 280^{0}F, leave to cook for 10 minutes.
3. Serve immediately.

Nutritional value per serving:

Calories: 165kcal, Fat: 2g, Carb: 33g, Proteins: 5g

Cocoa Cake

The cocoa seed is rich in polyphenol and has many nutritional benefits. It is used to make cocoa powder, cocoa butter, and chocolate.
Prep time and cooking time: 30 minutes|
Serves: 6

Ingredients To Use:

- 1 tsp. of cocoa powder
- 3 egg
- 1/2 tsp. of lemon juice
- 3.5 ounces of butter
- 3 ounces of flour
- 3 ounces of sugar

Step-by-Step Directions to Cook It:

1. Mix the cocoa powder and 1 tbsp of butter in a bowl.
2. In a separate bowl, put sugar, flour, remaining butter, and lemon juice. Mix thoroughly. Pour half of the mixture into a pan that fits the air fryer.
3. Spread half of the cocoa mixture on the pan, put the remaining flour mixture. Pour the remaining cocoa mixture.
4. Set the air fryer to 360^{0}F, cook for 17 minutes.
5. Serve immediately or leave to cool before serving.

Calories: 340kcal, Fat: 12g, Carb: 26g, Proteins: 6g

Chocolate Cake

Chocolate is one of the end-product of cocoa. It has a sweet taste and great smell.
Prep time and cooking time: 40 minutes| Serves: 11

Ingredients To Use:

- 1 tsp. of baking soda
- 8 ounces of pumpkin puree
- 3/4 cup of white flour
- 3/4 cup of sugar
- 2 tbsp. of canola oil
- 1 egg
- 3/4 cup of wheat flour, whole
- Cooking spray
- 1/2 cup of Greek yogurt
- 1 banana
- 2/3 cup of chocolate chips
- 1/2 tsp. of vanilla extract

Step-by-Step Directions to Cook It:

1. Mix the whole wheat flour, powder, salt, and pumpkin spice in a bowl. Add the white flour and baking soda. Stir well.
2. Get another bowl, put in banana, vanilla, egg, and oil. Add the pumpkin puree, sugar, and yogurt. Stir well.
3. Transfer the 2 mixtures into another bowl, put chocolate chips and mix. Pour the mixtures on a greased pan that fits the air fryer.
4. Set the air fryer to 330^0F and cook for about 30 minutes.
5. Allow cooling before serving.

Nutritional value per serving:

Calories: 233kcal, Fat: 8g, Carb: 30g, Proteins: 5g

Apple bread

Apple is a healthy fruit that reduces the risk of disease. It benefits the heart and is rich in vitamins and antioxidants.
Prep time and cooking time: 50 minutes| Serves: 6

Ingredients To Use:

- 1 cup of sugar
- 1 cup of water
- 3 cups of canned apple
- 1 tbsp. of baking powder
- 2 eggs
- 1 tbsp. of apple pie spice
- 1 stick of butter
- 1 tbsp. of vanilla

Step-by-Step Directions to Cook It:

1. Mix sugar, 1 butter stick, and egg in a bowl. Add the apple pie spice. Mix thoroughly or use a mixer.
2. Add cubed apples and mix.
3. Mix the flour and baking powder in another bowl.
4. Transfer the 2 mixtures into another bowl and stir. Pour the mixture into a spring pan.
5. Set the spring pan in the air fryer at a temperature of 320^0F. Cook for 40 minutes.
6. Serve immediately or let it cool before serving.

Nutritional value per serving:

Calories: 193kcal, Fat: 7g, Carb: 15g, Proteins: 8g

Banana Bread

Bread is made from a mixture of water and flour dough. Banana bread is the combination of mashed banana with water and flour.

Prep time and cooking time: 50 minutes|
Serves: 6

Ingredients To Use:

- 1 egg
- 1/3 cup of milk
- 1-1/2 cups of flour
- 1 tsp. of vanilla extract
- 2 bananas
- 1-1/2 tsp. of cream tartar
- 1 tsp. of baking powder
- 1/2 tsp. of baking soda
- Cooking spray
- 1/3 cup of butter

Step-by-Step Directions to Cook It:

1. Mix sugar, egg, bananas, and butter in a bowl. Add in cream tartar and vanilla. Stir well.
2. Get another bowl, mix the baking powder, flour, and baking soda.
3. Transfer the 2 mixtures into another bowl. Pour the mixture on a greased cake pan using cooking spray.
4. Place the pan in the air fryer, set the temperature to 320^0F, leave to cook for about 40 minutes.
5. Leave to cool. Serve by slicing.

Nutritional value per serving:

Calories: 293kcal, Fat: 8g, Carb: 30g, Proteins: 5g

Lava Cakes

Lava cake can be made in different ways by using a combination of different ingredients. In this recipe, the major ingredient is cocoa powder.
Prep time and cooking time: 30 minutes|
Serves: 3

Ingredients To Use:

- 1 tbsp. of cocoa powder
- 4 tbsp. of milk

- 1 egg
- 2 tbsp. of olive oil
- 4 tbsp. of flour
- 1/2 tsp. of baking powder
- 4 tbsp. of sugar
- 1/2 tsp. of orange zest

Step-by-Step Directions to Cook It:

1. Mix the oil, salt, baking powder, and milk in a bowl. Add sugar, cocoa powder, orange zest, and egg. Mix thoroughly and transfer to a greased baking dish.
2. Put the baking dish to the air fryer. Cook at a temperature of 320^0F for about 20 minutes.
3. Serve immediately or allow to cool.

Nutritional value per serving:

Calories: 200kcal, Fat: 8g, Carb: 25g, Proteins: 5g

Crispy Apples

This dessert is made from sliced apple and cinnamon powder. The cinnamon powder makes the air-fried apple crispy.
Prep time and cooking time: 20 minutes|
Serves: 4

Ingredients To Use:

- 1 tbsp. of maple syrup
- 2 tsp. of cinnamon powder
- 1/4 cup of flour
- 5 cored and chunk apples
- 3/4 cup of rolled oats
- 4 tbsp. of butter
- 1/4 cup of brown sugar
- 1/2 cup of water
- 1/2 tsp. of nutmeg powder

Step-by-Step Directions to Cook It:

1. Place apples in an air fryer sized pan. Add maple syrup, cinnamon, water, and nutmeg.
2. Mix sugar, flour, oat, salt, and butter in a

bowl. Put a tbsp. of the mixture on the apples. Set the air fryer to 320^{0}F. cook for 10 minutes.

3. Serve immediately.

Calories: 201kcal, Fat: 7g, Carb: 30g, Proteins: 13g

Carrot Cake

Carrot cake is yummy and delicious. It also tastes great with yogurt.
Prep time and cooking time: 55 minutes| Serves: 6

Ingredients To Use:

- 1 egg
- 1/2 tsp. of baking soda
- 1/3 cup of grated carrot
- 3 tbsp. of yogurt
- 1/2 tsp. of cinnamon powder
- 1/2 cup of sugar
- 4 tbsp. of sunflower oil
- 1/2 tsp. of allspice
- 1/3 cup of chopped pecans
- Cooking spray
- 1/4 cup of pineapple juice
- 1/2 tsp. of baking powder
- 1/3 cup of shredded coconut flakes
- 1/4 tsp. of nutmeg
- 5 ounces of flour

Step-by-Step Directions to Cook It:

1. Mix allspice, powder, nutmeg, and baking soda in a bowl. Add flour, salt, and cinnamon. Stir well.
2. To a separate bowl, add the sugar, carrots, pecans, oil, pineapple juice, yogurt, and coconut flakes. Mix thoroughly.
3. Transfer the 2 mixtures to another bowl. Pour the mixture on a cooking spray greased pan that fits the air fryer. Set the

air fryer temperature to 320^{0}F, leave to cook for 45 minutes.

4. Serve immediately or let it cool down.

Nutritional value per serving:

Calories: 201kcal, Fat: 7g, Carb: 24g, Proteins: 5g

Ginger Cheesecake

Ginger is a powerful medicinal plant that can be used as a spice. This Ginger cheesecake recipe contains ginger spice and cream cheese.
Prep time and cooking time: 2 hours 30 minutes| Serves: 7

Ingredients To Use:

- 1 tsp. of run
- 2 eggs
- 16 ounces of cream cookies
- 2 tsp. of butter
- 1/2 tsp. of vanilla extract
- 1/2 cup of sugar
- 1/2 cup of ginger cookies
- 1/2 tsp. of nutmeg

Step-by-Step Directions to Cook It:

1. Spread butter on a pan. Place cookies on the pan.
2. Mix nutmeg, rum, cream cheese, eggs, and vanilla in a bowl. Spread the mixture over the cookies.
3. Set the air fryer to a temperature of 340^{0}F. Cook for 20 minutes.
4. Allow the cheesecake to cool for about 2 hours.

Nutritional value per serving:

Calories: 415kcal, Fat: 13g, Carb: 22g, Proteins: 7g

Strawberry Pie

Strawberry pie is an excellent traditional dessert. The gelatine makes the flavor

lasting and improves the taste.
Prep time and cooking time: 30 minutes|
Serves: 12

Ingredients To Use:

- 1 tsp. of gelatin
- 2 tbsp. of water
- 1/4 tsp. of stevia
- 1 cup of coconut oil
- 12 ounces of strawberries
- 1/2 tbsp. of lemon juice
- 1/4 cup of butter
- 1 cup of sunflower seeds
- 8 ounces of cream cheese
- 1/2 cup of heavy cream

Step-by-Step Directions to Cook It:

1. Mix butter, a pinch of salt, sunflower seeds, coconut in a food processor. Transfer it to a pan that fits the air fryer.
2. Put water in a pan and heat over medium heat. Put in gelatine and stir till the gelatine dissolves. Allow it to cool down.
3. Add the mixture to the food processor. Add lemon juice, 4 ounces of strawberries, stevia, and cream cheese and blend.
4. Put in heavy cream and stir. Spread the mixture over the crust. Put 8 ounces of strawberries on it.
5. Set the air fryer to 330^0F, cook for 15 minutes.
6. Serve immediately or leave to cool.

Nutritional value per serving:

Calories: 235kcal, Fat: 25g, Carb: 7g, Proteins: 8g

Coffee Cheesecakes

Coffee powder is gotten from the coffee bean and has a lot of nutritional benefits. It is also the main ingredient of this amazing dessert. Try it out now, and you will not be disappointed.
Prep time and cooking time: 30 minutes|
Serves: 6

Ingredients To Use:

- 4 tbsp. of caramel syrup
- 3 tbsp. of coffee
- 8 ounces of mascarpone cheese
- 8 ounces of cream cheese
- 1/3 cup of sugar
- 3 tbsp. of butter
- 2 Tbsp. of sugar
- 3 eggs

Step-by-Step Directions to Cook It:

1. Put 2 tbsp. of butter, 1/3 cup of sugar, and eggs in a blender. Add in 1 tbsp. of caramel syrup, cream cheese, and coffee. Pour the mixture into the cupcakes pan on the air fryer.
2. Set the air fryer at a temperature of 320^0F, bake for about 20 minutes.
3. Mix 2 tbsp. of sugar, 3 tbsp. of butter, mascarpone in a bowl. Add in 3 tbsp. of caramel syrup. Blend the mixture well. Top the mixture on the cake and serve.

Nutritional value per serving:

Calories: 255kcal, Fat: 24g, Carb: 22g, Proteins: 6g

Cocoa Cookies

Who doesn't love cocoa cookies? They're perfect comfort foods and are always there for you when things get rough.
Prep time and cooking time: 25 minutes|
Serves: 12

Ingredients To Use:

- 6 eggs
- 2 tsp. of vanilla
- 4 ounces of cream cheese
- 6 ounces of coconut oil

- 3 ounces of cocoa powder
- 5 tbsp. of sugar
- 1/2 tsp. of baking powder

Step-by-Step Directions to Cook It:

1. Pour the cocoa powder, vanilla, and coconut oil into a blender. Add eggs, cream cheese, and baking powder. Mix thoroughly.
2. Transfer the mixture to a baking dish that fits the air fryer. Set the temperature to 320^{0}F, leave to bake for about 14-15 minutes.
3. Serve cookies immediately.

Nutritional value per serving:

Calories: 180kcal, Fat: 15g, Carb: 4g, Proteins: 6g

Special Brownies

The taste of this special brownie recipe is intensified by the walnut and peanut butter.
Prep time and cooking time: 30 minutes| Serves: 4

Ingredients To Use:

- 1 tbsp. of peanut butter
- 7 tbsp. of butter
- 1/4 cup of chopped walnut
- 1/3 cup of cocoa powder
- 1/2 tsp. of baking powder
- 1/3 cup of sugar
- 1/4 cup of white flour
- 1/2 tsp. of vanilla extract
- 1 egg

Step-by-Step Directions to Cook It:

1. Add 6 tbsp. of butter to a medium pan placed over medium heat. Add sugar and stir. Cook for 5 minutes. Put the mixture in a bowl, add egg, walnut, vanilla extract, and salt. Add cocoa powder, flour, and stir. Return the mixture to the pan that fits the air fryer.

2. Get another bowl, mix peanut butter, and 1 tbsp. of butter. Heat the mixture in the microwave for some seconds. Line it over the brownies.
3. Set the air fryer to a temperature of 320^{0}F, bake the brownies for about 18 minutes.
4. Allow cooling before serving.

Nutritional value per serving:

Calories: 225kcal, Fat: 33g, Carb: 4g, Proteins: 7g

Blueberry Scones

Succulent blueberry scones are wonderful deserts. It is also a rare desert because of the dearth of blueberry.
Prep time and cooking time: 20 minutes| Serves: 10

Ingredients To Use:

- 1 cup of blueberries
- 1/2 cup of butter
- 2 tbsp. of vanilla extract
- 2 eggs
- 2 tbsp. of baking powder
- 1 cup of flour
- 5 tbsp. of sugar
- 1/2 cup of heavy cream

Step-by-Step Directions to Cook It:

1. Mix baking powder, flour, blueberries, and salt in a bowl.
2. Get another bowl, put vanilla extract, eggs, heavy cream, sugar, and butter. Mix well.
3. Transfer the 2 mixtures into another bowl and mix until it forms a dough. Cut the dough into 10 pieces in triangle shapes. Line them on the pan that fits the air fryer.
4. Set the air fryer to a temperature of 320^{0}F. Cook for 10 minutes.

5. Serve when it is cool.

Nutritional value per serving:

Calories: 134kcal, Fat: 3g, Carb: 5g, Proteins: 4g

Chocolate Cookies

The is just the kind of cookie you want on a boring day to spice up your mood.
Prep time and cooking time: 35 minutes|
Serves: 12

Ingredients To Use:

- 1 egg
- 2 cups of flour
- 1 tsp. of vanilla extract
- 1/2 cup of chocolate chips, unsweetened
- 1/2 cup of butter
- 4 tbsp. of sugar

Step-by-Step Directions to Cook It:

1. Put butter in a pan and heat over medium heat. Cook for about 1 minute.
2. Mix sugar, egg, and vanilla extract in a bowl.
3. Add half of the unsweetened chocolate chips and flour to the melted butter, stir well. Add the 2 mixtures together.
4. Pour the mixture on the pan that fits the air fryer. Put the remaining half of the chocolate chips.
5. Set the air fryer temperature at 330^0F, leave to bake for about 25 minutes.
6. Serve when cool.

Nutritional value per serving:

Calories: 490kcal, Fat: 30g, Carb: 60g, Proteins: 8g

Tasty Orange Cake

This dessert is sweet, delicious, and healthy.
Prep time and cooking time: 43 minutes|
Serves: 13

Ingredients To Use:

- 1 tsp. of vanilla extract
- 2 ounces + 2 tbsp. of sugar
- 1 tsp. of baking powder
- 2 tbsp. of orange zest
- 4 ounces of yogurt
- 9 ounces of flour
- 1 orange
- 6 eggs
- 4 ounces of cream cheese

Step-by-Step Directions to Cook It:

1. Put the orange in a food processor and pulse until well-combined.
2. Add eggs, vanilla extract, flour, baking powder, and 2 tbsp of sugar. And pulse.
3. Place the mixture into spring pans that fit the air fryer. Set the air fryer to a temperature of 330^0F. Cook for about 15 minutes.
4. Get a bowl, mix yogurt, orange zest, and cream cheese. Add the remaining sugar and stir.
5. Put one layer of the cake on a plate. Put half of the cream cheese mixture. Put another layer of cake on it, pour the remaining cream cheese on it.
6. Serve immediately.

Nutritional value per serving:

Calories: 201kcal, Fat: 15g, Carb: 10g, Proteins: 9g

Macaroons

Macaroons are small cakes or cookies made from coconut or almond; they can also be made from any kind of nuts.
Prep time and cooking time: 20 minutes|
Serves: 20

Ingredients To Use:

- 1 tsp. of vanilla extract
- 4 egg whites

- 2 tbsp. of sugar
- 2 cups of shredded coconut

1. Use a mixer to whisk stevia and egg whites.
2. Add vanilla extract with coconut. Whisk with mixer. Shape the mixture into a small ball in 20 pieces, put it in your pan that fit your air fryer. Set the air fryer to 340^0F. Cook for 9 minutes.
3. Serve when cold.

Nutritional value per serving:

Calories: 56kcal, Fat: 7g, Carb: 3g, Proteins: 2g

Lime Cheesecake

Lime is a fruit with a sour taste; though it is acidic, it has many nutritional benefits. Lime gives the meal a lasting flavor.
Prep time and cooking time: 4 hours 15 minutes| Serves: 10

Ingredients To Use:

- 1 pound of cream cheese
- 2 tbsp. of butter
- 1 lime zest
- 2 tsp. of sugar
- 2 cups of hot water
- 4 ounces of flour
- 2 sachets of lime jelly
- 1/4 cup of shredded coconut
- 1 lime juice

Step-by-Step Directions to Cook It:

1. Mix the butter, flour, sugar, and coconut in a bowl. Stir and transfer it to the pan that fits the air fryer.
2. Get another bowl, pour hot water and jelly sachets in it. Mix until the jelly sachet dissolves.
3. Add lime zest, cream cheese, and lime juice to the mixture. Pour the mixture on

the crust in the pan.
4. Set air fryer to 300^0F. Cook for 5 minutes.
5. Allow cooling for about 4 hours.

Nutritional value per serving:

Calories: 262kcal, Fat: 24g, Carb: 6g, Proteins: 8g

Easy Granola

Granola can be served as a breakfast or a dessert.
Prep time and cooking time: 45 minutes| Serves: 4

Ingredients To Use:

- 1 tsp. of ground nutmeg
- 2 tbsp. of sugar
- 1/2 cup of almonds
- 2 tbsp. of sunflower oil
- 1 cup of shredded coconut
- 1/2 cup of pumpkin seed
- 1 tsp. of apple pie spice
- 1/2 cup of chopped pecan
- 1/2 cup of sunflower seeds

Step-by-Step Directions to Cook It:

1. Mix sunflower seeds, pecans, nutmeg, and almond in a bowl. Add in pumpkin seeds and apple pie spice, stir thoroughly.
2. Put oil in a pan and heat over medium heat. Put sugar and mix. Pour it on the coconut mixture. Stir.
3. Pour the mixture on a baking dish that fits the air fryer. Set the air fryer to 300°F. Bake for about 20-25 minutes.
4. Serve when cool.

Nutritional value per serving:

Calories: 325kcal, Fat: 8g, Carb: 14g, Proteins: 8g

Strawberry Cobbler

Cobbler is a dessert that contains different kinds of fruits. It is mostly baked but not fried.
Prep time and cooking time:35 minutes|
Serves: 6

Ingredients To Use:

- 1 tbsp. of lemon juice
- 6 cups of halved strawberries
- A pinch of baking soda
- 3/4 cup of sugar
- 1/8 tsp. of baking powder
- 3-1/2 tbsp. of olive oil
- Cooking spray
- 1/2 cup of water
- 1/2 cup of flour

Step-by-Step Directions to Cook It:

1. Mix half of the sugar, lemon juice, and strawberries. Sprinkle flour, mix well. Pour the mixture on a greased baking sheet that fits the air fryer with cooking spray.
2. Get another bowl, put in baking powder, soda and sugar. Add in olive oil and mix. Put 1/2 cup of water. Spread the mixture over the strawberries.
3. Set the air fryer to 355^0F, leave to bake for 25 minutes.
4. Set the cobbler down and let it cool before serving.

Nutritional value per serving:

Calories: 222kcal, Fat: 4g, Carb: 8g, Proteins: 10g

Black Tea Cake

The black tea cake is produced by adding black tea to the ingredients of a yellow pound cake. It is a wonderful dessert.
Prep time and cooking time: 45 minutes|
Serves: 12

Ingredients To Use:

- 1 tsp. of baking soda
- 2 cups of milk
- 6 cups of sugar
- 4 eggs
- 1-1/2 cups of butter
- 6 tbsp. of black tea powder
- 3-1/2 cups of flour
- 2 tsp. of vanilla extract
- 6 tbsp. of honey
- 1/2 cup of olive oil
- 3 tsp. of baking powder

Step-by-Step Directions to Cook It:

1. Heat the milk over medium heat. Put in tea and stir. Stop the heat and leave to cool.
2. Mix 2 cups of sugar, vanilla extract, baking soda, and 1/2 cup of butter in a bowl. Add in eggs, baking powder, 1/2 cups of flour, and vegetable oil. Mix well.
3. Transfer the mixture to a greased pan that fits the air fryer. Set the air fryer to 330^0F, bake for 20-25 minutes.
4. Mix 4 cups of sugar, 1 cup of butter, and honey in another bowl. Stir well.
5. Place the cake on a dish, pour cream over it, place another cake over it. Allow to cool down before serving.

Nutritional value per serving:

Calories: 201kcal, Fat: 5g, Carb: 7g, Proteins: 3g

Plum Cake

Plum cake is prepared by mixing dried fruit with cake ingredients. It is generally called fruit cake.
Prep time and cooking time: 2 hours | Serves: 8

Ingredients To Use:

- 1 ounce of butter

- 1 ounce of almond cake
- 5 tbsp. of sugar
- 7 ounces of flour
- 1 grated lemon zest
- 1 dried yeast
- 1-3/4 pounds of pitted plum
- 3 ounces of warm milk

1. Mix 3 tbsp. of sugar, butter, and flour in a bowl. Add egg with milk, mix well until it forms a dough.
2. Place the dough on a butter greased spring pan that fits the air fryer. Cover it and leave for about 1 hour.
3. Sprinkle sugar on the plums. Transfer the pan to the air fryer and set it to 350^0F. Leave to bake for 35 minutes.
4. Allow cooling before serving. Spray almond flakes on it and top with lemon zest.

Nutritional value per serving:

Calories: 195kcal, Fat: 5g, Carb: 8g, Proteins: 9g

Lentils Cookies

Lentils are edible legumes. They contains high protein and can also be called fiber powerhouse.
Prep time and cooking time: 35 minutes|
Serves: 30

Ingredients To Use:

- 1 cup of white flour
- 1 cup of butter
- 1 cup of raisins
- 1 cup of canned lentils
- 1 tsp. of baking powder
- 1 cup of shredded coconut
- 1/2 cup of brown sugar
- 1 cup of rolled oat
- 1 tsp. of cinnamon powder

- 1 egg
- 1 cup of whole wheat flour
- 2 tsp. of almond extract
- 1/2 cup of white sugar
- 1/2 tsp. of ground nutmeg
- 1 cup of water

Step-by-Step Directions to Cook It:

1. Mix the cinnamon, white flour, and baking powder in a bowl. Add whole wheat flour, nutmeg, and salt. Stir well.
2. Get another bowl, mix brown sugar, and white sugar. Whisk using kitchen mixer for about 2 minutes.
3. Add in lentil mix, oats, coconut, egg, flour mix, almond extract, raisins, and stir.
4. Use a tablespoon to scoop part of the dough and line it on the baking dish that fits the air fryer. Set the air fryer to 350^0F, bake for 15 minutes.
5. Serve immediately.

Nutritional value per serving:

Calories: 155kcal, Fat: 3g, Carb: 4g, Proteins: 10g

Lentils and Dates Brownies

This is an incredible dessert. The honey gives the brownies an awesome feel and also makes the flavor lasting.
Prep time and cooking time: 25 minutes |
Serves: 8

Ingredients To Use:

- 1 tbsp. of honey
- 4 tbsp. of almond butter
- 12 dates
- 2 tbsp. of cocoa powder
- 28 ounces of canned lentils
- 1 chopped banana
- 4 tbsp. of almond butter
- 1/2 tsp. of baking soda

Step-by-Step Directions to Cook It:

1. Mix banana, baking soda, butter, honey, lentils in a food processor. Blend well.
2. Add the dates to the processor and continue blending. Transfer the mixture to a greased pan that fits the air fryer.
3. Set the air fryer to a temperature of 360°F. Bake for 16 minutes.
4. Cut the brownies and serve.

Nutritional value per serving:

Calories: 163kcal, Fat: 5g, Carb: 4g, Proteins: 5g

Maple Cupcake

The flavor of maple syrup gives the cake a great taste. Adequately whisked Butter and eggs also make the cake fluffy.
Prep time and cooking time: 30 minutes | Serves: 4

Ingredients To Use:

- 1 tsp. of vanilla extract
- 1/2 tsp. of baking powder
- 1/2 cup of pure applesauce
- 4 tsp. of maple syrup
- 1/2 chopped apple
- 2 tsp. of cinnamon powder
- 3/4 cup of white flour
- 4 eggs
- 4 tbsp. of butter

Step-by-Step Directions to Cook It:

1. Put butter in a pan and heat over medium heat. Add eggs, applesauce, maple syrup, and vanilla. Whisk well. Remove the heat and allow it to co0l.
2. Add in baking powder, flour, apples, and cinnamon. Mix well.
3. Transfer the mixture to a cupcake pan that fits the air fryer. Set the air fryer at 350°F. Bake for about 15-20 minutes.
4. Serve immediately or allow to cool down.

Nutritional value per serving:

Calories: 165kcal, Fat: 5g, Carb: 4g, Proteins: 5g

Rhubarb Pie

Rhubarb pie may have extra sugar than appropriate, but the calories are definitely worth it.
Prep time and cooking time: 1 hour 15 minutes | Serves: 6

Ingredients To Use:

- 9 tbsp. of butter
- 3 cups of chopped rhubarb
- 1/2 tsp. of nutmeg
- 2-1/2 cups of sugar
- 2 tbsp. of low-fat milk
- 5 tbsp. of cold water
- 3 tbsp. of flour
- 1-1/2 cups of almond flour
- 2 eggs

Step-by-Step Directions to Cook It:

1. Mix cold water, 1 tsp. of sugar, 1-1/4 cup of flour, and 8 tbsp. of butter in a bowl. Mix until it forms a dough.
2. Put the dough on a floured flat surface and cut. Put inside the fridge and allow it to stay for about 30 minutes. Bring it out and place it in a pie pan that suits the air fryer.
3. In another bowl, mix 3 tbsp. of flour, 1-1/2 cups of sugar, rhubarb, and nutmeg. Mix well.
4. Get another bowl, put milk, and egg. Whisk well. Put it inside the rhubarb mix. Pour all the mixture into the pie crust. Set the air fryer to 390°F. Bake for about 45 minutes.
5. Serve when cold.

Nutritional value per serving:

Calories: 201kcal, Fat: 3g, Carb: 7g, Proteins: 4g

Lemon Tart

This lemon tart recipe contains lemon zest and lemon juice.

Prep time and cooking time: 1 hour 40 minutes| Serves: 6

Ingredients To Use:

- 12 tbsp. of cold butter
- 2 lemon zest
- 2 tbsp. and 1-1/4 cups of sugar
- 10 tbsp. of chilled, melted butter
- 2 cups of white flour
- 2 lemon juice
- 3 tbsp. of ice water
- 2 eggs
- Salt, a pinch

Step-by-Step Directions to Cook It:

1. Mix 2 tbsp. of sugar, 2 cups of white flour, and salt in a bowl. Whisk well.
2. Add water and 12 tbsp. of butter. Mix until it forms a dough. Give it a ball shape and wrap it in a foil. Leave in the refrigerator for 1 hour.
3. Put the dough on a floured flat surface. Transfer it to a tart pan that fits the air fryer. Set to 350^{0}F, bake for 16 minutes.
4. Get another bowl, put 10 tbsp of butter, lemon zest, 1-1/4 cup of sugar, lemon juice, and eggs. Whisk well.
5. Pour the mixture on the pie crust. Set the air fryer to 360^{0}F temperature. Cook for 19 minutes.
6. Serve immediately.

Nutritional value per serving:

Calories: 185kcal, Fat: 5g, Carb: 3g, Proteins: 5g

Mandarin Pudding

Mandarin is a tiny fruit that originates from China. It is readily available in local grocery stores.

Prep time and cooking time: 60 minutes | Serves: 8

Ingredients To Use:

- 2 eggs
- 2 mandarins juice
- 3/4 cup of sugar
- 1 peeled, sliced mandarin
- 3/4 cup of ground almond
- 2 tbsp. of brown sugar
- Honey
- 4 ounces of soft butter
- 3/4 cup of white flour

Step-by-Step Directions to Cook It:

1. Put the butter in a pan, put slices of mandarin in it and sprinkle with brown sugar.
2. Mix eggs, almond, mandarin juice, and sugar in a bowl. Add flour and stir. Pour the mixture on the mandarin slices. Put the pan in the air fryer. Set the air fryer to 360^{0}F temperature. Cook for 35-40 minutes.
3. Serve immediately and top with honey.

Nutritional value per serving:

Calories: 165kcal, Fat: 5g, Carb: 5g, Proteins: 8g

Strawberry Shortcake

Shortcake is a crumbly sweet biscuit or cake that's crunchier than shortbread. It is less dense; it has contains more carbonhydrate.

Prep time and cooking time: 65 minutes | Serves: 7

Ingredients To Use:

- 1 tbsp. of rum
- 1-1/2 cups of flour
- 1/2 cup of whipping cream
- 1/4 cup of sugar and 4 tbsps.
- 1 tsp. of grated lime zest
- 1/3 cup of butter

- 1 egg
- 1 tbsp. of chopped mint
- 1 tsp. of baking powder
- 2 cups of strawberries
- 1 cup of buttermilk
- 1/4 tsp. of baking soda
- Cooking spray

1. Mix the baking powder, flour, baking soda, and 1/4 cup of sugar in a bowl and stir.
2. Get another bowl, mix egg, flour mix, and buttermilk. Whisk well.
3. Shape the dough into 6 greased jar with cooking spray. Place foil on it. Transfer it to the air fryer and cook for 45 minutes at 360^0F.
4. In a bowl, put in rum, strawberries, lime zest, 3 tbsp. of sugar, and mint. Mix well and leave in a cold place.
5. Get another bowl, put 1 tbsp. of sugar, whipping cream, and stir.
6. Bring the jars out. Put on strawberry mix and top with whipped cream.

Nutritional value per serving:

Calories: 350kcal, Fat: 15g, Carb: 50g, Proteins: 8g

Sponge Cake

Sponge cake is also called a naked cake because it is not covered with icing sugar.
Prep time and cooking time: 30 minutes | Serves: 11

Ingredients To Use:

- 1 cup of olive oil
- 1-1/2 cup of milk
- 1-2/3 cup of sugar
- 3 cups of flour
- 2 tsp. of vanilla extract
- 3 tsp. of baking powder

- 1/4 cup of lemon juice
- 2 cups of water
- 1/2 cup of cornstarch
- 1 tsp. of baking soda

Step-by-Step Directions to Cook It:

1. Mix baking powder, sugar, flour, baking soda, and cornstarch in a bowl and whisk.
2. Get another bowl, mix vanilla, oil, water, lemon juice, and milk. Whisk well.
3. Mix the 2 mixtures. Transfer it to a greased baking dish that fits the air fryer. Set the air fryer at 350^0F temperature. Bake for 20 minutes.
4. Allow cooling before serving.

Nutritional value per serving:

Calories: 300kcal, Fat: 5g, Carb: 60g, Proteins: 8g

Ricotta and Lemon Cake

Ricotta cake is a fluffy, rich cake with good density due to the great number of eggs used to make the cake.
Prep time and cooking time: 1 hour 20 minutes | Serves: 4

Ingredients To Use:

- 1 grated lemon zest
- 3 pounds of ricotta cheese
- Butter
- 1 grated orange zest
- 8 eggs
- 1/2 pound of sugar

Step-by-Step Directions to Cook It:

1. Mix the cheese, orange zest, eggs, lemon zest, and sugar in a bowl.
2. Put butter in the baking pan that fits the air fryer. Pour the mixture into the pan at bake at 390^0F for 30 minutes.
3. Lower the air fryer heat to 380^0F, leave to bake for another 40 minutes.

4. Bring out of the oven and allow to cool before serving.

Calories: 113kcal, Fat: 5g, Carb: 5g, Proteins: 8g

Tangerine Cake

Tangerine is a fruit that belongs to the citrus family. It is rich in vitamin C, and intensifies the taste of tangerine cake.
Prep time and cooking time: 30 minutes | Serves: 8

Ingredients To Use:

- 1 tsp. of apple cider vinegar
- 2 cups of flour
- Tangerine segment
- 3/4 cup of sugar
- 2 lemon juice and zest
- 1/4 cup of olive oil
- 1 tangerine juice and zest
- 1/2 cup of milk
- 1/2 tsp. of vanilla extract

Step-by-Step Directions to Cook It:

1. Mix the sugar and flour in a bowl.
2. Get another bowl, mix vinegar, lemon juice, milk, oil, and lemon zest. Add vanilla extract, flour, and tangerine zest. Whisk well.
3. Transfer the mixture to a cake pan. Set the air fryer to 360^0F, bake for 20 minutes.
4. Serve immediately. Top with tangerine segments.

Nutritional value per serving:

Calories: 189kcal, Fat: 3g, Carb: 6g, Proteins: 6g

Blueberry Pudding

Blueberry pudding is made from a mixture of blueberries, maple syrup, and other important ingredients.
Prep time and cooking time: 35 minutes | Serves: 6

Ingredients To Use:

- 1 cup of chopped walnut
- 2 cups of rolled oats
- 3 tbsp. of maple syrup
- 1 stick of melted butter
- 2 cups of flour
- 2 tbsp. of chopped rosemary
- 8 cups of blueberries

Step-by-Step Directions to Cook It:

1. Put the blueberries in the greased baking pan.
2. Mix the walnut, rosemary, and rolled oats in a food processor. Add in flour, maple syrup, and butter and blend. Pour the mixture on the blueberries.
3. Set the air fryer to 350^0F temperature. Cook for 20-25 minutes.
4. Allow cooling before serving.

Nutritional value per serving:

Calories: 155kcal, Fat: 10g, Carb: 20g, Proteins: 15g

Almond and Cocoa Bars

Almond is an amazing nut and adds an incredible flavor to a chocolate bar.
Prep time and cooking time: 35 minutes | Serves: 6

Ingredients To Use:

- 1 cup of soaked, drained almond
- 1/4 cup of goji berries
- 1/4 cup of cocoa nibs
- 8 soaked dates
- 1/4 cup of hemp seeds
- 2 tbsp. of cocoa powder
- 1/4 cup of shredded coconut

Step-by-Step Directions to Cook It:

1. In a food processor, blend the almonds, cocoa powder, hemp seeds, coconuts, cocoa nibs, and goji. Blend well.
2. Put dates and blend again.
3. Transfer the mixture to a baking dish that fits the air fryer. Set it at 320⁰F, cook for 5 minutes.
4. Put in the refrigerator for 30 minutes, serve.

Nutritional value per serving:

Calories: 145kcal, Fat: 8g, Carb: 10g, Proteins: 20g

Pomegranate and Chocolate Bars

Pomegranate is delicious even eaten alone, and when added to a chocolate bar, it tastes incredible.
Prep time and cooking time: 2 hours 10 minutes | Serves: 6

Ingredients To Use:

- 1 tsp. of vanilla extract
- 1/2 cup of pomegranate seeds
- 1/2 cup of milk
- A pinch of salt
- 1-1/2 cups of dark chocolate
- 1/2 cup of chopped almond.

Step-by-Step Directions to Cook It:

1. Pour the milk into a pan and heat over medium heat. Put chocolate and stir for about 4-5 minutes. Add 1/2 of nut, 1/2 of pomegranate seeds, and vanilla extract. Stir.
2. Put the mixture in a baking pan. Sprinkle salt. And the rest of pomegranate nuts and arils. Set the air fryer to 300⁰F, bake for 5 minutes.
3. Put in the refrigerator for about 2 hours.

Nutritional value per serving:

Calories: 70kcal, Fat: 3g, Carb: 8g, Proteins: 3g

Tomato Cake

Tomato is rich in antioxidants and improves your general well-being. Try this recipe now for a truly nutritious dessert.
Prep time and cooking time: 40 minutes | Serves: 4

Ingredients To Use:

- 1 tsp. of baking soda
- 1/2 cup of olive oil
- 1 tsp. of baking powder
- 1 cup of chopped tomato
- 1 tsp. of cinnamon powder
- 1-1/2 cups of flour
- 2 tbsp. of cider vinegar
- 3/4 cup of maple syrup

Step-by-Step Directions to Cook It:

1. Mix the baking soda, maple syrup, baking powder, and cinnamon powder in a bowl. Stir.
2. Mix vinegar, tomato, and olive oil in another bowl. Stir.
3. Mix the 2 mixtures. Transfer it to a greased pan that fits the air fryer. Set the air fryer to 360⁰F temperature. Cook for 30 minutes.
4. Allow cooling before serving.

Nutritional value per serving:

Calories: 155kcal, Fat: 4g, Carb: 30g, Proteins: 10g

Berries Mix

Blueberries and strawberries are juicy, delicious, and yummy. A great dessert for days when you desire a sweet snack.
Prep time and cooking time: 12 minutes |

Serves: 4

- 1 pound of strawberries
- 1-1/2 tbsps. of maple syrup
- 2 tbsp. of lemon juice
- 1 tbsp. of olive oil
- 1-1/2 cup of blueberries
- 1-1/2 tbsps. of champagne vinegar
- 1/4 cup of basil leaves

Step-by-Step Directions to Cook It:

1. Mix the maple syrup, lemon juice, and vinegar in a pan that fits the air fryer. Boil for about 2 minutes. Add blueberries, strawberries, and oil. Stir well.
2. Set the air fryer to 310^{0}F. Cook for 6 minutes.
3. Top with basil while serving.

Nutritional value per serving:

Calories: 165kcal, Fat: 8g, Carb: 15g, Proteins: 5g

Passion Fruit Pudding

Passion fruit, also known as passiflora eduli, is a sweet and seedy fruit rich in antioxidants. It is a good fiber source for a pudding.
Prep time and cooking time: 50 minutes | Serves: 5

Ingredients To Use:

- 3 eggs
- 4 pulped and seeded passion fruits
- 3-1/2 ounces of almond milk
- 1 cup of passion fruit curd
- 2 ounces of melted ghee
- 1/2 tsp. of baking powder
- 3-1/2 ounces of maple syrup
- 1/2 cup of almond flour

Step-by-Step Directions to Cook It:

1. Mix the passion fruit seeds and pulp and half of the fruit curd in a bowl. Stir well.

Share it to 5 proof ramekins.
2. Get another bowl, put baking powder, maple syrup, milk, eggs, ghee, flour, and the remaining curd. Mix well.
3. Share into 5 ramekins. Set the air fryer to 200^{0}F temperature. Cook for about 40 minutes.
4. Allow cooling before serving.

Nutritional value per serving:

Calories: 435kcal, Fat: 30g, Carb: 10g, Proteins: 15g

Fried Apples

There are several fried apple recipes, but this recipe transcends a normal one because of the cinnamon used to spice things up.
Prep time and cooking time: 30 minutes | Serves: 4

Ingredients To Use:

- 1 tbsp. of ground cinnamon
- 4 large cored apples
- Honey
- 1 handful raisins

Step-by-Step Directions to Cook It:

1. Put the raisins in the apples. Drizzle with honey and sprinkle cinnamon on it.
2. Set it in the air fryer, set the air fryer to 367^{0}F. Cook for 18 minutes.
3. Allow cooling before serving.

Nutritional value per serving:

Calories: 225kcal, Fat: 10g, Carb: 15g, Proteins: 20g

Pumpkin Cookies

Pumpkin is a fruit that helps the body fight infections. It is rich in vitamin A, high in antioxidants. It also contains low calories.
Prep time and cooking time: 25 minutes | Serves: 23

- 1/2 cup of meshed pumpkin flesh
- 2-1/2 cups of flour
- 2 tbsp. of butter
- 1/2 tsp. of baking soda
- 1 tsp. of vanilla extract
- 1 tbsp. of ground flax seed
- 1/2 cup of black chocolate chips
- 3 tbsp. of water
- 1/4 cup of honey

Step-by-Step Directions to Cook It:

1. Mix the water and flaxseed in a bowl. Stir and put aside.
2. Get another bowl, mix baking powder, flour and salt and stir.
3. Get the third bowl, put pumpkin puree, vanilla extract, honey, flaxseed, and butter. Stir well.
4. Add the flour and chocolate chips to the honey mixture.
5. Scoop part of the dough on the put it on the baking pan that suits the air fryer. Do the same for the remaining dough.
6. Set the air fryer to 350^{0}F. Bake for 16 minutes.
7. Allow cooling before serving.

Nutritional value per serving:

Calories: 141kcal, Fat: 5g, Carb: 10g, Proteins: 20g

Coconut and Figs Butter Mix

Coconut and figs butter mix is a great dessert to try. Simply Delicious!
Prep time and cooking time: 10 minutes | Serves: 3

Ingredients To Use:

- 1 cup of chopped almonds
- 12 halved figs
- 2 tbsp. of coconut butter
- 1/4 cup of sugar

Step-by-Step Directions to Cook It:

1. Grease the pan with butter and place over medium heat.
2. Add the almond, figs, and sugar. Mix well.
3. Set the air fryer to 300^{0}F temperature. Cook for 5 minutes.
4. Serve when cold.

Nutritional value per serving:

Calories: 172kcal, Fat: 8g, Carb: 10g, Proteins: 15g

Lemon Bars

Lemon is a citrus fruit that's good for weight loss. It is rich in vitamin C, and improves hydration.
Prep time and cooking time: 35 minutes | Serves: 6

Ingredients To Use:

- 1 cup of soft butter
- 4 eggs
- 2 lemon juice
- 2 cups of sugar
- 2-1/4 cups of flour

Step-by-Step Directions to Cook It:

1. Mix 2 cups of flour, butter, and a half cup of sugar in a bowl and stir well.
2. Put the mixture in a pan that suits the air fryer. Set it to 350^{0}F temperature. Cook for 8-10 minutes.
3. In a separate bowl, mix the egg, remaining sugar, lemon juice, and remaining flour. Mix and pour the mixture on the crust.
4. Set the air fryer to 350^{0}F temperature and cook for 15 minutes.

Nutritional value per serving:

Calories: 130kcal, Fat: 5g, Carb: 20g, Proteins: 7g

Espresso and Pears Cream

This is an outstanding and rare desert. It is mostly prepared for a special occasion.
Prep time and cooking time: 40 minutes | Serves: 4

Ingredients To Use:

- 1/3 cup of sugar, 1 tbsp
- 4 pears
- 2 tbsp. of water
- 1 cup of mascarpone
- 2 tbsp. of lemon juice
- 2 tbsp. of butter
- 2 tbsp. of cold espresso
- 1 cup of whipping cream

Step-by-Step Directions to Cook It:

1. Mix 1 tbsp. of sugar, water, halved pear, butter, and lemon juice in a bowl. Stir well. Pour the mixture into the air fryer. Set the air fryer to 360°F temperature. Cook for 30 minutes.
2. In a separate bowl, mix the mascarpone, expresso, whipping cream, 1/3 cup of sugar, and stir. Put it in the refrigerator till the pear is ready.
3. Serve the pear and put espresso cream on top.

Nutritional value per serving:

Calories: 212kcal, Fat: 10g, Carb: 12g, Proteins: 13g

Poppyseed Cake

Poppyseed is also known as an oilseed. It is rich in antioxidants. It is also rich in fiber. This makes it an excellent ingredient for a healthy dessert.
Prep time and cooking time: 40 minutes | Serves: 6

Ingredients To Use:

- 1 tbsp. of grated orange zest
- 1-3/4 cup of sugar
- 1-1/4 cup of flour
- 2 whisked egg
- 4 egg yolks
- 2 tsp. of grated lemon zest
- 2 tbsp. of poppy seeds
- 1/2 cup of passion fruit puree
- 1 cup of milk
- 3 tbsp. of melted butter
- 1/2 cup of soft butter
- 1 tsp. of baking powder
- 1-1/2 tsp. of vanilla extract

Step-by-Step Directions to Cook It:

1. Mix 3/4 of cup sugar, flour, lime zest, baking powder, and orange zest in a bowl.
2. Add the vanilla, poppy seeds, 1/2 cup of butter, milk, and eggs to the same bowl.
3. Grease a cake pan that suits the air fryer with 3 tbsp of butter. Add sugar. Pour the mix into the cake pan. Bake at 350°F for 30 minutes.
4. Remove from heat. Add egg yolk and passion fruit puree gradually.
5. Allow cake to cool down. Horizontally cut into 2 equal halves. Put 1/4 passion fruit cream on it. Put another half slice of cake on it. Put cream on top.
6. Serve immediately.

Nutritional value per serving:

Calories: 212kcal, Fat: 10g, Carb: 20g, Proteins: 10g

Sweet Square

Lemon is a popular ingredient used in many great desserts, and this recipe is no different.
Prep time and cooking time: 40 minutes | Serves: 6

Ingredients To Use:

- 1 cup of sugar

- 2 eggs
- 1/4 cup of powdered sugar
- 2 tbsp. of lemon juice
- 1 cup of flour
- 1/2 tsp. of baking powder
- 2 tsp. of grated lemon peels
- 1/2 cup of soft butter

Step-by-Step Directions to Cook It:

1. Mix the butter, flour, and powdered sugar in a bowl. Pour the mixture on a pan that fits the air fryer.
2. Set the air fryer to 350^0F, bake for 15 minutes.
3. Get another bowl, mix lemon juice, baking powder, eggs, sugar, and lemon peels. Spread the mixture over the baked crust.
4. Bake for another 15 minutes. Allow to cool, cut into square, and serve.

Nutritional value per serving:

Calories: 100kcal, Fat: 15g, Carb: 20g, Proteins: 10g

Plum Bars

Plum may be a scarce ingredient, but it adds great flavor to the food. Try it out now in this delicious plum bar recipe.
Prep time and cooking time: 30 minutes | Serves: 8

Ingredients To Use:

- 1 tsp. of cinnamon powder
- 2 cups of rolled oats
- 2 cups of dried plums
- Cooking spray
- 1/2 tsp. of baking soda
- 2 tbsp. of butter
- 6 tbsp. of water
- 1 egg
- 2 cups of dried plums

Step-by-Step Directions to Cook It:

1. Blend the plums and water in a food processor until it is sticky.
2. Get a bowl, mix baking soda, butter, oats, sugar, cinnamon, and eggs. Whisk well.
3. Pour half of your oat mixture into a baking dish that fits the air fryer. Pour plum mixture on the crust and pour the remaining half of the oat mixture.
4. Set the air fryer to 350^0F. Cook for 15 minutes.
5. Allow cooling before serving.

Nutritional value per serving:

Calories: 112kcal, Fat: 15g, Carb: 25g, Proteins: 18g

Currant and Plum Tart

Currants, like plum, are great additions to a dessert recipe. Try this beautiful recipe that combines both ingredients to make a flavor-rich tart.
Prep time and cooking time: 65 minutes | Serves: 6

Ingredients To Use:

- 3 tbsp. of milk
- 1/2 tsp. of cinnamon powder
- 1 cup of white currants
- 1/4 cup of millet flour
- 10 tbsp. of butter
- 1/2 tsp of vanilla extract
- 1 cup of brown rice flour
- 2 tbsp. of cornstarch
- 1/4 cup of almond flour
- 3 tbsp. of sugar
- 1/2 cup of cane sugar
- 1 pound of halved and pitted plums
- 1 tsp. of lime juice
- 1/4 tsp. of ginger powder

Step-by-Step Directions to Cook It:

1. Mix the millet flour, butter, brown rice

flour, and milk in a bowl. Add almond flour, 1/2 cup of sugar, and stir until you get dough-like sand.

2. Take 1/4 of the dough aside. Pour the remaining dough into a tart pan that fits the air fryer. Leave in the refrigerator for about 30 minutes.

3. Get another bowl, mix vanilla extract, currant, cornstarch, and lime juice. Add cinnamon, plum, and ginger. Stir.

4. Pour the mixture on the tart crust. Sprinkle the 1/4 reserved dough on it. Set the air fryer to 350^0F, cook for about 30-35 minutes.

5. Allow cooling before serving.

Nutritional value per serving:

Calories: 202kcal, Fat: 8g, Carb: 16g, Proteins: 12g

Orange Cookies

It is no new thing that orange is a citrus fruit, and it is a good source of vitamin C. This recipe takes advantage of its dulcet taste to make a tropical snack.

Prep time and cooking time: 25 minutes | Serves: 8

Ingredients To Use:

- 1 tsp. off vanilla extract
- 4 ounces of cream cheese
- 1 tsp. of baking powder
- 2-3/4 cup of sugar
- 1 tbsp. of orange zest
- 2 cups of flour
- 1 cup of butter
- 1 egg

Step-by-Step Directions to Cook It:

1. Mix 1/2 cup of butter, cream cheese, and 2 cups of sugar in a bowl. Use a mixer to stir.

2. Get another bowl, put baking powder and flour, and mix.

3. Get the third bowl, mix egg, 3/4 cup of sugar, orange zest, 1/2 cup of butter, and vanilla extract. Mix well.

4. Combine the orange mixture and flour mixture in one bowl. Scoop the mixture with a tablespoon and put in a baking dish that fits the air fryer.

5. Do the same for the remaining orange batter. Set the air fryer to 340^0F, bake for 12 minutes.

6. Allow it to cool before serving. Top with cream fillings and serve.

Nutritional value per serving:

Calories: 156kcal, Fat: 14g, Carb: 21g, Proteins: 11g

Cashew Bars

Though cashew has a sour taste, it tastes incredible when used in this recipe to make cashew bars.

Prep time and cooking time: 25 minutes | Serves: 6

Ingredients To Use:

- 1 tbsp. of almond butter
- 3/4 cup of shredded coconut
- 1/3 cup of honey
- 1-1/2 cup of chopped cashews
- 4 chopped dates
- 1 tbsp. of chia seeds
- 1/4 cup of almond meal

Step-by-Step Directions to Cook It:

1. Mix almond butter, honey, and almond meal in a bowl and stir.

2. Add dates, cashew, chia seeds, and coconuts and stir well.

3. Pour the mixture on a baking dish that fits that air fryer.

4. Set the air fryer temperature to 300^0F. Bake for about 15 minutes.

5. Allow cooling before service.

Nutritional value per serving:

Calories: 122kcal, Fat: 7g, Carb: 9g, Proteins: 11g

Brown Butter Cookies

Brown butter is also called beurre noisette. It is gotten from cooking butter until it turns brown.
Prep time and cooking time: 20 minutes| Serves:

Ingredients To Use:

- 2 cups of brown sugar.
- 2 tsp. of vanilla extract
- 2/3 cup of chopped pecan
- 1-1/2 cups of butter
- 3 cups of flour
- 1/2 tsp. of baking powder
- 2 eggs
- 1 tsp. of baking soda

Step-by-Step Directions to Cook It:

1. Put butter in a pan and heat over medium heat. Put brown sugar and stir.
2. Get another bowl, mix vanilla extract, flour, eggs, baking soda, and pecans. Add baking powder and brown butter. Stir and scoop with a spoon and line it on the baking pan that suits the air fryer.
3. Set the air fryer to 340^{0}F, bake for 10 minutes.
4. Allow cookies to cool before serving.

Nutritional value per serving:

Calories: 150kcal, Fat: 7g, Carb: 10g, Proteins: 20g

Sweet Potato Cheesecake

Each cheesecake recipe has a secret ingredient that makes it unique. Cinnamon gives this recipe extra boost.
Prep time and cooking time: 15 minutes|

Serves: 5

Ingredients To Use:

- 1 tsp. of vanilla extract
- 6 ounces of soft mascarpone
- 3/4 cup of milk
- 2/3 cup of sweet potato puree
- 8 ounces of soft cream cheese
- 1/4 tsp. of cinnamon powder
- 2/3 cup of crumbled graham crackers
- 4 tbsp. of melted butter

Step-by-Step Directions to Cook It:

1. Mix the crumbled crackers and butter in a bowl. Pour it into a cake pan that suits the air fryer.
2. Get another bowl, mix sweet potato puree, cream cheese, and cinnamon. Add vanilla extract, mascarpone, and milk.
3. Pour the mixture on the crust. Set the air fryer to 300^{0}F. Bake for 4 minutes.
4. Allow to cool down in the refrigerator before serving.

Nutritional value per serving:

Calories: 173kcal, Fat: 12g, Carb: 18g, Proteins: 15g

Peach Pie

Peach pie is a traditional pie that is prepared in a traditional home. It has always tasted great for generations and still tastes great.
Prep time and cooking time: 45 minutes| Serves: 4

Ingredients To Use:

- 1 tbsp. of dark rum
- 1/2 cup of sugar
- 2 tbsp. of cornstarch
- Ground nutmeg, a pinch
- 2-1/4 pounds of chopped peaches
- 2 tbsp. of melted butter

- 1 pie dough
- 2 tbsp. of flour
- 1 tbsp. of lemon juice

1. Put the pie dough into a pie pan that suits the air fryer.
2. Mix the sugar, nutmeg, cornstarch, rum, butter, peaches, and lemon juice in a bowl. Stir.
3. Pour the mixture into the pie pan. Set the air fryer at 350^{0}F. Cook for 30-35 minutes.
4. Serve immediately or allow to cool.

Nutritional value per serving:

Calories: 230kcal, Fat: 10g, Carb: 15g, Proteins: 10g

Conclusion

With this cookbook, you're going to enjoy your favorite meals without worrying about the portion, fat, and calorie. We hope this comprehensive cookbook, with more than 500+ recipes, will meet all your needs for breakfast, lunch, dinner, snacks, appetizers, and side dishes. All the recipes above can be your keys to having a healthy and fulfilling eating lifestyle.

Keep exploring! You won't regret it.

Good Luck!

CPSIA information can be obtained
at www.ICGtesting.com
Printed in the USA
BVHW021016150223
658569BV00004B/41